Alabama
CURIOSITIES

Quirky characters,
roadside oddities &
other offbeat stuff

2nd Edition

Andy Duncan

Guilford, Connecticut

The prices, rates, and hours listed in this guidebook were confirmed at press time. We recommend, however, that you call establishments to obtain current information before traveling.

To buy books in quantity for corporate use
or incentives, call **(800) 962–0973**
or e-mail **premiums@GlobePequot.com.**

Photos by Andy Duncan unless otherwise noted.

Text design: Bret Kerr
Layout: Casey Shain
Project manager: John Burbidge
Maps: Daniel Lloyd © Morris Book Publishing, LLC

Library of Congress Cataloging-in-Publication data is available on file.

ISBN 978-0-7627-4931-7

Printed in the United States of America

10 9 8 7 6 5 4

To Sydney, again and always

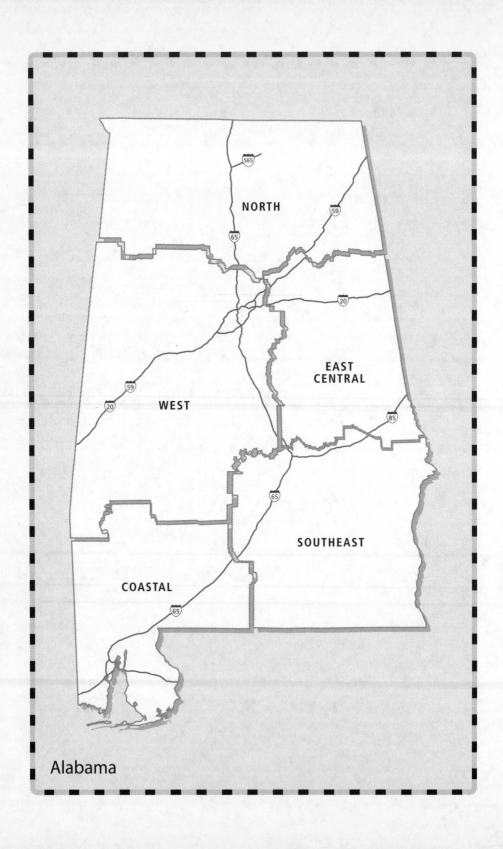

NORTH

WEST

EAST CENTRAL

SOUTHEAST

COASTAL

Alabama

contents

✦ ✦

acknowledgments

* *

Many publications, Web sites, and organizations are referenced throughout this book, but several are so valuable to any student of Alabama curiosities, and curiosities in general, that they merit special mention and special thanks at the outset. I commend to your attention all of the following: Alabama Folklife Association and its journal, *Tributaries* (http://alabamafolklife.org); *Alabama Heritage* magazine, published by the University of Alabama and the Alabama Department of Archives and History (www.alabamaheritage.com); the Kentuck Museum Association and the Kentuck Festival of the Arts (www.kentuck.org); The *Tuscaloosa News* in general and columnist Ben Windham in particular (www.tuscaloosanews.com); and the University of Alabama Press, especially its books *Stars Fell on Alabama* by Carl Carmer (1934), *Place Names in Alabama* by Virginia O. Foscue (1989), and *An Alabama Songbook*, edited by Robert W. Halli Jr. (2004). I also highly recommend the works of Jan Harold Brunvand, beginning with his *Encyclopedia of Urban Legends* (www.janbrunvand.com); Barbara and David Mikkelson's Urban Legends Reference Pages (www.snopes.com); the Roadside America Web site by Doug Kirby, Ken Smith, and Mike Wilkins (www.roadsideamerica.com); Jane and Michael Stern's Roadfood Web site (www.roadfood.com); and the Internet Movie Database (www.imdb.com). My personal thanks extend as well to Sydney Duncan, Connie Johnston, Julie Marsh, Shawna McCarthy, Russ Ringsak, Alex Sartwell, Laura Strom, and all the cheerful informants on the listserv of the Tuscaloosa Science Fiction Society (http://bama.ua.edu/archives/tsfs.html).

introduction

✦ ✦

*I*n the Marx Brothers' movie *Animal Crackers*, Groucho Marx plays a big-game hunter named Captain Spaulding. His speech about his adventures in Africa includes this passage:

> One morning I shot an elephant in my pajamas. How he got in my pajamas I don't know. We tried to remove the tusks, but they were imbedded so firmly, we couldn't budge them. Of course in Alabama the Tuscaloosa, but that's entirely irr-elephant to what I was talking about.

How true that is!

Like Captain Spaulding, two of Alabama's most famous citizens never existed. In 2003 the American Film Institute named "the greatest hero in 100 years of film history." It wasn't James Bond; he was number three. Nor was it Indiana Jones, who was number two. The winner was small-town Alabama lawyer Atticus Finch, hero of Harper Lee's novel *To Kill a Mockingbird*, played on-screen by the Oscar-winning Gregory Peck.

Surprising numbers of lawyers and judges across Alabama say their career choice was inspired by the example of Atticus. The Alabama Bar Association erected the statue of Atticus that stands at the old court-house in Harper Lee's hometown of Monroeville. Alabama politicians, like politicians everywhere, like to fulminate against "trial lawyers," but none ever criticizes Atticus, the most famous trial lawyer of all.

The other famous nonexistent Alabamian is the hero of Winston Groom's novel *Forrest Gump*, played on-screen by the Oscar-winning Tom Hanks. Surprising numbers of people call the University of Alabama to ask, in all seriousness, for copies of Forrest's yearbook photo and have to be let down gently. As yet no Forrest Gump statue stands in Tusca-loosa, but the Bubba Gump Shrimp Company exists. However, it's based in California and has no restaurants in Alabama.

★ ★

Many other illustrious Alabamians are real people, not inventions: Hank Aaron, Hugo Black, Rick Bragg, Zelda Fitzgerald, Fannie Flagg, Helen Keller, Jesse Owens, Condoleezza Rice. Some famous figures loom so large in the state's history that it's easy to forget they weren't Alabama natives to begin with: Wernher von Braun, Paul W. "Bear" Bryant, Truman Capote, George Washington Carver, Jefferson Davis, Martin Luther King Jr., Joe Namath, Sequoyah, Booker T. Washington.

American music would be hard to imagine without Alabamians such as Nat King Cole, W. C. Handy, Sam Phillips, and Hank Williams. Also born in Alabama were Clarence Carter, the Delmore Brothers, Emmylou Harris, the Louvin Brothers, Wilson Pickett, Martha Reeves, Lionel Richie, Percy Sledge, Sun Ra, and Dinah Washington. The original Commodores were Richie's classmates at Tuskegee. A Birmingham beautician named Tammy Wynette got her start singing on a local TV show called *Country Boy Eddie*. Eddie Kendricks and Paul Williams were Birmingham schoolboys when they formed a singing group called the Cavaliers. They took the act to Detroit, where they added personnel and became the Temptations.

TV Land viewers should note the actors who played Mr. Haney on *Green Acres*, Flo on *Alice*, and Gomer and Goober on *The Andy Griffith Show* are all from Alabama, too.

While most Presidents' Day observations in February honor George Washington and Abraham Lincoln, Alabama's is the only one that specifically honors only Washington and a fellow southerner, Thomas Jefferson—who was born in April.

Another Alabama distinction is an enormous and unwieldy state constitution. At press time the Alabama constitution had 799 amendments. (When the first edition of this book was published in 2005, it had only 742.) Every fall a handful of new amendments is on the ballot. Many of the amendments have amendments themselves. For example, Amendment 799 amended Amendment 756; the revision allows Shelby County to enforce traffic laws on private roads, or something like that. Why this sort of local issue needs to be put to a statewide vote is a mystery, but Alabamians enjoy the opportunity each fall to crush some faraway county's bingo sales, just out of spite.

introduction

Alabama towns include The Bottle, Bug Tussle, Burnt Corn, Chigger Hill, Graball, Hustleville, Intercourse, Needmore, Pull Tight, Scant City, Scratch Ankle, Smuteye, and Zip City.

Alabama's forests cover more acres than the states of Connecticut, Delaware, Maryland, Massachusetts, New Hampshire, and Rhode Island combined. A twelfth of all the water going to the ocean in the United States flows through Alabama, on waterways such as Hells Creek, Murder Creek, Peckerwood Creek, and Polecat Creek. Alabama eminences include Penitentiary Mountain, Rattlesnake Mountain, Straight Mountain, and Turkey Heaven Mountain.

Other states make do with state birds and state flowers, but Alabama has all sorts of officially recognized state symbols. Alabama has a state reptile (the Alabama red-bellied turtle), a state American folk dance (the square dance), and a state soil (the Bama Soil Series). The state fossil is the basilosaurus, a carnivorous 70-foot-long prehistoric whale. Its bones first were dug up on an Alabama plantation in 1834, and the two most complete basilosaurus skeletons ever unearthed were dug up in Alabama.

The state shell is Johnstone's Junonia, named for Mobile shell enthusiast Kathleen Yerger Johnstone. The camellia was named the state flower in 1959, ending the thirty-two-year reign of the previous state flower, the goldenrod, to which many Alabamians were allergic.

The monarch butterfly is the state insect, but the state butterfly is the eastern tiger swallowtail. The state game bird is the wild turkey, but Wild Turkey is not the state spirit. That honor goes to Clyde May's Conecuh Ridge Whiskey, which is made in Kentucky.

The legislature confused itself when it named the largemouth bass, *Micropterus salmoides*, the state freshwater fish. The official legislation calls it *Micropterus punctulatus*, which as everyone knows is not the largemouth bass but the spotted bass. If this were in the state constitution, it would have been amended by now.

The state nut is the pecan, though it has plenty of competition.

The state motto is "We dare defend our rights," but many Alabamians find that not half so inspiring as "In Alabama the Tuscaloosa."

Interesting Town Names in Alabama

Active (Bibb County)

Aimwell (Marengo County)

Alabaster (Shelby County)

Allgood (Blount County): Named for the Allgood family.

Arab (Marshall County): Pronounced "A-rab," with the emphasis on the first syllable. The post office was supposed to be named Arad after the first postmaster's son, but federal officials misread the handwritten application.

Axis (Mobile County)

Ballplay (Etowah County): Native American sportsmen had a playing field here.

Benevola (Pickens County)

Black Diamond (Jefferson County)

Blues Old Stand (Bullock County): Named for Mr. Blue's nineteenth-century general store, or "stand."

Bon Air (Talladega County): French for "good air."

Boot Hill (Barbour County)

The Bottle (Lee County): Named for a large sign in the shape of a Coca-Cola bottle.

Brilliant (Marion County): Named for the Brilliant Coal Company.

Bug Tussle (Cullman County)

Burnt Corn (on the Monroe County/Conecuh County line): Early settlers came upon a burnt cornfield here.

Carbon Hill (Walker County)

Chance (Clarke County): The first postmaster kept recommending names for his post office, all of which were rejected by the federal government. Saying he'd give it one more chance, he wrote down *Chance*, and it was accepted.

Chigger Hill (DeKalb County): Named for a mite infestation.

Consul (Marengo County)

Dog Town (DeKalb County): Coon hunting and coonhounds were popular here.

Dolomite (Jefferson County)

Duck Springs (Etowah County)

Echo (Dale County): Early settlers heard an echo as they built their cabin.

Eclectic (Elmore County): The town founder, having taken an "eclectic" course of study in school, believed "eclectic" meant "best."

Eight Mile (Mobile County)

Elsanor (Baldwin County): Named not for Hamlet's Elsinore but for Elsa Norton, whose philanthropist husband donated land and money for a school here.

Excel (Monroe County)

Flomaton (Escambia County): "Flo" from Florida, "ma" from Alabama, "ton" for town.

Florala (Covington County): "Flor" from Florida, "ala" from Alabama.

Fort Deposit (Lowndes County): Andrew Jackson built a supply depot here during his 1813 extermination of the Creeks.

Froggy Bottom (Montgomery County)

Fruithurst (Cleburne County): Named by the Alabama Fruit Growers.

Graball (Henry County): When the law raided a cockfight here, someone yelled, "Grab all the money and run!"

Half Acre (Marengo County): The full name was originally Hell's Half Acre, named by the disgusted surveyors after they discovered they were off by a half acre.

Hazel Green (Madison County): Named for the hazelnut groves.

Hedgeman Triplett's Ferry (Randolph County)

Hightogy (Lamar County)

Holy Trinity (Russell County)

Honoraville (Crenshaw County): Named for a character in John Dryden's long poem "Theodore and Honoria."

Hope Hull (Montgomery County): Named for a circuit-riding Methodist preacher named Hope Hull.

Hopeful (Talladega County)

Hurricane (Baldwin County)

Hustleville (Marshall County)

Hytop (Jackson County)

Ino (Coffee County): When the postmaster asked the citizens to suggest names, everybody spoke at once. One person kept saying, "I know. I know. I know."

Intercourse (Sumter County): This was a crossroads community, where travelers could exchange, uh, information with one another.

(Continued)

Land (Choctaw County): Named for the Land family.

Lavaca (Choctaw County): *La vaca* is Spanish for "the cow."

Leggtown (Limestone County): Named for the Legg family.

Level Road (Randolph County)

Listerhill (Colbert County): Named for U.S. Senator Lister Hill (1894–1984).

Loango (Covington County): Farmers at the store here used to "load and go."

Locust Fork (Blount County)

Lower Peach Tree (Wilcox County)

Lubbub (Pickens County)

Majestic (Jefferson County)

Marvel (Bibb County): Named for poet Andrew Marvell.

Muscle Shoals (Colbert County): Named for Tennessee River shellfish. *Muscle* is the Middle English spelling of *mussel*.

Nectar (Blount County)

Needmore (Pike County)

New Site (Tallapoosa County): According to legend, people moved here because they found neighboring Goldville, an 1842 gold rush town, to be sinful.

Normal (Madison County): Named for the state Normal and Agricultural School, now Alabama A&M.

Octagon (Marengo County): Named for the eight-sided Bethlehem Baptist Church, built in 1868.

Old Texas (Monroe County)

Paragon (Choctaw County): Once was named Drag, the nickname of a lazy resident.

Peeks Corner (DeKalb County)

Perdido Beach (Baldwin County): *Perdido* means "lost" in Spanish, hence "Lost Beach."

Phenix City (Russell County) Named for the Phenix Mills, the major employer across the river in Columbus, Georgia. Once known as Lively.

Phil Campbell (Franklin County): Named for the contractor who built the railroad through here.

Pine Level (Montgomery County): Once known as Pine Tucky.

Potash (Randolph County)

Pull Tight (Marion County)

Pyriton (Clay County): Named for pyrite, a.k.a. "fool's gold."

Rabbit Town (Marshall County)

Rainbow City (Etowah County)

Rash (Jackson County): Named for William Rash.

Reform (Pickens County): The sinful residents ran an evangelist out of town. As he went, the evangelist hollered over his shoulder, "Reform! Reform!"

Robjohn (Choctaw County): Named for Rob Edwards and John Hodges.

Rodentown (DeKalb County): Named not for a rodent, but for Billy Roden.

Rural Home (Pike County)

Scant City (Marshall County): Moonshiners here sold their product in "scant pint" bottles (twelve ounces).

Scratch Ankle (Monroe County)

Six Mile (Bibb County)

Sledge (Sumter County): Named for murderer Simms Sledge.

Smuteye (Bullock County): Another Smut Eye, in Coffee County, now is named Victoria.

Sunny South (Wilcox County): Named for the Alabama River steamboat the *Sunny South,* which burned in 1867.

Susan Moore (Blount County): Community near Susan Moore High School and Susan Moore Elementary School in Blountsville.

Sylacauga (Talladega County): From the Creek phrase *suli kagi,* meaning "buzzards' roost."

Three Notch (Bullock County): Three notches on the trees marked the trail through here.

Toadvine (Jefferson County): Named for a man with the surname Toadvine.

Trickem (Cleburne County): Pronounced "trick 'em," but derived from "Tri-Com," for Three Communities Church.

Twin (Marion County)

Vestavia Hills (Jefferson County): Named for the goddess Vesta and the Vestal Virgins of ancient Rome.

Vinegar Bend (Washington County)

Zip City (Lauderdale County): Named by Alonzo Parker in the 1920s because of all the cars zipping through on their way to buy legal liquor in Tennessee.

Coastal

1

Coastal

The beaches and bays, *rivers and swamps of coastal Alabama have a mythic quality, and the history of the area includes more than its share of larger-than-life figures: Railroad Bill the outlaw; former slave Cudjo Lewis; future Alamo hero William Barrett Travis; and Atticus Finch, a universally beloved lawyer who is, of course, fictional. Both Steven Spielberg and Steven Seagal made arguably their best movies here, though in the second Steven's case that may not be saying much. The Mobile area is serious about its Mardi Gras and serious about honoring the memory of good-time guys Joe Cain and the Goat Man, who always knew where the party was. The coast has more unique festivities, too, such as Jubilee, in which the fish fling themselves; and the Interstate Mullet Toss, in which the fish are flung by others, being already dead. The Junior Miss Pageant is still around, but we haven't had a Nutria Rodeo Queen, alas, in years. Aaron Burr's dream of ruling North America west of the Appalachians died here, as did the thriving nineteenth-century port of Blakeley, now vanished, and the ill-fated inhabitants who gave Dauphin Island its early name, Isle of Bones. The descendants of the original fire ants that the young Edward O. Wilson studied are still around, of course, as is the oak tree that sprang from a cursed grave. The earth of coastal Alabama is rich in pests and legends.*

★ ★

The Legend of Railroad Bill
Atmore

On March 7, 1897, while eating crackers and cheese in Tidmore and Ward's general store in Atmore, a fugitive African-American train robber named Morris Slater was shot and killed by Sheriff Leonard McGowan. Slater's life was over, but his legend was just beginning. Slater was better known, in life and in death, as "Railroad Bill."

According to the police Railroad Bill had bedeviled trainmen in Alabama and Florida for years and had murdered at least two people, including the sheriff of Escambia County, who had failed to heed Bill's handwritten warning: "I love you and do not want to kill you so do not come after me."

But to the poor African Americans who lived along the L&N (Louisville and Nashville) tracks, Railroad Bill was a hero. In their version of the story, he was a law-abiding worker in the turpentine camps that dotted the piney woods, until the police came for him on trumped-up charges. He grabbed his guns, disappeared into the swamps, and spent the rest of his days robbing trains and helping the poor, often by leaving crates of groceries on the porch. To his fans he was the black Robin Hood of Alabama.

As Railroad Bill continued to elude capture, wild stories were told about him: He was a hoodoo man, a sorcerer; he caught bullets in his hands and shot holes through dimes; he transformed himself into a bloodhound and ran with the pack that was hunting him; only silver bullets could kill him.

Three thousand people, it is said, came to see Railroad Bill's body on view in nearby Brewton. Later it was put on display in Pensacola and Montgomery. Curiosity seekers were charged admission, and hawkers did a brisk business in souvenir photos of Sheriff McGowan posing with Railroad Bill's corpse.

And yet the wild stories persisted: Railroad Bill's white enemies had stuffed his corpse's mouth with bitterweed and later dropped dead under mysterious circumstances. Railroad Bill was not dead at all, but still out there in the swamps, helping the poor, terrorizing the railroad men, and guarding his vast hoard of loot that no one would ever find.

Before long people were singing a song about Railroad Bill, parts of which almost certainly are older than Morris Slater. Versions of "Railroad Bill" have been recorded by Etta Baker, Ramblin' Jack Elliott, Cisco Houston, Taj Mahal, Van Morrison, and the New Christy Minstrels, among many others. The old song's many verses include these:

Railroad Bill lived on a hill
He never worked and he never will
Railroad Bill going down the hill
Lighting cigars with a five-dollar bill
Railroad Bill went out West
Shot all the buttons off a brakeman's vest

Tidmore and Ward's general store is long gone, but it was located on the 100 block of Ashley Street downtown. There is no historical marker, alas, for the site of Railroad Bill's last meal.

That Other River Styx

Baldwin County

In Greek mythology a ferry carries the dead across the River Styx en route to Hades. In Baldwin County, Highway 64 carries tourists across the River Styx en route to Interstate 10. Okay, in Baldwin County they call it the Styx River, not the River Styx, but isn't it more fun to say it the old Greek way?

The excellent reference book *Place Names in Alabama*, from the University of Alabama Press, notes that the Styx River is "probably named for the mythical river in Hades." Or the Chicago-based rock band. No, wait, "Lady" charted in 1974, and the river in Alabama was named long before, so that's out. Never mind.

Despite its ominous name the Styx is a gentle, shady river with a sandy shoreline. Kicks on the Styx, on U.S. Highway 90 east of Elsanor, offers canoeing, tubing, and overnight camping trips. For information call (251) 942-1807.

Stolen County Seat
Bay Minette

Bay Minette wasn't always the county seat of Baldwin County. That honor used to be held by Daphne, on Mobile Bay, 30 miles to the southwest. When the legislature voted in 1901 to move the county seat to Bay Minette, so the story goes, the folks in Daphne ignored the order. About twenty Bay Minette folks finally got tired of waiting. On the night of October 1, 1901, they made up a story about a fugitive murderer that was good enough to get the Daphne sheriff out of town on a "snipe hunt," or wild-goose chase. When the sheriff was gone, the Bay Minette folks broke into the Daphne courthouse by night, packed up the judge's desk, as well as all the county records and the county's one prisoner, and trundled them all back to Bay Minette in buggies and wagons. When the sun rose, Bay Minette was the new county seat, and so it has been to this day.

This episode is commemorated in the Bay Minette post office by a mural with the sexy title *Removal of the County Seat from Daphne to Bay Minette*, painted for the old post office in 1939 by Hilton Leech, a well-known Sarasota, Florida, artist commissioned by the Roosevelt administration. The post office is at 601 McMeans Avenue (Highway 59).

Don't mention any of this to anyone from Daphne.

Trust me.

Blueberry Drop
Brewton

Without capital letters a blueberry drop is a type of cookie. With capital letters a Blueberry Drop is what happens every New Year's Eve in downtown Brewton, on U.S. Highway 29 just north of the Florida line.

New York City and Brewton signal the start of a new year simultaneously, New York by dropping a 6-foot ball made of Waterford crystal, Brewton by dropping a giant cluster of blueberries.

In warmer weather Brewton salutes its favorite crop with a Blueberry Festival every June on the campus of Jefferson Davis Community

College. For more information call the Brewton Chamber of Commerce, (251) 867-3224, or log onto www.brewtonchamber.com.

Ellicott's Stone
Bucks

One of North America's most historically significant rocks is Ellicott's Stone, an unlovely, lopsided sandstone pyramid 2 feet high, placed in 1799 to mark the east-west boundary between Spanish Florida and the United States.

On the south side is the inscription DOMINIO DE S.M. CARLOS IV, LAT. 31, 1799. On the north side is the inscription KILROY WAS HERE. Just kidding. The north side says U.S. LAT. 31, 1799.

The marker is named for Andrew Ellicott, the surveyor who placed the rock on instructions from George Washington. Ellicott intended to place it on the thirty-first parallel of the Earth's latitude. Using only the stars and his homemade instruments, he missed the line by a mere 500 feet, a remarkable achievement for its day and plenty close enough for government work even now.

Mobile, which lies just to the south of Ellicott's Stone, remained a Spanish city until 1813. Ask Mobile residents whether they live "south of the rock" and bask in their funny looks.

Ellicott's Stone is at the end of a 900-foot path in a small roadside park on U.S. Highway 43. Watch for the historical marker.

The Improbable Voyage of the LST-325
Chickasaw

On January 10, 2001, accompanied by the cheers of thousands of well-wishers, a rusty, battered, sixty-year-old warship, the LST-325, sailed into Mobile Bay, crewed mostly by sailors older than she was. Thus ended one of the strangest and noblest voyages of recent maritime history.

LSTs (landing ship, tanks), much used by U.S. forces during World War II, were amphibious vessels that carried troops and vehicles across open ocean directly to shore. For many years the 10,000-member U.S.

★ ★

L.S.T. Association, all veterans of LST crews, looked for an LST they could restore as a floating museum. The Pentagon didn't have a single one left. They all had been sold, given away, or scrapped decades ago.

Finally the veterans learned that the Greek navy had acquired a number of LSTs after the war and was planning to scrap all of them. The veterans worked out a deal with the Greek government for LST-325, which had been part of the Allied invasion of Sicily in 1943. Greece would give them the ship free of charge. The catch? They had to come get it.

The veterans recruited a full crew of volunteers under Capt. Robert Jornlin of Earlville, Illinois. The average age of the twenty-eight sailors was seventy-two, all of them World War II and Korean War veterans. Skeptics said not even a hale and hearty crew of young men could get

On the LST-325's last voyage, the average age of the crew was seventy-two. NIKI SEPSAS

across the wintertime Atlantic in that scrapyard-bound rust bucket, but the skeptics were wrong. Two months after setting sail from Crete, LST-325 reached its destination, Mobile Bay, 6,500 miles away.

Jornlin and his crew were surprised to discover that en route, they had become celebrities. "We never figured on this being anything great or heroic," Jornlin said. "All of us guys just wanted to bring back an LST."

Formerly docked at Hooks Terminal north of Chickasaw, LST-325 since has sailed from Alabama and is permanently berthed in Evansville, Indiana. For more information on its trans-Atlantic voyage, visit www.lstmemorial.org. "Please don't call," the ship's Web site notes, "just to chew the rag or to ask how things are going."

Got Any Wrestlers by Monet?

Daphne

If you thought "sport art" was limited to snazzy team insignias, the dance routines of the Laker Girls, and baseball-card photography, you need to visit the American Sport Art Museum.

Opened in 1998 and dedicated to "artistically rendering the human expression that is sport," this serious art museum has a single theme: It claims to house "the largest collection of sport art in the world."

The collection includes a two-story outdoor mural dedicated to baseball legend Jackie Robinson, a sculpture of golfer Hale Irwin, and a portrait of hockey star Wayne Gretzky by Stephen Holland, official artist of the Los Angeles Kings. (Wealthy organizations always have been patrons of the arts: during the Renaissance, the Borgias; today, pro hockey teams.)

Outside, the brick Walk of Fame honors donors such as Yankees owner George Steinbrenner, tennis champion Martina Navratilova, and the world's most famous bobsledder, Prince Albert of Monaco. Your name can join theirs underfoot, for only $25 per brick. Other supporters on the museum's advisory board include golfer Arnold Palmer, *Sports Illustrated* writer Frank Deford, and John Kelly, former president of the Goodwill Games.

The breathtaking Interstate 65 bridge, 125 feet above the Mobile River at Creola, is officially named for Walter K. "Weary" Wilson of the U.S. Army Corps of Engineers. The locals took one look at the double arches and nicknamed it the Dolly Parton Bridge. NIKI SEPSAS

★ ★

Out back, a sculpture resembling a giant leaning pinecone is made of hundreds of diamond-tipped drill bits. This sculpture commemorates oil drilling, which is not yet an Olympic sport but nevertheless, according to the museum's Web site, has been very good to "several Middle Eastern countries" that "were instrumental in the establishment of the institution financially."

The museum is a half mile south of I-10, on U.S. Highway 98 between Spanish Fort and Fairhope, just inland from Mobile Bay. It's open from 9:00 a.m. to 4:00 p.m., Monday through Friday. Admission is free, though donations are encouraged. Call (251) 626-3303, extension 7103, or log onto www.asama.org.

Jubilee!
Daphne

When residents of the Eastern Shore of Mobile Bay are awakened in the wee hours by shouts of "Jubilee!" they know to grab whatever containers they can find—nets, buckets, washtubs, sacks, baskets, even pillowcases—and run for the shoreline.

"Jubilee!" means that all the sea creatures that normally live in the deep waters in the middle of the bay—flounder, eel, catfish, stingray, shrimp, and especially blue crab—have swarmed into the shallows along the water's edge so that even the dullest angler can wade in and catch a seafood haul of biblical proportions.

For years jubilees were mysterious events, and some outsiders doubted they happened at all. Scientists now believe they occur in summertime when winds, tides, and runoff force a layer of oxygen-poor water to rise and head toward shore, forcing all the fish to come in, too. Scientists also believe this happens occasionally all over the world but that Mobile Bay may be the only place in North America where it occurs regularly.

Still, jubilees are unpredictable. Sometimes a jubilee affects only a few hundred feet of shoreline, sometimes 15 miles of it, from Point Clear north to Daphne, which calls itself the "Jubilee City." And once

the tide or the wind changes, the jubilee ends as quickly as it began, and thousands of fish become, once again, the ones that got away.

Isle de Bones
Dauphin Island

The first French explorers to land on this lovely spit of sand in 1699 made a horrible discovery on the southwest corner of the island: piles of human bones, thousands of them, bleaching in the sun. They assumed the worst and named the place—ominous drumroll, please— Massacre Island.

Despite its less-than-inviting name, a lot of French people happily settled on Massacre Island. In 1707 they finally changed the island's name to Dauphin, to honor the son of Louis XIV, thus doing wonders for the non-French tourist industry. Face it, who other than a reality-TV producer would consider a beach vacation at a place called—ominous drumroll, again—Massacre Island?

That first French landing party was led by Pierre Le Moyne d'Iberville (whose brother, Jean-Baptiste Le Moyne de Bienville, founded New Orleans nineteen years later). Pierre wrote in his journal that judging from the bones, "more than sixty men or women had been slain" on Massacre Island.

Later legends greatly inflated the number of bones found. By the time an MTV crew came to Dauphin Island in 2001 to film an episode of *Fear*—which, if you've forgotten it, was like a weekly *Blair Witch Project* without fatalities—the claim had been inflated to 40,000 human skulls!

Anthropologists say Pierre probably just stumbled upon a Native American cemetery or battle site. So much for—one last, somewhat less ominous drumroll—Massacre Island!

Massacre, uh, Dauphin Island is easy to find. Just drive south on Highway 193, along the western shore of Mobile Bay, until you reach the beach.

★ ★

Don't Ask How It's Made . . .
Evergreen

If you're not up for the drive to the annual Sausage Festival in Bekesc-saba, Hungary, next October, come to the one in Evergreen, on U.S. Highway 84 just off I-65. In Alabama as in Hungary, October was the traditional month when swine were slaughtered and their meat put up for the winter.

Hungary's Sausage Festival puts on "pig-killing shows," according to its Web site (www.kolbaszfesztival.eu/index_en.htm), but the Evergreen Chamber of Commerce promises to do no such thing. For more info call the Evergreen/Conecuh Chamber of Commerce at (251) 578-1707.

Surreal Surfaces
Fairhope

Artist Luke Gontarek specializes in faux and decorative painting and trompe l'oeil, French for "fool the eye." That means he can make a concrete floor look like inlaid marble or make a plaster urn shine like the purest gold or make a brand-new set of kitchen cabinets look like heirlooms. He can festoon a bathroom with permanently blooming irises and magnolias and turn a dead-end hallway into a room with a view—of a Tuscan hillside or a moonscape or anything you want, really.

It would not, however, be accurate to call Gontarek a professional faker. He does what all artists do: He takes the materials of the world around him and gives them style. He also does not accept faux money.

Gontarek's studio is at 323 De La Mare, 1 block south of Fairhope Avenue between South Church Street and South Section Street. For more information call (251) 990-3226 or visit www.lukedward.com.

The Tax Radicals of Mobile Bay

Fairhope

Today Fairhope is known for its shops and restaurants, its parks and pier, its beautiful shaded houses overlooking Mobile Bay. A century ago, however, Fairhope was known as an experiment in radical government.

Fairhope was founded by transplanted Iowans in 1894 as "a model community or colony, free from all forms of private monopoly," according to the original charter. The founders were disciples of reformer Henry George, a Philadelphia native who never lived in Alabama. Beginning in the 1870s, George told anyone who would listen, and many who wouldn't, that land was the source of all monopoly privilege and should be taxed accordingly.

In fact, George argued that the land tax should be the only tax—no income taxes, business taxes, or sales taxes, just a single land tax, an annual rent paid by the land "owner" to the community for the privilege of using a plot of land for another year. (Henry George had a lot of wacky notions. For example, he was one of the first Americans to call for the secret ballot, having the audacity to argue that whom you voted for was no one else's business. Because George pointed to how well the secret ballot worked in Australia, his critics derided the secret ballot as "kangaroo voting." Resistance was such that the secret ballot didn't become law in all states until 1950, more than fifty years after George's death.)

By creating the Fairhope Single Tax Corporation, the founders implemented George's tax ideals as best they could. They felt they had a "fair hope" of success, hence the town's name. They had no control, however, over all those other taxes that the county, state, and federal governments still wanted someone to pay. The founders also couldn't prevent outsiders from buying adjacent land and doing as they pleased with it.

So the Fairhope experiment never caught on, as its founders had fairly hoped. In fact, Alabama thumbs its nose at Henry George by taxing just about everything *except* land. (Timberland, for example, accounts for 71 percent of Alabama's real estate but less than 2 percent of its property tax revenue.)

But the Fairhope Single Tax Corporation is still around, and it still owns 4,500 acres of land in and around Fairhope, issuing ninety-nine-year leases and occasionally donating tracts to the town for parks and such. The corporation's office, which includes some historical exhibits, is at 336 Fairhope Avenue, west of U.S. Highway 98, and is open 9:00 a.m. to 5:00 p.m., Monday through Thursday, and 9:00 a.m. to 4:00 p.m. on Friday. For more information call (251) 928-8162, or visit www.fairhopesingletax.com.

Move Those Clams—I'm Trying to Bowl

Foley

Mobile Bay has many good seafood restaurants, but at only one of them can diners work up an appetite by bowling.

Captain's Choice is a well-regarded seafood restaurant located in a bowling alley, the Gulf Bowl in Foley. The food—such as oyster loaf with homemade tartar sauce—has been recommended in the upscale *Coastal Living* magazine. One wonders how often the phrase "bowling alley" has appeared in *Coastal Living*.

Both the sixteen Brunswick lanes and the restaurant are run by Butch and Sonya Cole. The Gulf Bowl is at 204 East Michigan Avenue, at the intersection with Highway 59. For more information call (251) 943-4575.

Throwed Rolls

Foley

"Not only fun to catch, but delicious to eat" are the "throwed rolls" at Lambert's Café on Highway 59 just south of Foley. "Throwed" refers not to their preparation but to the waitstaff's technique in serving them. "Dozens of hot rolls are flying through the air every few

Lambert's Café in Foley is a great place to catch lunch—literally.

minutes at Lambert's, so be alert and have a roll," says the restaurant's Web site, www.throwedrolls.com. The late Norman Lambert started this odd tradition, we are told, decades ago at the original Lambert's in Sikeston, Missouri, when he was passing out extra hot rolls but couldn't reach the guy in the corner. "Just throw the #@$#@ thing," the customer said, and Lambert's rolls have been "throwed" ever since. Known for down-home fare such as black-eyed peas, fried okra, frog legs, hog jowls, chicken gizzards, and turnip greens, the Lambert's in Foley opened in 1996. One of its many slogans is "Come on in and eat or we'll both starve." Hours are 10:30 a.m. to 9:00 p.m. Call (251) 943-7655.

St. Nick's Knife Factory

Foley

Women love the Christmas collectibles, and men love the knives. That's the business principle behind this startling two-in-one emporium, which conjures images of Santa crawling wild-eyed down the chimney with a dagger in his teeth.

Owner Kenny Winters says the store is designed to appeal to vacationing couples. Women will find beach-themed Christmas ornaments, Harbour Lights collectible lighthouses, and ceramic Santas. And men browse items such as the $300 Harsey Tactical Knife with Desert Camouflage from Lone Wolf Knives, which (says the catalog) "provides a

At 15 feet, can it truly be a pocket knife? NIKI SEPSAS

low visual profile in both daylight and night-vision environments." After loading their shopping bags, happy female and male shoppers can reunite on the beach and get their photos snapped wearing Santa hats.

Founded in Orange Beach, St. Nick's Knife Factory now is eight miles north, in the Tanger Outlets shopping center on Highway 59 in Foley, and is open from 9:00 a.m. to 9:00 p.m. Monday through Saturday, 11:00 a.m. to 6:00 p.m. Sunday. For more information call (251) 981-2724.

A Bath for Bossie
Gateswood

One of the few remaining cow-dipping vats built during the great tick-eradication program of the early twentieth century can be found in Propst Park in this community.

The vats were basically big stone or concrete troughs in the ground. Tick eradicators poured an arsenic solution into the trough, and cattle were walked through it. Cow dippings often drew big crowds of spectators (this was before cable). By World War II tickborne "cattle fever" had pretty much been eradicated in the United States.

If you've read this far, you'll probably be interested to know that the U.S. government still employs sixty mounted cattle inspectors to patrol the Mexican border to make sure the ticks don't come back. These inspectors are known as "tick riders."

Propst Park (say that five times fast) is located on Highway 112 halfway between Bay Minette and Gateswood.

Alabama Bedrock
Jackson

At Salt Mountain, near Jackson, is the world's only known outcrop of a distinctive white limestone. Since its discovery in 1891, geologists worldwide have known it, naturally enough, as Salt Mountain limestone.

Salt Mountain limestone underlies much of south Alabama and north Florida. Everywhere but here, though, you have to dig for it.

Scientists believe the limestone is the remains of an ancient coral reef, evidence that all of Alabama south of Montgomery once was submerged by the Gulf of Mexico. Inside the limestone have been found fossils of tiny creatures, including two species previously unknown to science.

During the Civil War the Union blockaded Alabama's ports, creating a shortage of salt, among other commodities. Resourceful locals boiled brine water to "make" salt. The furnaces in which the salt water was heated were built from Salt Mountain limestone, which is soft enough to be cut by a regular wood saw.

Salt Mountain is located about 6 miles southeast of Jackson on County Road 15. Watch for a granite historical marker that describes Central Salt Works.

Mail Boat
Magnolia Springs

Magnolia Springs, on US 98 near the Gulf of Mexico, may be the only town in the United States where the postal service still delivers mail year-round by boat. Magnolia Springs novelist Thomas Lakeman beautifully described the process in a 2002 posting on his Web site:

> The postman is Huey, a lean and hard-boned man who looks like he would not tolerate being called a "postal carrier" by anybody. His official vehicle is a speedboat that looks like it's spent more time trawling for mullet than hauling Val-Pak coupons; its only mark of admiralty is a banged-up sign reading "U.S. Postal Service" on the starboard bow. In other words, do not hinder him: Huey's boat is a federal vessel, just like the U.S.S. *Nimitz*.

★ ★

A Demon by Any Other Name
McIntosh

For many years the sports teams at McIntosh High School on US 43 were known as the Demons. In 2001, however, a pastor complained, and the school board decided the teams couldn't be the Demons anymore. Students were asked to vote on what they'd like to call themselves instead.

The students voted to call their teams the Players. The school board then realized that in hip-hop culture, a "player" is a playboy, a man-about-town who's interested in only one thing, that one thing not being basketball. So the school board nixed the McIntosh Players, too.

For a while thereafter, the McIntosh athletic teams had no nickname, no mascot at all. A group of McIntosh parents and grandparents sued the school board to get the Demons back. Today, McIntosh High's athletes are all Demons again.

According to the Alabama High School Athletic Association, eight Alabama schools have the Blue Devils as their mascots, seven the Red Devils, one the Purple Devils—and only four the Saints. Final score: Devils 16, Saints 4. When the first edition of this book was published in 2005, there were twenty-six "Devil" schools, suggesting that a number of towns recently have found the mascot too hot to handle.

Founding Father and Really Sore Loser
McIntosh

The dead town of McIntosh Bluff exists today only as a roadside historical marker. But this rather ordinary spot represented the end of Aaron Burr's dreams of empire.

Burr, a New York lawyer and U.S. senator, was one of the great early leaders of the United States, but he never got over losing the 1800 presidential election to Thomas Jefferson. The electoral college vote was a tie between him and Jefferson, which threw the election into the House of Representatives, which finally went for Jefferson on the thirty-sixth ballot.

Burr blamed another founding father, Alexander Hamilton, for his defeat and killed him in a duel. Then, just to show the United States, Burr plotted to raise a private army, conquer Mexico, and rule everything west of the Appalachians, on the old schoolyard principle of "I don't want to be in your old club anyway!"

His coconspirator, Gen. James Wilkinson, squealed to President Jefferson, and Burr took off for Spanish Florida with the law at his heels. He nearly made it but was arrested at McIntosh Bluff in 1807. He went on trial for treason before Chief Justice John Marshall in Virginia, who ruled there weren't enough witnesses and thus acquitted him.

Burr traveled abroad for a few years and then went home to New York City and settled back into his law practice. He did pretty well. Clients saw he clearly had a knack for getting out of trouble!

Mardi Gras and Joe Cain Day
Mobile

Which Mardi Gras carnival is older, the one in Mobile or the one in New Orleans, is a matter of some dispute—if you live in New Orleans.

Mobile folks are content with the fact that theirs began in 1703, fifteen years before New Orleans even existed. You'd think that would settle things, but no, residents of the Big Easy claim a 1699 Mardi Gras that was held a "few" miles from the site of the future New Orleans. Mississippians say this was a few miles away, all right—in Gulfport, Mississippi, about 80 miles away as the crow flies.

Best not to bring any of this up if you're partying in Mobile in the days preceding Lent. Just know that Mobile's Mardi Gras celebration peaks not on Fat Tuesday but two days earlier, on Shrove Sunday. In Mobile this is known as Joe Cain Day, after the reveler who in 1866 revived the Mardi Gras street festival that had been interrupted by the Civil War. With six of his friends, Cain, a store clerk and fireman, dressed as a Chickasaw Indian and paraded around in a borrowed coal wagon.

In 1966 Mobile observed the Joe Cain centennial by having Cain's

Accept no substitutes: Mobile dates its Mardi Gras from 1703. COURTESY OF MOBILE BAY CVB

body exhumed from its resting place in Bayou La Batre and rein-
terred in Mobile's historic Church Street Graveyard, behind the public
library. The event was marked with a jazz funeral procession, and this
was the beginning of the annual Joe Cain parade. The whole thing
was the brainchild of another Mobile character, the late Julian Lee
"Judy" Rayford, who claimed Joe Cain appeared to him in dreams
and urged him to start a "people's parade." Fittingly, Rayford is now
buried next to Joe Cain.

Everyone is welcome to walk in the Joe Cain procession, which
begins at Joe's house at 906 Augusta Street and ends at Joe's grave,
just east of the cemetery's north gate. The parade is led by Joe's wail-
ing "widows," actually men in mourning drag who quarrel loudly over
which was Joe's favorite and wind up dancing on his grave. (In life

Joe was happily married to only one woman, Elizabeth, who is buried beside him.) The widows take joke names such as Sola Cain and Nova Cain. Each year, more than 150,000 visitors crowd into Mobile for Joe Cain Day.

The history of Mobile's Mardi Gras traditions is well told at the Mobile Carnival Museum at 355 Government Street downtown. Hours are 9:00 a.m. to 4:00 p.m. Monday, Wednesday, Friday, and Saturday, and admission is charged. Visit www.mobilecarnivalmuseum.com.

For more information on taking part in Joe Cain Day itself, contact the Mobile Convention and Visitors Bureau at (800) 566-2453 or visit www.mobile.org.

Oak Tree Proves Innocence . . . a Little Late

Mobile

Other than Joe Cain's grave, the chief attraction in the Church Street Graveyard is the Boyington Oak, and not just because it provides a shady spot on a hot day.

The oak grew from the grave of one Charles Boyington. According to legend Boyington was condemned for murder in 1835 but swore on the scaffold that an oak tree with a hundred roots would sprout from his grave to prove him innocent. The tree stands tall to this day.

Founded in 1819 during a yellow-fever epidemic, the Church Street Graveyard is Mobile's oldest surviving cemetery. It is divided into three sections: Catholics in the east, Protestants in the north, and paupers in the south. (Paupers, presumably, were by definition un-Christian.) The entrance is at Church and Scott Streets, behind the public library.

Row, Row, Row Your Boat

Mobile

The late Lawrence Stauter was raised in a stilt house on Conway Creek in the Mobile Delta. Not surprisingly, since his family could scarcely step off the porch without one, he grew up with a deep and abiding respect for boats. Spurning the traditional family pursuits of trapping, fishing, and moonshining, Stauter started making and selling wooden boats in 1947. That first year he sold a hundred of them for $25 each.

For a generation Mobile outdoorsmen swore by their green and white "Stauter boats," handcrafted of cypress, mahogany, oak, and marine plywood. "If you keep 'em under a shed, hell, they'll last forever," Stauter used to say.

Stauter retired after Hurricane Frederic washed away his inventory in 1979, but he passed the business on to relatives. Wooden Stauter boats still are made the old-fashioned way and still are status symbols among those who ply the waters around Mobile.

Stauter Boat Works welcomes visitors to the shop at 4549 Clearview Drive. Clearview is off Three Notch Road west of I-10, southwest of downtown. For more information call (251) 666-1152 or (251) 666-7897 or visit www.stauterboats.com.

Wintzell's Oyster House
Mobile

Cigar-chomping oyster chef Oliver Wintzell long ago went to that great half shell in the sky, but some of the founder's eccentricities linger at Wintzell's Oyster House on Dauphin Street, which has served 'em up "fried, stewed, or nude" since 1938.

Judging from the photos all around, Wintzell would have been an easy Halloween costume to put together: Clark Kent eyeglasses, apron, scowl. The menu boasts a photo of the corpulent Wintzell asleep in his favorite booth. The food must be good!

The menu is a winning combination of high-minded instruction and shameless huckstering:

> Oysters are rich in protein; they also contain vitamins A, B, C, and D, plus phosphorus, copper, sulphur, manganese, and iodine. So rich in nutritive value are they that, with the addition of only one food, milk, as in oyster stew, they make a practically complete diet on which one can live and thrive.

✦ ✦

Wintzell's serves oysters on the half shell, oysters Rockefeller, oysters Buffalo, oysters Alfredo, oysters Parmesan, oysters Bienville (with shrimp and crabmeat in a Parmesan sauce), steamed oysters, oyster stew, and, of course, fried oysters, one of Oliver Wintzell's original secret recipes. During happy hour at the bar (4:00 p.m. to 7:00 p.m., Monday through Friday), raw oysters are 25 cents each. Other house specialties include fried pickles, fried oyster salad (for dieters), and West Indies salad, a pile of tender crabmeat in a tangy sauce, served with crackers.

Wintzell's interior walls are covered in witticisms coined or endorsed by the late owner:

HE WHO THINKS HE KNOWS IT ALL IS MOST ANNOYING TO THOSE OF US WHO DO.

BLUNT PEOPLE MAKE THE MOST POINTED REMARKS.

GOSSIP: LETTING THE CHAT OUT OF THE BAG.

DONALD DUCK IS A QUACK!

EVEN THE BEST FAMILY TREE HAS ITS SAP.

Other Wintzell's locations around Mobile and elsewhere in Alabama and Mississippi have the same menu and signs, but natives accept no substitutes for the original downtown eatery at 605 Dauphin Street, where you can watch the city pass by and listen for the ghost of Oliver Wintzell, snoring. Hours are from 11:00 a.m. to 10:00 p.m., Sunday through Thursday, and 11:00 a.m. to 11:00 p.m. on Friday and Saturday. For more information call (251) 432-4605 or visit www.wintzellsoysterhouse.com.

Edward O. Wilson and the Original Fire Ants

Mobile

Thirteen-year-old Edward O. Wilson of Mobile was one of those kids who would happily spend hours watching living things. A childhood accident had cost him his sight in one eye, and he seemed determined to see as much as possible out of the remaining one. He was especially fascinated by ants, in particular the ants in the vacant lot next to his

family's house on Charleston Street, near the docks on the western edge of Mobile Bay.

He didn't know it at the time, but young Wilson had made a breakthrough scientific discovery. That ant colony he studied and documented so carefully in 1942 turned out to be one of the first two recorded colonies of the red imported fire ant, *Solenopsis invicta*, in the United States.

Native to central South America, fire ants probably came ashore in North America on cargo unloaded at the Mobile docks, practically within sight of Wilson's boyhood home. Today, fire ants—so called because of their painful poisonous bite—infest hundreds of millions of acres in the Southeast and continue to spread across the nation.

Meanwhile, Edward O. Wilson, the kid from Mobile, has become what *New Scientist* calls "the world's leading authority on ants." (He was distracted only briefly, at age sixteen, by houseflies, but he decided against studying them because of a wartime shortage of pins.) As a young experimenter at Harvard, he proved that ants communicate chemically, telling one another, for example, to march single-file across long distances to reach a picnic. The communicative chemicals Wilson discovered in ants are now called pheromones, and they are known to operate in many other species as well.

Wilson also founded the science of sociobiology, the study of the social systems of animal species, and he is sometimes called "the father of biodiversity" for his long insistence that a multitude of plant and animal species is vital to life on Earth, including human life. To date he has won two Pulitzer Prizes for nonfiction, most recently for a book titled simply *The Ants*. And as he explains in his memoir, *Naturalist*, he started it all in a vacant lot in Mobile, staring at ants.

Close Encounters and Closer Encounters at Brookley

Mobile

To film his 1977 science fiction blockbuster *Close Encounters of the Third Kind*, director Steven Spielberg wanted the largest indoor stage he could find in the United States so his crew could build a convincing "runway for UFOs." He selected an old aircraft hangar at the former Brookley Air Force Base in Mobile.

For weeks Spielberg and his crew, including stars Richard Dreyfuss, Teri Garr, and François Truffaut, worked inside the vast, uncomfortable hangar, where eighty high-energy arc lights raised temperatures to 120 degrees. The set was 100 yards wide and 150 yards long, with an eight-story scaffold to hold the immense black backdrop that doubled as the night sky.

Few of the millions who saw the movie realized that some of Spielberg's most spectacular outdoor scenes were filmed indoors. The mountaintop highway where careening UFOs spook the townspeople actually was a set built inside the hangar. So was the Devil's Tower landing field that the mother ship visits at the movie's climax. In long shots all the outdoor landscapes surrounding the floodlit field are painted special effects.

The movie's other stars left Alabama long ago, but Georgia native Cary Guffey, who was four years old when he played the most famous UFO abductee in Hollywood history, graduated from Jacksonville State University in Jacksonville, Alabama, and became a financial planner in Birmingham.

Though it's not mentioned in the documentary on the *Close Encounters* DVD, for Spielberg to choose Brookley for his blockbuster UFO movie was an eerie coincidence. Between April 1950 and June 1954, a quarter century before Spielberg came to town, Brookley was the site of a series of UFO sightings later made famous by the air force investigation named Project Blue Book. The August 28, 1952, sighting was especially noteworthy because the objects were spotted both visually and on radar—suggesting that whatever they were, they were real.

Much of the old Brookley Air Force Base now is the 1,700-acre Brookley Complex, an industrial park between I-10 and Mobile Bay. Its Web site, www.brookleycomplex.com, mentions neither its UFO history nor its contributions to Spielberg's movie.

Steven Seagal's Most Expensive Movie Set
Mobile

The battleship U.S.S. *Alabama* is the star attraction at Battleship Memorial Park in Mobile. Its crews fought with great distinction in the Atlantic and Pacific during World War II and led the American fleet into Tokyo Bay. Thousands of visitors tour the great old ship in the spirit of patriotism, even reverence. But some are there only because they're Steven Seagal fans.

Under Siege, filmed mostly aboard the U.S.S. *Alabama* in Mobile Bay in 1992, is widely regarded as the best Steven Seagal action movie, among fans who don't mind using the words *best* and *Steven Seagal*

The sequel to the movie *Under Siege* was set aboard a train, but it couldn't compare to the U.S.S. *Alabama*.
COURTESY OF MOBILE BAY CVB

* *

movie in the same sentence. In *Under Siege,* terrorists led by Tommy Lee Jones and Gary Busey hijack a battleship but are foiled by the ship's cook, who just happens to be a one-man Special Forces unit (that would be Seagal). Also in the movie is Erika Eleniak, who was *Playboy*'s Miss July 1989. In the movie she plays *Playboy*'s Miss July 1989 and is surprisingly good at it. In one scene she hides in a giant cake, just like Debbie Reynolds in *Singin' in the Rain*. In another scene the cook tears out a bad guy's larynx. This movie was nominated for two Oscars: Best Picture and Best Actor. Just kidding. Actually, *Under Siege* was nominated for Sound and Sound Effects Editing but was robbed, man. It's who you know.

Battleship Memorial Park is on the bay just east of Mobile at 2703 Battleship Parkway, also known as US 90. From I-10, exits 27 or 30 will take you there. The park opens at 8:00 a.m. daily except Christmas and closes at 6:00 p.m. April through September and 4:00 p.m. during winter. Admission is charged. For more details call (251) 433-2703 or visit www.ussalabama.com.

More than Just a Pretty Face
Mobile

The America's Junior Miss Pageant traces its history back to the azalea queens crowned by the Mobile Jaycees in the 1920s, part of the Azalea Trail promotion that planted azaleas all over Mobile as a tourist lure.

The azalea queens led to the Azalea Trail Maids, which led in 1958 to the first Junior Miss America Pageant in Mobile's Saenger Theatre, with contestants from fifteen states. The winner was Phyllis Whitenack of West Virginia, who received a $5,000 scholarship. The next year, the program changed its name to the America's Junior Miss Pageant and has been going strong ever since.

Famous America's Junior Miss winners include *Newhart* costar Mary Frann (Junior Miss Missouri, 1961) and *Good Morning America* host Diane Sawyer (Junior Miss Kentucky, 1963). Other contestants who didn't win the national event but did just fine nonetheless include

Oscar-winning actress Kim Basinger (Junior Miss Georgia, 1969), *Inside Edition* host Deborah Norville (Junior Miss Georgia, 1976), and *Will & Grace* star Debra Messing (Junior Miss Rhode Island, 1986).

The pageant takes place each June at the Mobile Civic Center Theater but has not been televised since 2005. To learn more log onto www.ajm.org.

They Don't Faint; They Just Seize Up

Mobile

Alan and Sharon Reeves of Mobile run R Fainting Farm (www.goat spots.com/rfaintingfarm.htm), where they raise fainting goats (a.k.a. "myotonic goats," "wooden leg goats," and "stiff leg" goats).

These rare goats, native to the United States, don't really faint, but they do tend to painlessly fall over when excited because of a muscle condition called myotonia congenita—hence "myotonic goats." Dr. D. Phillip Sponenberg explains how this muscle condition works at the Web site of the International Fainting Goat Association (www.fainting-goatsite.com/myotonia.htm):

> When muscles fire rapidly in a myotonic animal, they cannot quickly relax, resulting in a prolonged contraction. . . . It is an interesting condition and is painless. . . . The animals do not truly "faint" in any sense of the word, as they never lose consciousness because of the condition. They remain fully conscious.

There are fewer than 10,000 fainting goats in the world, but Alabama has its share. The Fainting Goat Directory at GoatFinder.com—yes, you can find everything online—lists among Alabama breeders not only the Reeveses but also Douglas Helms of Louisville and Sarah Matthews of Pleasant Hill Acres in Decatur (www.pleasanthillacres.com).

Cudjo Lewis and Africatown
Mobile

In front of Union Baptist Church in the section called Africatown is a bust of the late Cudjo Lewis, who for many years was this neighborhood's most famous resident: He was the last survivor of the last slave ship to reach the United States.

The African slave trade had been outlawed by Congress in 1808, but as the Civil War approached, proslavery forces in the South agitated to start it up again. A wealthy Mobile secessionist sent one of his schooners, the *Clotilde*, to Africa with orders to bring back slaves. By the time the *Clotilde* returned to Mobile Bay with more than a hundred captive members of the Turkbar tribe, from what is now known as Ghana, the federal government had learned of the plan. The skipper eluded arrest just long enough to secretly unload his human cargo, then burn and sink his own vessel one night in 1859.

The West Africans settled north of Mobile and preserved as much of their tribal society as they could. A chieftain arbitrated differences, and a tribal healer did their doctoring. Lewis, the last survivor of the original group, became a celebrity during the Harlem Renaissance of the 1920s, as writers and folklorists such as Zora Neale Hurston traveled to Mobile to interview him. Hurston called him Kossula, an approximation of his African name. Anthropologists excavated the wreck of the *Clotilde* and presented wooden fragments of it to Lewis, who gave them in turn to visitors he especially liked. *Clotilde* fragments sell today for as much as $25,000.

To the end of his long life, Lewis said he missed his home in West Africa. "I lonely for my folks," he told one visitor. He died in 1935.

In recent years civic leaders, including Lewis's descendants, have promoted the old Africatown neighborhood as a tourist attraction. Union Baptist Church is in the middle of Africatown, at 506 Bay Bridge Road at the corner of Timothy Avenue. Bay Bridge Road connects US 43 and Interstate 165 north of downtown Mobile.

Exhibits about Africatown and the survivors and descendants of the

This memorial to Cudjo Lewis marks the centennial of his arrival in Mobile Bay. COURTESY OF MOBILE BAY CVB

Clotilde can be found at the National African-American Archives and Museum at 564 Martin Luther King Jr. Drive in Mobile. For more information call (251) 433-8511.

Mock Me, Bird, and I'll Kill You

Monroeville

The two most famous Alabama writers of the twentieth century— Harper Lee, who wrote *To Kill a Mockingbird*, and Truman Capote, who wrote *In Cold Blood*, *Breakfast at Tiffany's*, and "A Christmas Memory"—were childhood neighbors in Monroeville who wrote about the place as adults. In 1997 the Alabama legislature proclaimed Monroeville the official Literary Capital of Alabama.

The Monroeville tourist industry peaks each spring, when a play based on *To Kill a Mockingbird* is staged downtown in the old Monroe County courthouse in the very courtroom where Harper Lee's father, the model for Atticus Finch, argued cases. Tickets for the play go on sale in March—earlier for members of the Monroe County Heritage Museums—and sell out immediately.

Contrary to popular opinion the celebrated movie of *To Kill a Mockingbird*, which won Gregory Peck an Academy Award, was filmed not in Monroeville but on a beautifully constructed set in California that duplicated the Monroeville courtroom. The movie did, however, star two Alabama child actors, Mary Badham and Phillip Alford, as the two Finch children. Alford became a businessman in Birmingham, Badham an art restorer and college administrator in Virginia. (Her brother, John Badham, became a successful Hollywood director of such movies as *Saturday Night Fever*.) Mary Badham typically comes to Monroeville for the final performance of *To Kill a Mockingbird* each spring.

Also contrary to popular opinion, the movie's Alabama premiere was in Mobile, not Monroeville. In spring 1963 *To Kill a Mockingbird* played for a week at the Monroe Theatre in Monroeville and another week at the nearby Grove Hill drive-in. The Monroe Theatre offered a $10 prize to the first five customers to bring in a live mockingbird.

Harper Lee's father argued cases in the old
Monroe County Courthouse, just like Atticus
Finch in Lee's novel *To Kill a Mockingbird.* NIKI
SEPSAS

Truman Capote died in 1984. Harper Lee, whose first name is Nelle and who is known as "Miss Nelle" to everyone in Monroeville, divides her time between New York City and her hometown, and her celebrated decades-long refusal to grant interviews makes visitors all the more determined to catch a glimpse of her. Good luck!

The Old Courthouse Museum is open from 8:00 a.m. to 4:00 p.m., Monday through Friday, and 10:00 a.m. to 2:00 p.m., Saturday. Admission is free. A gift shop sells *Mockingbird* memorabilia such as posters, T-shirts, handheld fans, and copies of the all-*Mockingbird* winter 1994 issue of the *Alabama Law Review*. Countless lawyers and judges in Alabama say they were inspired by Atticus Finch's fictional example, and the Alabama Bar Association paid for the statue of Atticus Finch on the courthouse lawn. The museum is located at 31 North Alabama Avenue.

Visitors often stop for a burger or a shake at Mel's Dairy Dream, 216 South Alabama Avenue, (251) 743-2483, which sits on the site of the long-gone house where Harper Lee grew up.

For more details on all things Monroeville, including play tickets, call the Monroe County Heritage Museum at (251) 575-7433 or visit www.tokillamockingbird.com.

Giant Metal Marlin

Orange Beach

The entrance to SanRoc Cay Marina is hard to miss, thanks to its giant sheet-metal marlin perpetually leaping over a fountain. Designed and built by brothers Larry and Ronald Godwin of Art Wurks in Brundidge, Alabama, the marlin had a police escort on its 150-mile trip to Orange Beach.

The marina has shops, restaurants (including the highly recommended SanRoc Delicatezza deli and gourmet shop), charter boats, fishing tournaments, and outdoor music in the courtyard on weekends.

The marina and its marlin are at 27267 Perdido Beach Boulevard, a.k.a. Coastal Highway 182. For more details call (251) 981-5423 or log onto www.sanroccay.com.

✦ ✦

Interstate Mullet Toss

Orange Beach

Throw a dollar across the Potomac, and you're minus a dollar. Throw a mullet from Alabama into Florida, and presto! You get one of the biggest annual parties on the Gulf Coast.

The Interstate Mullet Toss is always held on the last full weekend in April at the Flora-Bama Lounge & Package Store, which calls itself "the last great American roadhouse." The Flora-Bama Web site, www.flora-bama.com, offers a helpful FAQ about the Mullet Toss:

What Is a Mullet?

A mullet is one of the more popular and plentiful fish indigenous to this area. It is the only fish with a gizzard and is said to possess mystical properties.

To paraphrase Jimmy Buffett: The Flora-Bama Lounge & Package Store is the place your parents warned you about. NIKE SEPSAS

What Is a Mullet Toss?

A Mullet Toss consists of individuals on the beach throwing a mullet from a 10-foot circle in Alabama across the state line into Florida. . . .

Are the Mullet Alive?

No.

What Happens to Mullet after the Mullet Toss?

We feed them to the birds.

The mullet-tossing record is held by Josh Serotum, who in 2004 hit 189 feet, 8 inches in his first toss and 174 feet, 3 inches in his second toss.

The Flora-Bama Lounge & Package Store is officially located at 17401 Perdido Key Drive in Perdido Key, Florida, but it has two phone numbers, an Alabama one (251-980-5118) and a Florida one (850-492-0611). While you're there, pick up a copy of the latest "Men of the Redneck Riviera" calendar. Like the Mullet Toss, it benefits charity. Really.

Maybe He Took Independence Too Literally

Perdue Hill

William Barrett Travis, the colorful rogue who became a Texas hero by dying in command of the Alamo in 1836, had been a pillar of the community of Claiborne, Alabama. He was an attorney, a newspaper publisher, a member of the Masonic lodge, and an officer in the Alabama militia. He also had a wife, a child, and a baby on the way.

Yet he abandoned career and family and skipped town, settling in Anahuac, Texas, in 1831. He told everyone he was single and started a bilingual diary detailing his sexual exploits with dozens of women. His wife, Rosanna Travis, finally showed up in Texas, children in tow, demanding a divorce on charges of desertion, which she got in 1834. By then her ex-husband was caught up in the armed struggle for Texas independence, a struggle that killed him at age twenty-six and, in a sense, made him immortal.

★ ★

Why Travis left Alabama has been gossiped about for nearly 200 years. Some people say he learned, or suspected, that his wife's unborn child was not his. Some say he killed a man whom he caught with his wife. Some say he got fed up with Alabama politics—always a possibility, today as then. Some say that he came home from a business trip to find that some scalawag had cut off his horse's tail, and that was the last straw. Some say he owed more money in Alabama than he felt like repaying. But the chief reason may have been simply that the Mexican government, to encourage immigration, was offering any American man 4,000 acres of land and Texas citizenship for a mere $30. Travis wasn't the only wayward husband who found that offer too good to pass up.

The two-room cottage where Travis and his family once lived now is on display on US 84 in Perdue Hill, a few miles east of Claiborne.

Those Pesky Mosquitos

Dr. Josiah Nott of nearby Mobile suggested in 1848—correctly, as it turned out—that the culprit behind the yellow fever epidemics that devastated Blakeley and countless other communities might be the mosquito, but no one in the medical community followed up on the suggestion until a Cuban doctor, Carlos Finlay, presented the same theory at a conference in 1881.

Proving Finlay's theory correct in the early twentieth century were Dr. Walter Reed and another Alabamian, Dr. William Crawford Gorgas, who eliminated yellow fever first from Cuba and then from Panama and made the building of the Panama Canal possible.

★ ★

Goat Man Parade
Prichard

A Mardi Gras celebration unique to this historic, mostly African American suburb of Mobile is the Goat Man Parade, which begins at noon on the Saturday before Fat Tuesday. Founded in 1996 and run by an organization that calls itself the Krewe of Goats, it commemorates the original Goat Man, a kindly 1920s eccentric who rolled around the dirt streets of Prichard each Mardi Gras in a cart pulled by a dozen goats, throwing homemade trinkets to the neighbors. No longer a one-person event, the Goat Man Parade now is a seventy-five-unit extravaganza led by a ceremonial Goat Master and, of course, two actual goats.

Nutria Rodeo
Spanish Fort

In William Goldman's comic-fantasy novel *The Princess Bride*, the hero and heroine are attacked in a swamp by ROUS, "Rodents of Unusual Size." Goldman might have been thinking of that infamous Alabama swamp critter, the nutria.

A nutria isn't exactly a rat. It has the tail of a rat, yes, but the head of a beaver and webbed hind feet. It's much bigger than a rat, too: An adult nutria can weigh twenty pounds and reach 2 feet long, not counting the tail. Nutria do breed like rats, though. So you begin to see the error of the various Gulf Coast entrepreneurs—including, in Louisiana, E. A. "Mr. Ned" McIlhenny, heir to the Tabasco sauce fortune—who got into the nutria business in the 1930s, hoping to raise the Argentinian critters in the United States and market their fur. The 1941 hurricane spread the nutria around a bit, and in their new quarters they happily set about doing that thing that nutria do so well. By the 1960s nutria had overrun the Gulf Coast and were literally devouring thousands of acres of marshland.

In the name of pest control, the Mobile County Wildlife and Conservation Association launched an annual nutria hunt, the Nutria Rodeo. Once a year, hundreds of hunters paddled into the swamps of the

★ ★

Mobile Delta, used fires and dogs to flush the nutria out of hiding, and then shot the critters from their boats. Then everyone headed back to Trader George's bar in Spanish Fort to party and crown a Nutria Rodeo Queen, a young woman typically wearing little but strategic nutria pelts, a la Raquel Welch in *One Million Years B.C.*

Like most such critter roundups nationwide, the Nutria Rodeo disappeared years ago, a casualty of changing attitudes toward animal rights—even the rights of nutria. Besides, the alligators came back, and more alligators mean fewer nutria. But Trader George's is still around. Now called Traders on the Causeway, the popular nightspot is at 4015 Battleship Parkway, a.k.a. US 98, just north of I-10 on Ducker Bay. Women wearing as little attire as that of a Nutria Rodeo Queen are still welcome. For more information call (251) 626-5630.

Ghost Town of Blakeley
Spanish Fort

Historic Blakeley State Park on the Tensaw River is a wilderness laced with hiking and biking trails, its 400-year-old oaks eerie reminders of how fleeting "civilization" can be. Only fliers and signs remind the visitor that this once was the site of a city that rivaled Mobile in size and importance. The park calls itself "the South's most beautiful ghost town."

Plantation owner Josiah Blakeley, a Connecticut native, moved to Mobile in 1806, when living there still meant swearing an oath of loyalty to the Spanish Crown. He bought land on the Tensaw and hired a surveyor to plot a town that was incorporated January 6, 1814. When Blakeley died the next year, his town looked well on its way to permanent success. By 1822 it had several thousand people—more than Mobile had across the bay—as well as mansions, churches, a newspaper, a hotel, a ferry service, and the first Baldwin County courthouse.

What killed the town, and many of its inhabitants, was yellow fever. Epidemics swept Blakeley in 1822, 1826, and 1828. No one yet understood what caused the disease, and they didn't stick around the seemingly cursed town to find out.

How Big Was It?

Washington County is the oldest county in Alabama, created in 1800 as the eastern half of the Mississippi Territory. At that time Washington County was 300 miles wide and 88 miles deep, with an area of more than 26,000 square miles.

Decade after decade, it was carved up into smaller counties, even bisected by a state line. Sixteen Mississippi counties and twenty-nine Alabama counties were created from Washington County, and does Washington County ever get a word of thanks? Do those younger counties ever call? Do they ever write?

The county seat, Chatom, lies on Highway 56 between U.S. Highways 43 and 45, two major north-south routes to Mobile and the beach. Wherever you cross the Washington County line, even if you're just driving through, be respectful. Remember, it used to be bigger than West Virginia.

By 1860 Blakeley was a ghost town, inhabited only by the soldiers who manned the earthen fortifications of Fort Blakely. (With military precision the second e had been struck from the record.) On April 9, 1865—the same day as a rather more famous battle in Appomattox, Virginia—Fort Blakely's 4,000 Confederate defenders were overrun by 16,000 Union attackers. These were amazing numbers, considering the entire population of Baldwin County in 1860 was a mere 8,000 people. More amazing to the locals was the fact that about half the Union troops were black. Alabamians note that the Battle of Blakely took place six hours after the Battle of Appomattox, making theirs the last major bloodletting of the Civil War.

Its 3,800 acres make Historic Blakeley State Park the largest National Historic Register site east of the Mississippi, with prehistoric Indian mounds, 15 miles of trails, and 5 miles of Civil War fortifications. Primitive campsites and cabins are available.

The entrance to Historic Blakeley State Park is on Highway 225 about 4 miles north of Spanish Fort and I-10. For more information call (251) 626-0798 or visit www.blakeleypark.com.

Cooling Board
Wagarville

One of the oldest buildings in Washington County is the four-bedroom log cabin built in Wagarville in 1874 by Civil War veteran Gibeon Sullivan. Still intact on its front porch is the three-plank "cooling board" that made the cabin a gathering place for the whole town.

In the days before funerals became an industry, cooling boards were the low tables on which the bodies of the recently deceased were laid out for public viewing. (Hence Blind Willie McTell's old blues song "Cooling Board Blues.") Sullivan's cooling board was detachable so that it could be loaded onto a wagon and used to transport the body back to the house.

Sullivan's "dogtrot" cabin, so called because dogs could trot through the open hallway that bisected the house, is on Sullivan's Lane on the banks of Bassett Creek, just off US 43 about a mile and a half north of Wagarville.

2

East Central

It would be *unjust to say the most interesting thing in east central Alabama is a big hole in the ground, but the Wetumpka Astrobleme—what nonscientists would call a meteor crater—is a truly remarkable 4-mile-wide reminder of the Earth's past and, just possibly, its future. Other area attractions are in a state of flux: The World's Largest Chair is now only the World's Largest* **Office** *Chair, while the Choccolocco Monster was recently captured, identified, and presented to a grateful world. (His name is Neal Williamson.) Anniston's World War I monument is notable not for being unique but for being so utterly commonplace; indeed, it may be the most often viewed U.S. statue, after the one on Liberty Island. Area sports legends include blind golfer Charley Boswell and trick archer Howard Hill, Errol Flynn's stand-in. We're told there's some sort of annual sporting event at Talladega, but readers of this book will be more interested in the town's possible claim as the site of the first manned airplane flight, years before what's-their-names at Kitty Hawk. Visitors to Lake Martin can stay overnight in the cabin where Hank Williams wrote "Your Cheatin' Heart," preferably with their own spouses. Speaking of tearjerkers, the playhouse on Nadine Earles's grave is surely the most heart wrenching attraction in the state, though the grave of Fred the Town Dog of Rockford may be a close second. The few remaining (and apparently misnamed) Alabama Indestructible Dolls are, to some, more creepy than poignant, but they're worth seeing, as are the World War II espionage artifacts at the Berman Museum; even Howard Hill at his showiest couldn't match the gun that fires around corners.*

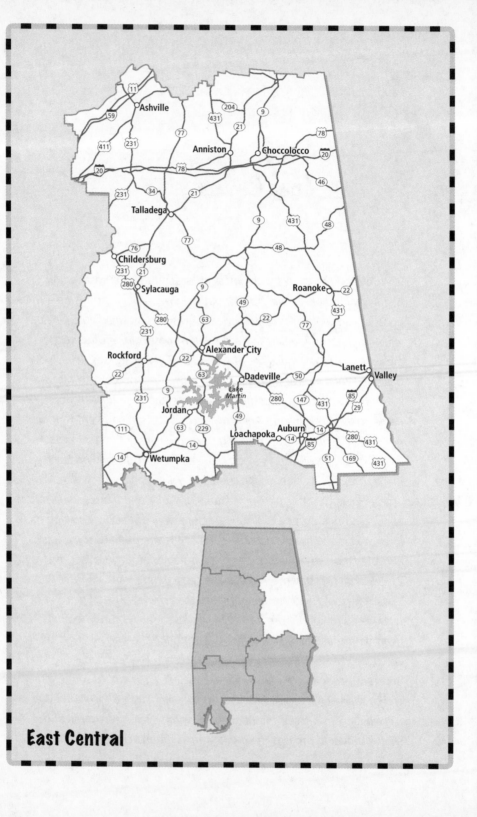

East Central

You Won't See These Islands on Survivor

Alexander City

The Tallapoosa River was dammed in the 1920s to form Lake Martin, then the world's largest man-made lake—44,000 acres, with 750 miles of shoreline. Three of the lake's many islands are especially interesting:

- Goat Island, just north of the dam, is home to a family of goats. Boaters like to bring them lettuce and fruit.
- Neptune Island in Parker Creek is marked by a statue of Neptune, the Roman god of the sea.
- Graveyard Island is an old cemetery protected by a circular seawall 30 yards across. The graves date from the 1880s to the 1920s, when the area was flooded to form the lake. Visible from the Bay Pines lake properties, it's popular with boaters who tether to the seawall and walk among the tombstones to read the inscriptions.

For more on Lake Martin's islands, and to purchase a map to help you find them, visit www.lakemartin.com/Islands.asp.

The Martin Hydro Plant's visitor center (800-525-3711) is located on Highway 50 east of the Tallapoosa River bridge. Or visit Wind Creek State Park (256-329-0845), 7 miles southeast of Alexander City off Highway 63; see www.stateparks.com/wind_creek.html.

This Chair Is Too Big!

Anniston

Ten tons of steel went into the 33-foot World's Largest Office Chair, erected by Miller's Office Furniture in 1981.

Once it was known as the World's Largest Chair, but since 1995 that title has been held by one in Manzano, Italy, where a third of the world's chairs are manufactured. The Manzano chair is 65½ feet tall, the height of a seven-story building. It's not an office chair, though.

The World's Largest Office Chair is outside Miller's Office Furniture, 625 Noble Street, at the corner of Sixth Street, 2 blocks west of U.S. Highway 431. For more information call (256) 237-1641.

★ ★

The Museum Paris Didn't Need
Anniston

Most of the people who walk into the Berman Museum have come to
see Hitler's tea service and only Hitler's tea service—which is a shame,
not because Hitler's tea service isn't cool (it is) but because it's only the
start of the cool stuff in this wholly unexpected small-town museum.

The Berman Museum displays the collection of artwork and artifacts
amassed through the decades by two of Anniston's most colorful residents, the late husband-and-wife team of Farley and Germaine Berman. They met in North Africa during World War II, when Germaine
was with French intelligence and Farley was with the U.S. Office of
Strategic Services, the predecessor of the CIA. "I was spying on her,
and she was spying on me," Farley liked to say.

After the war they continued to travel the globe collecting things,
until the city of Anniston built a museum to house it all. When out-
of-towners expressed surprise that the Bermans elected to keep their
collection in Anniston, Farley replied that their favorite cities were
Anniston and Paris, and Paris "doesn't need any more museums."

Given the Bermans' line of work, it's unsurprising to find that the
Berman collection is particularly strong in espionage devices: a German
bent-barrel gun that fires around corners; guns disguised as door keys,
flutes, ink pens, cigarette lighters, walking canes, even a box of throat
lozenges; a Liberator pistol, one of a million mass-produced by General
Motors and smuggled to resistance fighters across Europe with a word-
less set of instructions drawn in the form of a comic strip; and the Holy
Grail of WWII cryptography, an Enigma machine. And, yes, Hitler's tea
service. Plus, as a nineteenth-century bonus, Napoleon's ivory-handled
grooming kit, right down to the great man's tweezers.

The Berman Museum is at 840 Museum Drive in Lagarde Park, at
US 431 and Highway 21, 7 miles north of Interstate 20 (exit 185). It's
open from 10:00 a.m. to 5:00 p.m., Tuesday through Saturday, and

from 1:00 p.m. to 5:00 p.m. on Sunday; in summer months it's open Monday, too. Admission is charged. For more details call (256) 237-6261 or log onto www.bermanmuseum.org.

Spirit of the American Doughboy
Anniston

A bronze statue titled *Spirit of the American Doughboy* stands atop the World War I memorial in Anniston. Its sculptor, E. M. Viquesney of Georgia, was clearly onto a good thing in the years after the Great War.

Viquesney used to claim that at least one of his Doughboys was on display in every state, but Earl D. Goldsmith of Texas, who has tracked the statue with an admirable degree of good-humored obsession (at http://doughboy_lamp.tripod.com/earlspages/), has found examples in only thirty-nine states—142 Doughboys in all, including three in Alabama, though Anniston's is the oldest.

Earl estimates that Viquesney's *Doughboy* accounts for more than 10 percent of all World War I statues in the United States and may be the most-viewed sculpture in America after the Statue of Liberty.

Alabama locations:

Anniston: Center of Quintard Avenue, a.k.a. U.S. Highway 431, between Twelfth and Thirteenth Streets. (Dedicated November 11, 1921)

Bessemer: DeBardeleben Park, bounded by Second and Third Avenues and Sixteenth and Seventeenth Streets. (Dedicated November 11, 1922)

Birmingham: Linn Park, Twentieth Street North and Park Place entrance. (Dedicated November 11, 1923)

Anniston's World War I statue is the opposite of unique. NIKI SEPSAS

The View from a Pew

Anniston

The Church of St. Michael and All Angels, an 1890 Episcopal church designed by William Hulsey Wood, has several unusual features.

The most striking element in the sanctuary may be the ceiling, hand-carved of Alabama longleaf pine in the shape of the ribs of a ship. This symbolizes the church as God's ark, a vessel that carries its members safely home. At the end of each beam is the head of an angel; all the heads face the altar.

The stained-glass windows on the east and west walls of the sanctuary depict incidents in the life of Christ. The Madonna and Child window, the second one on the east, is by Louis Comfort Tiffany, son of the famous jeweler. The back wall, bereft of windows, symbolizes the eighteen years of Christ's life for which there is no biblical record.

The church also houses a Coptic cross that was a gift from the late Ethiopian emperor Haile Selassie.

The Church of St. Michael and All Angels is at 1000 West Eighteenth Street, 12 blocks west of Quintard Avenue, a.k.a. US 431, and is open daily from 8:00 a.m. to 4:00 p.m. For more information call (205) 237-4011 or visit www.stmaaa.org.

How Ty Cobb Became an "Overnight" Success

Anniston

For generations Zinn Park has been a popular green space in downtown Anniston, but it's especially interesting to baseball fans. Long ago Zinn Park had a resident Southeastern League baseball team, the Anniston Steelers. And in 1904 Zinn Park briefly was the home field of a ferocious eighteen-year-old center fielder from Narrows, Georgia: Tyrus Raymond "Ty" Cobb.

Cobb had been let go by the Augusta, Georgia, minor-league club after playing two whole games, and he tagged along to Anniston with his friend Thad Hayes, who was in a similar predicament. Just

★ ★

before he left Augusta, Cobb called his father on the telephone and told him he was going to try again in Alabama. According to Cobb's memoirs his father said: "Go after it. And I want to tell you one other thing—Don't come home a failure."

Cobb's memories of his time with the Steelers included "one of the best fights I was ever in." In a game against the Oxford, Georgia, team, Cobb hit for the cycle—meaning he got a single, a double, a triple, and a home run in the same game, a rare achievement for any player. Late in the game, he thought he had hit a second home run, but he was called out, either because (according to the umpire) the Oxford outfielder intercepted the ball just before it cleared the fence or (according to Cobb) because the Oxford outfielder pulled a spare ball from his pocket to make it look as if he had caught Cobb's liner. Either way, the indignant Cobb slugged the outfielder, and a battle royal ensued. For the first time in his career, Cobb was ejected from a game.

Cobb played well during his three months in Anniston, but word of his exploits did not reach Georgia. At the time the Southeastern League was at the bottom of the baseball barrel, beneath the notice of sportswriters and major league scouts. The sports editor of the *Atlanta Journal* in those days was Grantland Rice, a twenty-four-year-old Tennessean who later would become a legendary sports figure himself. To get Rice's attention, Cobb started sending him postcards and telegrams, all signed with different fake names, bragging on the talents of this wonderful kid Cobb in Anniston. Finally, Rice ran a small item in the paper, and the Augusta Tourists sent Cobb a telegram, asking him to return.

In fall 1905 the Augusta team sold Cobb's services to the Detroit Tigers. Thirty-one years later—after 4,191 hits, 2,245 runs, 892 stolen bases, and a career batting average of .367—the Georgia Peach became one of the first players elected to the Baseball Hall of Fame.

Zinn Park is at West Fourteenth Street and Gurnee Avenue, a few blocks west of US 431.

Howard Hill's tombstone ought to depict his cool splitting-an-arrow-with-an-arrow trick. NIKI SEPSAS

Errol Flynn's Stunt Double

Ashville

In the Ashville City Cemetery is a simple headstone for one Howard Hill, 1899–1975. To either side of the name are two engraved long-bows, each with arrows cocked and ready to fire. It's a fitting memorial for an internationally renowned athlete best remembered as Robin Hood's stand-in.

Hill was the prototype of what we now would call an extreme sportsman. A burly man who stood 6-foot-2, he was a football, basketball, and baseball star at Auburn University who later made a living as a golf pro and a semiprofessional baseball player. He took up archery relatively late, after reading a book about it, and became a tireless promoter of the sport and of his own talents.

He gave trick-shot performances not only at sportsmen's gatherings but at world's fairs and Wild West shows. He spent years in Hollywood, letting arrows fly in a number of movies starring his friend Errol

49

Flynn. All the trick shots seemingly done by Flynn in the 1938 classic
The Adventures of Robin Hood were really done by Hill, who also had
a small role as the captain of the archers. Hill starred in twenty-three
Warner Bros. short subjects and one RKO feature, *Tembo*. In Chicago
in 1941 he drew a crowd of 35,000 and had his shirt ripped off by
adoring fans.

But Hill was most interested in the bow and arrow as a weapon,
and during his many hunting trips in Africa and North America, he
bagged many thousands of animals, keeping careful record of the
tally by species: one elephant seal, two black mambas, two Thomson's
gazelles, two greater bustards, three bat-eared foxes, four gila monsters, six lesser bustards, six loggerhead turtles, twelve wild jackasses,
thirteen crocodiles, forty sharks, and so forth. He lost count of rabbits,
penciling in an estimated career total of 1,500. On February 27, 1950,
Hill became the first white man on record to kill an elephant with a
bow and arrow; he later downed two more.

Hill's nickname was Ol' One-Shot, a nickname fellow Alabamian
Harper Lee later bestowed on Atticus Finch, hero of her novel *To Kill
a Mockingbird*. Hill wrote a book about his exploits titled *Wild Adventure*, with a foreword by Flynn, who knew something about wild
adventures himself. The 2003 two-disc special-edition DVD release of
The Adventures of Robin Hood has footage of Hill in a behind-the-
scenes documentary.

You'll find the cemetery on Highway 23 just southwest of downtown.

Tigers on the Prowl

Auburn

Tigers on the Prowl was a 2001 public art project sponsored by the
City of Auburn Chamber of Commerce and inspired by Chicago's 1999
Cows on Parade project. Twenty-five life-size fiberglass tigers, variously
decorated, went on display all over town and then were auctioned
off for charity. Why tigers? Because the tiger is the mascot of Auburn
University and Auburn High School, of course.

This Auburn tiger would only be camouflaged in one cra-a-a-a-azy jungle, man. NIKI SEPSAS

Since fiberglass isn't heavy, stealing tigers by dark of night became a popular Auburn pastime among pranksters and souvenir hunters, but some of the tigers are still on public display.

The fire department (359 East Magnolia Avenue) has one with red, white, and blue legs, as if it waded through a Fourth of July parade. The public library (749 East Thach Avenue) has a black one with a red and white ladybug design on its back. The one atop the high school (405 South Dean Road) is blue. City Hall (144 Tichenor Avenue) has a gray one. The Hilton Garden Inn (2555 Hilton Garden Drive, at exit 57 off Interstate 85) has a blue-green hippie tiger covered with colorful flowers. And Arby's (1711 South College Street) has a tiger that's colored like a tiger. Imagine.

★ ★

All the Kudzu You Can Drink
Auburn

In the 1930s and 1940s, the federal government paid Southern farmers to plant kudzu, touting the Japanese vine as a miraculous forage
crop that controlled erosion. It proved miraculous, all right: It grows 60
feet a year, smothers the native plants, and is impervious to herbicides.

The late novelist Oxford Stroud, author of *Marbles* and *To Yield a
Dream*, taught for many years in Auburn University's English depart-
ment. One way Stroud ensured students' admiration and allegiance
was by serving them kudzu tea. Stroud's recipe is preserved in Max
Shores's documentary *The Amazing Story of Kudzu*, produced for the
University of Alabama Center for Public Television and Radio.

Stroud advises the selection of tender kudzu leaves in spring or early
summer, with the caution to avoid herbicides as well as poison oak
and poison ivy, as they can resemble kudzu. After drying the leaves,
steep them in boiling water. Variations include adding salt for a savory
pot-liquor flavor, honey for sweetening, or molasses for medicinal pur-
poses. Stroud called the molasses elixir "healthy but horrible!"

Hernando's Hideaway
Childersburg

The Spanish explorer Hernando de Soto is no hero to Native Americans, whose ancestors he enslaved and killed as he plundered the
Southeast looking for gold. But at DeSoto Caverns Park, one of
Alabama's oldest tourist attractions, de Soto has become a Disneyfied
mascot, a grinning cartoon conquistador named Happy Hernando.

Though de Soto did visit this area in 1540, there is no evidence he
visited the cave, which held the sacred burial grounds of a local tribe.
One I. W. Wright did visit the cave in 1723, carving his name and the
year into the rock before the Indians killed him for intruding. Wright
would be forgotten today if not for his dubious achievement of creating the earliest cave graffiti in the United States (still on display today).

During Prohibition the cave housed an infamous speakeasy known
as the Bloody Bucket. Revelers with snootfuls used to shoot stalactites

off the ceiling. The cave opened to tourists in 1965 as KyMulga Onyx Cave. Ten years later, the owner, tired of telling people how to pronounce "KyMulga Onyx," renamed it DeSoto Caverns.

The cave's biggest room, the Great Onyx Cathedral, is larger than a football field and has a ceiling higher than a twelve-story building. The waterfall is man-made, the cave fish are store bought, and the subterranean laser show has a different Christian message for each holiday season. Aboveground there are other rides and attractions, including Happy's Potty Racers, which are wheeled toilets with handlebars.

DeSoto Caverns Park is on Highway 76, 5 miles east of Childersburg. It's open from 9:00 a.m. to 5:30 p.m. every day but Sunday, when the hours are 1:00 to 5:30 p.m.; in winter the park closes an hour earlier. Cavern tours leave hourly on the half hour. Admission is charged. For more details call (800) 933-2283 or visit www.desotocavernspark.com.

Move Over, Pilgrims
Childersburg

Childersburg claims to have been continuously occupied since at least 1540, when the Spanish conquistador Hernando de Soto discovered a Coosa Indian town on the site. If you squint, that makes Childersburg the oldest community in the United States; St. Augustine, Florida, wasn't founded for another twenty-five years.

The Coosa chief treated de Soto and his men with great hospitality for a month, after which the well-fed, well-rested de Soto seized the chief and a number of his tribesmen as slaves and marched off with them, never to return. But the Coosa town was still there 250 years later, when an emissary from President George Washington visited it.

Childersburg became a World War II boomtown thanks to the 13,000-acre ammunition plant built there, in great secrecy, by the Pentagon. More than 25,000 people from all over the United States worked in Childersburg for the duration of the war, five times the town's present population. Today, the old Alabama Army Ammunition Plant is a wilderness along the Coosa River north of town, along Highway 235.

Interesting Alabama Town Names That Were Changed (for Good Reason)

Bankston (Fayette County) once was Bucksnort.

Brownville (Tuscaloosa County) once was Hog Eye, as in "small as a hog eye."

Cullomburg (Choctaw County) once was Redemption, named by a poor man who made good.

Delmar (Winston County), **Elyton** (Jefferson County), **and Fayette** (Fayette County) all once were named Frog Level.

Gardendale (Jefferson County) once was Jugtown, home of a jug factory.

Kellys Crossroads (Coosa County) once was Devil's Half Acre, site of an infamous saloon

Monterey (Butler County) once was Gobblersville.

Natural Bridge (Winston County) once was Low Die.

Oxford (Calhoun County) once was Lickskillet.

Pleasant Grove (Jefferson County) once was Frog Pond.

Prices (Calhoun County) once was Savages. The Prices and Savages were both local families.

Santuck (Elmore County) once was Flea Hop.

Stanley Crossroads (Escambia County) once was Sardine.

Southside (Etowah County) once was Smoke Neck.

Summit (Blount County) once was Shanty.

Hey! That Monster Looks Like Neal

Choccolocco

In May 1969 spooked drivers started calling the sheriff's office and the newspaper to report a monster in the woods between Choccolocco and Iron City, on the lonely road known as the Iron City Cutoff.

As headlights approached, the awful thing would rear up on its hind legs and threaten to jump into the road. "I just knowed the booger had me for sure," one terrified witness reported. At least eight people reported seeing the thing. They agreed it had big teeth, a huge head, and a shaggy pelt and was about the size of a cow.

Most locals scoffed, saying a cow was exactly what it was, or at worst a bear. But the whole United States had Bigfoot fever in 1969—the infamous "Patterson film," since discredited, had surfaced two years before—and shaggy monsters in the woods were newsworthy. The Choccolocco Monster made headlines, and both locals and out-of-towners took to cruising the Calhoun County backroads, hoping to photograph, capture, or kill the beastie.

None ever succeeded. Soon the sightings petered out, the out-of-towners went home, and the monster became one of those abiding mysteries remembered only by locals and connoisseurs of "cryptozoology" (the pursuit of creatures unknown to science).

More than thirty years later, on Halloween 2001, Neal Williamson confessed to the *Anniston Star* newspaper that he had been the Choccolocco Monster. At the time he was only fifteen and didn't have a driver's license, much less parental permission to take the family's 1950 Ford out at night; he had to hot-wire it so he could drive far enough into the countryside. Wearing a bedsheet or a long black coat, holding a cow skull over his head, and dancing by the side of the road, the young prankster had a high old time scaring drivers for several nights until a driver scared him back by firing a rifle at him, whereupon the Choccolocco Monster turned tail and ran into permanent retirement.

"Back then, you didn't have nothing to do, really," Williamson told

★ ★

the newspaper. "You didn't have computers. You just had to create your own fun."

Williamson's confession made him a brief celebrity. He appeared on Comedy Central's *The Daily Show* and was applauded at his high school class reunion.

To go monster hunting yourself, take exit 199 from I-20, go north on Highway 9 and turn left onto Dry Hollow Road; the next right is the Iron City Cutoff, which takes you into Choccolocco through Neal Williamson's old hunting grounds.

Fictional Scoundrel Simon Suggs
Dadeville

The infamous nineteenth-century con artist Simon Suggs was known around Dadeville—then a frontier settlement—as the Chief of Sinners. Suggs's motto? "It is good to be shifty in a new country."

Suggs once crashed a revival meeting, faked a conversion experience so dramatic that it made him do somersaults, and then passed the hat, swearing on his newly saved soul that he wanted to raise money for a new church. He pocketed the proceeds, of course. During an Indian war Suggs persuaded his panicky neighbors to appoint him their military commander, whereupon he declared martial law, confiscated all the whiskey, and played poker while his inept "soldiers" shot up the town.

Suggs was a fictional character created by Montgomery lawyer, politician, and newspaper editor Johnson Jones Hooper (1815–1862) in his book *Adventures of Captain Simon Suggs, Late of the Tallapoosa Volunteers* (1845). Hooper was often in Dadeville on legal business, and he conducted Tallapoosa County's first census, in 1840. His stories, populated by lecherous preachers, stupid farmers, hypocritical slave owners, and crooked businessmen, made fun of every aspect of frontier life. Many readers took Suggs to be a parody of Andrew Jackson, whom the Republican Hooper disliked intensely.

Hooper's book was a best seller, and it made Dadeville nationally famous—or infamous, depending on your point of view. One of Hooper's big fans was Samuel Clemens, who later wrote about many a Suggs-like frontier scoundrel in *Adventures of Huckleberry Finn* and other books under the pen name Mark Twain.

Hooper's stories have not one good thing to say about Dadeville, but the town has decided to be proud of them nonetheless. Dadeville is on U.S. Highway 280, east of Lake Martin. For more information call the Dadeville Area Chamber of Commerce at (256) 825-4019 or log onto www.dadeville.com. (*Adventures of Captain Simon Suggs* is available in paperback from the University of Alabama Press, www.uapress.ua.edu.)

Kowaliga Cabin
Jordan

In August 1952 singer-songwriter Hank Williams was in a bad way. He had just been fired from the Grand Ole Opry, he was strung out on booze and pills, and his girlfriend, Bobbie Jett, was pregnant. Small wonder Hank wanted to retreat from the world, get away from stardom for a while.

Back home in Alabama, Hank's long-suffering mother, Lillian, called Alexander City disc jockey Bob McKinnon, a family friend. McKinnon arranged for Bobbie and Hank, an avid fisherman, to hole up at Lake Martin in the lakeside cabin owned by local car dealer Darwin Dobbs.

While living at the cabin, Hank wrote two of his most famous songs, "Your Cheatin' Heart" and "Kaw-Liga"—the second one inspired by McKinnon, who told Hank about Kowaliga, a long-gone Creek Indian town in the area.

The lakeside vacation didn't last long. A month later Hank married for the second time, and his bride was not Bobbie Jett. Three months after that, Hank Williams was dead, at age twenty-nine. Five days after he died, the jilted Bobbie Jett gave birth to their daughter, who as an adult would prove her paternity and take the name Jett Williams.

On June 21, 2002, the cabin where Hank Williams holed up was

formally dedicated as the Kowaliga Cabin, its interior restored by Ben and Luanne Russell to look exactly as it did in August 1952, down to the gingham curtains and knotted-pine floor. "It's nothing short of a flat miracle," said Jett Williams, on hand for the ceremony.

The Kowaliga Cabin is off Highway 63 on the south shore of Lake Martin, just south of the Kowaliga Bridge on Kowaliga Bay. The property is part of Children's Harbor, a local nonprofit that helps troubled and ill children, and while the cabin is not open for tours, it can be rented for overnight stays. To learn more call (334) 857-2133 or visit www.childrensharbor.org or the Alabama Bureau of Tourism's Hank Williams Trail brochure at www.hankwilliamstrail.com.

Across the road from the cabin is Sinclair's Kowaliga Restaurant. The restaurant displays Hank-related memorabilia, including, of course, a wooden Indian, though not one Hank ever saw; it was bought after Hank's death from a Pontiac dealership in Sylacauga. Call (334) 857-2889 or visit http://sinclairsrestaurants.com.

Farther up Highway 63, on the other side of the lake in Alexander City, is the Darwin Dobbs GM dealership, now owned by Fred Dobbs, the third generation. You can call (256) 234-3435.

Nadine Earles's Grave
Lanett

The most heart-wrenching roadside attraction in Alabama is the grave of Nadine Earles.

Nadine was four years old when she died just before Christmas in 1933. She had wanted Santa to bring her a dollhouse, so her grieving parents built a miniature redbrick house around her grave and filled it with all her toys and personal belongings. Today the local Town and Country Garden Club maintains the dollhouse and its contents, switching old toys for new from time to time, so through the windows visitors still can see a tea set and dolls sitting atop the marble slab.

Nadine's grave is located in the Lanett City Cemetery on First Street.

Syrup Sopping Day

Loachapoka

In the Creek Indian language, *Loachapoka* means "place of turtles." Today this tiny town (population 135) is known not for turtles but for syrup. This is not your New England, maple-tree-tapping syrup, but cane syrup, made by crushing sugarcane and capturing and then boiling the juice.

Every fall on the last Saturday in October, 15,000 visitors pour in for Syrup Sopping Day, which celebrates syrup making and other old-time rural crafts.

"Thank you for a great sop!" says the official Syrup Sopping Day Web site at www.soppin.org, which features recipes for syrup cookies, syrup pie, syrup pudding, syrup corn pone, and syrup popcorn balls.

Loachapoka is located on Highway 14, north of I-85 and west of Auburn. For more information call the Auburn-Opelika Convention and Visitors Bureau at (866) 880-8747.

Alabama Indestructible Dolls

Roanoke

In December 1897 a neighbor child asked seamstress Ella Gauntt Smith of Roanoke to repair her doll. This was the humble start to one of the great woman-run businesses of the early twentieth century.

The child must have been patient because the repairs took the painstaking Smith two years. When Smith was done, she had perfected a doll-making technique that involved painted heads of stiffened fabric filled with solid plaster. Smith patented her technique through her husband in 1901, since women weren't eligible for patents in those days, and she won a blue ribbon for doll making at the 1904 St. Louis World's Fair.

Back home in Roanoke, Smith turned entrepreneur, employing up to twelve women in her doll factory and turning out 8,000 dolls a year, selling them nationwide by mail order. The dolls were hand-painted,

Of all the artifacts at the Museum of East Alabama,
only one can stare at you all day. PHOTO BY
CHARLES JERNIGAN JR.; COPYRIGHT MUSEUM OF EAST ALABAMA

each with a slightly different facial expression. About a tenth of the
dolls she made were painted black, which was unheard of in the South
at that time. Most of the black dolls, however, like most of the white
ones, were sold to white families, and the black dolls retained Cauca-
sian facial features.

Ever the saleswoman, Smith claimed a delivery truck had driven over
one of the dolls without even cracking the paint. Her dolls became

known as Alabama Indestructible Dolls. They are also known among collectors as Roanoke Dolls and Alabama Babies.

Smith died in 1932, and no one carried on her work. Original Ella Smith dolls are now rarities that fetch as much as $20,000 apiece. A black Ella Smith doll appeared on a commemorative 32-cent U.S. postage stamp in 1997.

Since 1996 Roanoke has had an annual Ella Smith Doll Show. A year-round rotating display of Ella Smith dolls is at the Randolph County Historical Museum, 809 Main Street, in Roanoke, but it's open only by appointment; call (334) 863-5534. In neighboring Lee County several Ella Smith dolls are on display at the Museum of East Alabama in Opelika, 121 South Ninth Street (off I-85 northwest of Auburn). Call (334) 749-2751 or visit www.eastalabama.org for more information.

Fred, the Beloved Town Dog

Rockford

The name on the tombstone is simply FRED. Beneath the name is inscribed:

THE TOWN DOG

ROCKFORD AL

DEC 23 2002

ROCKFORD'S BELOVED

COMPANION

Above the name is an engraved picture of a happy black and white pooch wearing a red bandana.

Fred was a stray Airedale mix who showed up in 1993, sick and hungry, at Ken's Package Store in the center of Rockford, population 450. He was so friendly and cute that he was adopted not only by the store owner but also by the whole town. Fred was made the grand marshal of the town's Fourth of July parade, and the town newspaper gave him his own column, "A Dog's Life." (A local police officer helped with the typing.)

★ ★

The most famous resident of Rockford even had his own newspaper column. NIKI SEPSAS

The town sold Fred T-shirts and Fred coffee mugs, and a sign was posted at the town limits: ROCKFORD, AL, HOME OF "FRED" THE TOWN DOG.

The cable channel Animal Planet even did a feature about Fred. "He brought the community together," explained *Birmingham News* columnist Kathy Kemp.

After nearly a decade as Rockford's favorite citizen, the aged Fred died and was buried behind the Old Rock Jail on Jackson Street, now a history museum. A Birmingham businessman donated the tombstone a few months later. In 2004 Fred was inducted into the Alabama Animal Hall of Fame.

Rockford is on U.S. Highway 231 about 37 miles north of Montgomery. For more information on the Old Rock Jail Museum, which is open on summer Sunday afternoons, contact the Coosa County Historical Society at 256-234-5437.

Gravity Hill
Sylacauga

Northwest of town is a spot where cars in neutral seem to roll uphill, a place known to generations of teenagers as Gravity Hill.

Like all the hundreds of other Gravity Hills in the United States, Sylacauga's is a simple optical illusion. The roadbed and the surrounding terrain intersect at such an angle that downhill looks like uphill and vice versa.

This Gravity Hill, like the others, has a body of folklore purporting to explain the phenomenon. The guilt-ridden claim Gravity Hill is the site of a Native American burial ground; cars roll the wrong way because ghosts are trying to push intruders off their land. Others claim Gravity Hill is the site of a buried meteorite with a powerful magnetic force. They may be thinking of the Sylacauga Meteorite, which isn't magnetic and is on display, aboveground, in Tuscaloosa.

Urban sprawl has destroyed many "Gravity Hills" as grading and paving smooth out the natural terrain, but Sylacauga's is still hanging on, for now. Take US 280/231 northwest from town and turn left at Fulton Gap Road onto Gravity Hill Lane.

The Joy of Wrecks
Talladega

NASCAR has long denied that fans go to the racetrack to see wrecks, but smashed-up cars behind velvet ropes are big attractions at the International Motorsports Hall of Fame and Museum. The museum used to advertise itself with a billboard featuring a photo of a car wadded up like tinfoil and the slogan: "They walked away!"

No fatal crashes are commemorated here, as that wouldn't be tasteful, but visitors can gawk all they like at the car Michael Waltrip wrecked at Bristol in 1990. His car disintegrated over hundreds of yards of track, leaving intact only the safety cage; Waltrip suffered minor injuries.

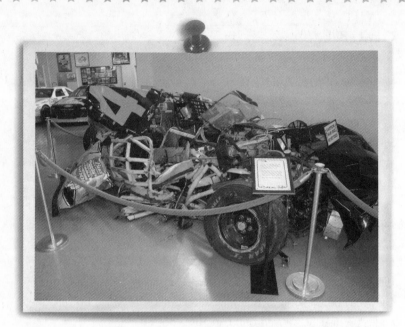

"The crowning achievements of man's abilities" include some totally cool wrecks. NIKI SEPSAS

The museum says its exhibits represent "the crowning achievements of man's abilities." Displays include the Budweiser rocket car that broke the sound barrier in 1979; the 1935 "Bluebird" driven by British racing pioneer Sir Malcolm Campbell, who set the land speed record nine times; cars driven by Dale Earnhardt, "Junior" Johnson, Richard Petty, "Fireball" Roberts, and Darrell Waltrip, as well as actor Gene Hackman and singer Marty Robbins; and the custom-built limousine that carried Governor George Wallace around the track to a standing ovation before the 1986 Talladega 500.

The museum, which opened in 1983, was the result of a deal between Wallace and NASCAR owner/founder Bill France. France donated the land, Wallace, the state's money to build it. For good measure the museum houses five additional halls of fame, including the Western Auto Mechanics Hall of Fame and the Alabama Sports-writers Hall of Fame.

The museum is at 3198 Speedway Boulevard on the grounds of the Talladega Superspeedway, which is just off that other celebrated speedway, I-20 (exit 168 eastbound, exit 173 westbound). Hours are 9:00 a.m. to 4:00 p.m. daily. Admission is charged. For details call (256) 362-5002 or log onto www.motorsportshalloffame.com.

Orville and Wilbur Who?

Talladega

Any schoolchild will tell you that Orville and Wilbur Wright invented the airplane and first flew it in 1903 at Kitty Hawk, North Carolina—unless the schoolchild is from Alabama.

North Carolina's "First in Flight" license plate notwithstanding, many Alabamians stubbornly insist the airplane was invented by Dr. Lewis Archer Boswell in the late nineteenth century, years before the Wright brothers packed their bags for the Outer Banks.

Boswell (1834–1909) was a Virginia native and a Confederate veteran who moved with his new bride to Red Hill, her family's Talladega County plantation, in 1869. He already had published articles on aeronautics and had built a toy-size flying machine. In Alabama he built a full-size version and—according to witnesses, some of whom lived well into the twentieth century—made several flights across his cotton fields, using a barn roof as a launching platform.

Unlike the Wright brothers, alas, Boswell left behind no written flight logs, no photographs, no concrete evidence whatsoever. He did patent two important aeronautical inventions, a propeller wheel (1874) and a steering mechanism (1903), so clearly he was up to something down on the farm. He also invented a tricycle-like undercarriage, the forerunner of the one still common on airplanes today. At the time of his death, his achievements had been eclipsed by the Wright brothers' worldwide fame.

Thanks to Boswell, some have called Talladega Municipal "the world's first airport"; it's been renamed Boswell Field in his honor. Boswell's plantation now is owned by the International Motorsports

Hall of Fame, which has an exhibit devoted to his work and legend.

Boswell is buried in Oak Hill Cemetery on Highway 77 west of Talladega. His gravestone mentions only his military service, but a historical marker at the site notes: INVENTED A FLYING MACHINE IN THE 1800S. RECORDED WITNESSES STATED THEY SAW IT AIRBORNE. So there.

Where There's a Mill, There's a Way

Valley

The old Riverdale Mill sticks out just far enough into the Chattahoochee River to cross the Georgia line. For generations lovers in a hurry got married in the Georgia end of the mill to avoid Alabama's mandatory thirty-day waiting period.

As another architectural oddity, the four-story mill was built on the side of a steep bluff so that each story had its own ground-floor entrance.

Built in 1866, Riverdale was the first cotton mill in the Chattahoochee Valley. It had no electricity, deriving all its power from the flow of the river. The mill's child laborers went barefooted, so the foreman carried a pocketknife to cut splinters out of their feet.

Today, the Riverdale mill building is part of the WestPoint Stevens textile empire and is used as a warehouse. It's located just south of I-85.

The Irish Struggle Comes to Alabama

Valley

In 1872 a fiery young Irishman named Charles Stewart Parnell spent three weeks in what is now Valley, Alabama, visiting his older brother, peach farmer John Howard Parnell.

Charles Stewart Parnell urged his brother to come home, to quit his two-room cabin in the wilderness. John Howard Parnell, in turn, urged his brother to stay on; he took him quail hunting and fox hunting and fed him catfish, to no avail.

The younger Parnell did, however, seriously consider investing in the Birmingham, Alabama, steel industry and changed his plans only when the train on which he was a passenger derailed outside the city. The superstitious Parnell took this as an ill omen and back to Ireland he went.

He became a member of Parliament (M.P.), where for more than a decade he led the political struggle for Irish independence. A scandalous affair with a married woman prematurely ended his career, but he remains one of the national heroes of Ireland.

John Howard Parnell prospered in Alabama; his Sunny South farm pioneered the packing and shipping of peaches by rail. Eventually, though, he too went home to Ireland and was himself an M.P. for twenty-five years. He also was on the parliamentary chess team that played members of the U.S. Congress by telegraph.

Part of Parnell's farm is now John Parnell Memorial Park on River Road. It's marked by a line of peach trees and clusters of misty-eyed, muttering Irishmen thanking St. Patrick that young Charles Parnell didn't stay in Alabama to eat catfish and grow peaches.

For more on all this, check out a book by Kieran Quinlan, a native of Ireland and longtime resident of Birmingham. It's titled *Strange Kin: Ireland and the American South*.

A Crater Unmasked
Wetumpka

"Structurally disturbed." For years that's how maps published by the Alabama Geological Survey identified the jagged landscape southeast of Wetumpka, across the rock-strewn Coosa River.

In these weird, forbidding badlands, older rocks lie on top of younger rocks, and rocks of many different ages are jumbled together like granola in a giant's breakfast bowl.

Not until 1972 did geologist Tony Neathery realize the whole area was a giant astrobleme—what nongeologists call a meteor crater. And what a crater this one is!

The famous Meteor Crater in Arizona is less than a mile across. The crater left by the gargantuan explosion of Krakatoa in 1883 was a mere 2 miles across. The Wetumpka crater is a startling 4 miles across, meaning the rock that created it eighty million years ago must have been a thousand feet wide, or, notes Auburn University geologist David King, about the size of the 85,000-seat Auburn football stadium.

Some speculate that the Wetumpka object may have been a fragment of the even larger rock that hit the Yucatán Peninsula, throwing up the global dust cloud that changed the Earth's climate and killed the dinosaurs, but more scientists think the Wetumpka impact was about fifteen million years too early.

"If the land of Alabama has a memory," writes John C. Hall in the fall 1996 issue of *Alabama Heritage* magazine, "then the fall of the Wetumpka meteorite must have been the most dreadful instant of its half-billion-year lifetime." Nevertheless and needless to say, the city of Wetumpka hopes to turn its big hole in the ground into a tourist attraction; log on to www.wetumpkacrater.com for more information.

Good places to view the rock formations include US 231 south of town; the Bibb Graves Bridge, which carries Highway 14 across the Coosa River at Wetumpka; and Bald Knob Road, which extends east from US 231 to climb the highest point on the crater's western rim.

Stuffed with Good Advice
Wetumpka

If you admire taxidermy, Al Holmes's place is a must-see. He has on display more than 800 mounted wild animals, from lions to sharks, plus a touch board for people who want to know what each animal pelt or hide or skin feels like.

Holmes writes a column of tips and advice titled "Why Didn't I Think of That, Al?" for the National Taxidermists Association (NTA) newsletter. Sample tips include "Always spray your studio for bugs and insects." "To remove blood stains, spray Shout stain remover." "When tagging migratory birds, always put a migratory bird tag on the specimen's feet before you place it in the freezer." Holmes also urges affiliation with the NTA: "It has been said over and over that 'a nation divided against itself cannot stand.' So it is with us as taxidermists."

High praise for famed taxidermist Al Holmes: "Don't they look natural!"
NIKI SEPSAS

★ ★

The museum is at 1723 Rifle Range Road, a.k.a. Highway 4 (a county road), east of US 231 south of Wetumpka. Hours are from 9:00 a.m. to 5:00 p.m., Monday through Friday. ("Keep definite shop and studio hours," advises "Why Didn't I Think of That, Al?" "Post your hours on the door and don't take callers after hours. . . . Remember, you must have time for yourself and your family.") Admission is charged. For more maxims call (334) 567-7966 or visit www. alholmestaxidermy.com.

3

Southeast

The giant boll *weevil in downtown Enterprise is rightly the most famous public statue in southeast Alabama, but it's not the only unlikely monument in the region, which also boasts monuments to bird dogs, roosters, and hogs—the last two, for good measure, made of scrap metal. The marble likeness of the largemouth bass Leroy Brown, on the other hand, probably should be classified with the area's grave sites and death sites, however public and festive some of them have become through the years—such as the drinker's tombstone shaped like a whiskey bottle, or the haunted and much-desecrated unresting place of Grancer the Dancer, or the two Hank Williams memorial sites in Montgomery: his elaborate tombstone in Oakwood Cemetery, and the blue 1952 Cadillac he died in, now parked permanently in a museum downtown. Though the fact is immaterial to Hank pilgrims, Montgomery is (who would have guessed it?) also the state capital, so it's not surprising to find politics cropping up occasionally on the next few pages of this book. Southeast Alabama can claim not only the last Confederate widow but also the original Black Panthers, and you can still walk the Phenix City pavement where a candidate for state attorney general was assassinated in 1954, leading the governor to declare martial law in the "Wickedest City in America"—one year before a rather better-remembered period of civil unrest began in Montgomery. But the most disruptive thing that ever happened in southeast Alabama may have been a tantrum fit by the Shawnee warrior Tecumseh, which according to legend caused the New Madrid earthquake of 1811. You can look it up.*

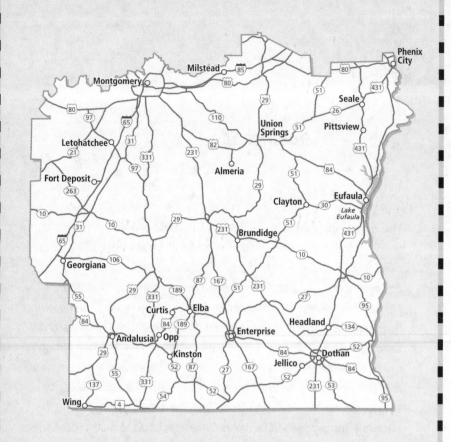

Milstead

Phenix City

Montgomery

Seale

Pittsview

Union Springs

Letohatchee

Almeria

Fort Deposit

Clayton

Eufaula

Lake Eufaula

Georgiana

Brundidge

Curtis

Elba

Headland

Andalusia

Opp

Enterprise

Kinston

Jellico

Dothan

Wing

Southeast

Hank Williams Shrine

Almeria

The Almeria Community Club is a 1907 schoolhouse turned honky-tonk turned community center in the Almeria community of Bullock County, between Troy and Union Springs. According to country-music legend, the Almeria Club was the site of a 1947 Hank Williams performance that ended in a table-clearing brawl—started not by Williams but by two jealous patrons fighting over a woman.

When one of the combatants pulled a gun, Williams and his wife, Miss Audrey, jumped out a window and fled into the woods, behavior consistent with the theme of Williams's song "Mind Your Own Business."

More than fifty years later, Williams's son, country star Hank Williams Jr.—who owns property nearby—recorded an album in this building, titled of course *The Almeria Club Recordings*. Critics called it his best work in years.

From Union Springs, take U.S. 82 southwest to Bruceville, then turn left onto Highway 15 to Almeria.

Dominoes Played Cordially

Andalusia

For two days every July, Andalusia becomes the Dominoes Capital of the World. For a $40 registration fee, hundreds of players in both singles and doubles divisions compete for first prizes of $3,000. A Miss World Domino is also crowned each year.

The official rules emphasize the civility of the event: "No drinking, smoking, loud talking, using profanity, or slapping dominoes down on the table. Those breaking dominoes will be required to pay for a new set."

In the years since the tournament began in 1976, it's amazing how often this world championship has been won by Alabama residents. The towns of Atmore, Dozier, Luverne, Montgomery, and Rainbow

★ ★

City all can boast of world dominoes champions. In 1980 both doubles champions were from Ozark. But no Alabama town can match
Andalusia's record: singles champions four times (1976, 1977, 1978,
2002), and doubles champions five times (1976, 1977, 1982, 1986,
2005). In three of those years, both doubles champions called
Andalusia home.

For more details call the Andalusia Area Chamber of Commerce at
(334) 222-2030 or visit www.worlddomino.com.

Cock-a-Doodle Crunch
Brundidge

A 15-foot chrome rooster made of car bumpers stands in front of
Art Wurks, the studio and gallery of brother artists Larry and Ronald
Godwin. Art Wurks used to be Bob's Feeds, the Godwin family's feed
store. The family's first giant metal animals were built to draw customers to the store. Through the years the menagerie has included a dog,
a pig, a horse, a bull, and a catfish.

Larry Godwin, an Auburn University graduate, was the first artist in
residence in Alabama's public schools. Ronald Godwin, a graduate of
Washington University in St. Louis, studied with famed outdoor sculptors Louise Kaisch and Theodore Roszak.

The Art Wurks studio is located on U.S. Highway 231, 4 miles south
of Brundidge. Call (334) 735-2341 to make an appointment. Meanwhile visit www.larrygodwin.com.

Other Art Wurks creations around Alabama include the giant metal
marlin at SanRoc Cay Marina in Orange Beach and the Carnival of the
Waterbugs at the KinderCare headquarters in Montgomery.

Whiskey-Bottle Tombstone
Clayton

The final resting place of W. T. Mullen (born June 18, 1834; died July
18, 1863) is known to locals as the "whiskey grave" because the
tombstone is shaped like a whiskey bottle.

According to legend Mullen drank himself to death at age twenty-nine, and his stern widow had the tombstone erected as a rebuke to the dead and a warning to others.

Clayton is at the intersection of Highways 51 and 30 in the middle of Barbour County, near the Chattahoochee River and the Georgia line. Mullen's grave is in the Clayton Town Cemetery on North Midway Street. For more information call the Eufaula Barbour County Chamber of Commerce at (800) 524-7529.

Twice as Many Walls to Paint

Clayton

The Octagon House in downtown Clayton, built between 1859 and 1861 as the home of store owner Benjamin Franklin Petty, is the oldest eight-sided house in Alabama.

More than a thousand octagonal houses were built in the United States during the nineteenth century, most of them in the ten years preceding the Civil War. The fad was launched by a New Yorker named Orson Squire Fowler (1809–1887), who argued that eight-sided houses with a central staircase and a central rooftop cupola were more healthful than traditional houses. They had better lighting and ventilation, Fowler claimed, and all the rooms were equally accessible from the stairs in case of fire. As a bonus they also offered greater square footage on the same plot of land.

The idea of octagon houses wasn't new. Thomas Jefferson designed and built his own eight-sided house on his plantation at Poplar Forest, Virginia, before the War of 1812. (Jefferson soon cheated by adding an office wing; see www.poplarforest.org.) Fowler was no Jefferson, was not even an architect, but he was a tireless self-promoter and a renowned medical man.

He was the nation's best-known phrenologist, which means he judged people's character traits and intelligence levels based on the shapes of their heads. In other words, he made big money traveling the nation, feeling skulls.

★ ★

Fowler's own sixty-room octagonal mansion in Fishkill, New York, "Fowler's Folly," no longer exists, but Clayton's Octagon House is a lovely reminder of the head-feeler's life and work. In April 1865 Union general Benjamin H. Grierson paid it a dubious compliment by making it his headquarters during the military occupation of Clayton.

The Octagon House is at 103 North Midway Street and is open by appointment. Admission is charged. Call (334) 775-3254.

The Last Confederate Widow

Curtis

Born December 4, 1906, at Danleys Crossroads, Alberta Stewart Farrow was only twenty-one when she married eighty-one-year-old Confederate veteran William Jasper Martin. Each needed looking after, the groom because of his age and the bride because she had an infant son to feed. Even before the Great Depression, Martin's $50 monthly pension looked like a godsend in rural Alabama. Many years later, Mrs. Martin explained her decision to marry: "It's better to be an old man's darlin' than a young man's slave."

Ten months after the wedding, Mrs. Martin gave birth to her second child. Her husband died in 1932; two months later, Mrs. Martin married her late husband's grandson, Charlie Martin, and that marriage lasted more than fifty years.

Mrs. Martin lived in obscurity most of her life, until the one-hundredth anniversary convention of the Sons of Confederate Veterans (SCV) in Richmond, Virginia, in 1996, where she was a guest of honor. This "coming-out party" made her a celebrity on the circuit of SCV conventions, Civil War reenactments, and League of the South meetings. She attended a pro-Confederate flag rally in Columbia, South Carolina, and cut the ribbon at the opening of the Jefferson Davis Presidential Library in Biloxi, Mississippi.

Ken Chancey, a dentist from nearby Enterprise, has a Web site devoted to Mrs. Martin at www.lastconfederatewidow.com, from which all this biographical material is drawn.

★ ★

Mrs. Martin died peacefully on May 31, 2004. Planning ahead, Chancey had put on the Web site years before all Mrs. Martin's funeral information. A Confederate heritage service with reenactors in period dress was conducted graveside. Mrs. Martin was laid to rest in the cemetery at New Ebenezer Baptist Church at 3132 Highway 141, west of Elba in the Curtis community.

Giant Peanuts and Other Statues

Dothan

"Everything in a nutshell" is the slogan of the Dothan Convention and Visitors Bureau, and that's only the start of the puns that abound in this Peanut Capital of North America.

About 65 percent of all U.S. peanuts are grown around Dothan. It's the home of the National Peanut Festival, which draws 160,000 people to the fairgrounds on US 231 South the first week of November (see www.nationalpeanutfestival.com). The fairgrounds has a monument to Alabama peanut pioneer George Washington Carver, who was the festival's first guest of honor in 1938.

Other statues around Dothan are, well, nuttier. The Peanut Monument is simply a giant golden peanut at the Dothan Visitor Information Center (334-794-6622) on the US 231 bypass.

The Peanuts around Town project placed about fifty giant, decorated peanuts, each 5 feet tall, all over Dothan. Each is made of concrete-filled fiberglass; a complete list, with descriptions and addresses, is available from the Visitor Information Center. These include:

- *Adventure Nut,* a caped and flying superhero at Adventureland on U.S. Highway 84 West;
- *Elvis Nut,* in sideburns and a white jumpsuit, at the Days Inn on the US 231 bypass;
- *Gone Shopping,* which wears a floral hat in the center court of Wiregrass Commons Mall, at Ross Clark Circle and US 231 North;
- *Mr. Peanut Head* in the Dothan Civic Center, 126 North St. Andrews Street, just off Business US 84;

Those with peanut allergies needn't worry; this goober is made of fiberglass. NIKI SEPSAS

- *The Paper Boy* at the *Dothan Progress* on US 231;
- *Sheriff Sam* in front of the Krispy Kreme on the US 231 bypass;
- *Savings Nut,* a peanut-shaped piggy bank at the AmSouth bank on US 84 downtown;
- *Wise Ol' Owl,* which wears a mortarboard at the US 231 entrance to Troy University's Dothan campus;
- *Violin Nut* outside the Dothan Opera House on St. Andrews Street, just north of US 84 downtown.

Also of interest is Dothan's Monument to the Hog, a giant scrap-metal porker on U.S. Highway 431 North. One of the first creations by Brundidge metal sculptor Larry Godwin, the giant hog—26 feet long and 13 feet high—originally was built to promote the family feed company; its original sign read GOING WHOLE HOG FOR BOB'S FEEDS.

The 10-foot bronze statue of the biblical prophet Joseph in Millennium Park on US 84 downtown, across from the art museum, is

★ ★

meant to depict Genesis 37:17—"For I heard them say, Let us go to Dothan"—the verse that inspired the leaders of Poplar Head to change the town's name to Dothan back in 1885. Since the biblical Dothan is the place where Joseph's brothers tore off his many-colored coat, threw him into a cistern, and sold him into slavery, the reasoning of the town leaders is unclear.

Two Driving Distinctions

Dothan

From US 84 downtown take Museum Street 1 block north to the intersection of Museum Street, North Appletree Street, and East Troy Street. This wholly uninteresting triangular traffic island is claimed by proud Dothan as the "World's Smallest City Block."

Much harder to avoid is the circular bypass around Dothan, numbered as both the US 231 bypass and the US 84 bypass. This four-lane divided highway is the oldest such "loop" in the United States. Begun in 1954, two years before President Eisenhower authorized an interstate highway system, it earned Dothan the truckers' nickname of "Circle City."

Klaatu Lands in Alabama

Dothan

The late British actor Michael Rennie is best remembered today as the dignified alien Klaatu in Robert Wise's *The Day the Earth Stood Still* (1951, remade in 2008). As a result, the first words of *The Rocky Horror Picture Show* are "Michael Rennie was ill / The day the Earth stood still."

The Internet Movie Database tells an interesting Rennie anecdote set in, of all places, Dothan, Alabama. Rennie already had played small roles in a number of movies when he joined the Royal Air Force (RAF). With other RAF pilots he was sent to the United States for flight training and wound up at Napier Field in Dothan. When his fellow pilots in Dothan asked him what he did for a living, he replied, truthfully enough, that he was a movie actor, and they all burst into disbelieving laughter.

A few nights later, they all went into town to take in a movie. It turned out to be *Ships with Wings*, a British war movie that starred John Clements, Leslie Banks . . . and, in a small role as Lieutenant Maxwell, none other than Michael Rennie, who presumably got the last laugh. One wonders how Rennie steered his friends to that particular movie theater!

Boll Weevil Monument
Enterprise

The most photographed monument in Alabama is at the intersection of College and Main in downtown Enterprise, a.k.a. the "Weevil City."

Because the boll weevil destroyed the county's cotton crop in 1915, farmers were forced to plant other crops, such as peanuts, to make ends meet. This proved so immediately successful that the leaders of Enterprise decided to erect a monument to the insect pest that had forced them to declare independence from King Cotton.

The Boll Weevil Monument was dedicated December 11, 1919, before a crowd of 5,000 people. Alabama peanut pioneer George Washington Carver was to have been the main speaker, but a washed-out railroad kept him away. Made in Italy and paid for mostly by Enterprise businessman Bon Fleming, the monument originally featured a stone woman in a flowing white gown, holding aloft a spouting fountain.

The inscription reads: IN PROFOUND APPRECIATION OF THE BOLL WEEVIL AND WHAT IT HAS DONE AS THE HERALD OF PROSPERITY. THIS MONUMENT WAS ERECTED BY THE CITIZENS OF ENTERPRISE, COFFEE COUNTY, ALABAMA.

Not until thirty years later did the town decide the Boll Weevil Monument needed an actual boll weevil on it somewhere. In 1949 the fountain in the woman's hands was replaced by a giant black metal boll weevil designed by local artist Luther Banks.

Though the giant weevil certainly draws the tourists, it also has been something of a headache for the town. It has been stolen at least four times and repeatedly vandalized by unsuccessful thieves. The current

Actual boll weevils seldom reach the size of the one on this monument. NIKI SEPSAS

monument is a replica unveiled in 1998; the damaged original is in the Depot Museum a few yards away.

The Pea River Historical and Genealogical Society runs a shop at 108 South Main Street that features all manner of Boll Weevil Monument souvenirs—desktop replicas, T-shirts, FEAR NO WEEVIL bumper stickers—as well as copies of Roy Shoffner's book *Pest of Honor: The Story of the World's Most Unusual Monument*. For details call (334) 393-2901 or order online at www.rootsweb.ancestry.com/~alprhgs/. The best online resource on the monument is Enterprise writer Shelley Brigman's invaluable Web site, www.weevilwonderland.com.

The Late Largemouth Bass Leroy Brown
Eufaula

When Tom Mann's pet largemouth bass, Leroy Brown, died in 1981, the governor sent a condolence letter. So did country singers Hank Williams Jr., Jerry Reed, Porter Wagoner, and Sonny James. More than 800 people attended the funeral, including the Eufaula High School Marching Band, which played the Jim Croce hit "Bad, Bad Leroy Brown." The pallbearers were all celebrity bass fishermen.

That night someone stole Leroy Brown's body. Mann offered a $10,000 reward. The first break in the case was a cryptic phone call from someone who demanded a ransom and claimed to be in the Tulsa, Oklahoma, airport, but who hung up without making any arrangements. Alerted by the police, a Tulsa baggage handler with a keen nose detected the pungent corpse inside an unclaimed piece of luggage.

Mann's $4,000 monument to Leroy Brown was the highlight of the Fish World Museum, which adjoined Tom Mann's Fish World, a sort of bait-shop superstore. Mann once told the *Montgomery Advertiser*: "My wife gave me a hard time about how much it cost, but I told her I'd make sure there was room for her name on the back of it."

The marble inscription on the monument read:

★ ★

MOST BASS
ARE JUST FISH
BUT LEROY BROWN
WAS SOMETHING SPECIAL

Mann caught Leroy Brown with a strawberry jelly worm in 1973
and put him in his 40-foot, 38,000-gallon breeding tank at the bait
shop. He even cut a hole in his office wall so that he could watch Leroy
Brown all day. Leroy Brown ran all the male fish out of his corner of
the tank, bred prodigiously with all the females, and spurned every test
lure Mann dropped into the water; he wouldn't be fooled a second
time. Whenever the other fish became sluggish, Leroy Brown bumped
them, as if to encourage them to keep going.

Mann trained the six-pound bass to eat out of his hand and jump
through a hoop like a porpoise. Mostly, Mann stared at Leroy Brown,
and Leroy Brown stared back, his eyes set high in his head and nearly
side by side, like a human's.

Mann was something special in the bass-fishing world even before
he landed Leroy Brown. He invented the jelly worm and the Humming-
bird depth finder, designed thousands of lures, wrote a book titled
Think Like a Fish, and held the record for the largest string of bass ever
caught in Lake Eufaula, Bass Fishing Capital of the World: twenty-five
bass weighing 155 pounds. A member of the Professional Bass Fishing
Hall of Fame, Mann died in 2005 at age seventy-two, two years after
closing Mann's Fish World and the adjacent museum. But at last report
Leroy Brown's tombstone was still there, behind the old buildings on
US 431 north of Eufaula; the address is 1951 North Eufaula Drive.

The Batman of Eufaula

Eufaula

Professional bat remover George "Batman" Perkins calls his business
Batbusters. He calls his Plymouth Prowler the Batmobile. Callers to his
home and office hear the theme to the 1960s' *Batman* TV show while

This Epitaph Is "D.O.A."

Dozens of Web sites devoted to "humorous epitaphs" feature this purported "actual epitaph of Elizabeth Rich, Eufaula, Alabama":

HONEY, YOU DON'T KNOW WHAT YOU DID FOR ME,

ALWAYS PLAYING THE LOTTERY.

THE NUMBERS YOU PICKED CAME IN TO PLAY,

TWO DAYS AFTER YOU PASSED AWAY.

FOR THIS, A HUGE MONUMENT I DO ERECT,

FOR NOW I GET A YEARLY CHECK.

HOW I WISH YOU WERE ALIVE,

FOR NOW WE ARE WORTH 8.5.

Some Web sites include the purported winning numbers, "36-33-01-24-17," as the first line of the epitaph. Some Web sites give the location as "Eufaula Historical Cemetery" (there's no such place). Some Web sites misspell *Eufaula* as *Eufala*. But no Web site provides any corroborating details of who Elizabeth Rich was, what her widower's

they're on hold. Perkins even has a Batman costume but swears he wears it only in parades, mostly.

In 1994 Perkins bought an 1840s-era house on West Broadway in Eufaula knowing that it was infested by 50,000 bats and that a woman who worked in the house had died of rabies. He ran off the bats, cleaned up the place, and has lived in it ever since, calling his home office Batcave 1. (Batcave 2 is his office in Union Springs.) One room is full of Batman memorabilia: toys, blankets, banners, posters.

Perkins's 2006 struggle against the bats infesting the historic district

name was, or when and where he supposedly won this $8.5 million jackpot. Presumably it would have been in the Georgia Lottery; Eufaula is on the Georgia line, and Alabama has no lottery. The Georgia Lottery opened for business in 1993, so this "actual epitaph" would have to have been written fairly recently. And if any Eufaula resident had won $8.5 million in the Georgia Lottery only days after his wife's death and then erected a "huge monument" to thank her in the form of a humorous poem, this odd set of circumstances certainly would have been widely covered by the press. In fact, no online news archive says anything about a posthumously lucky Elizabeth Rich or the tongue-in-cheek monument erected in her honor.

The endlessly repeated phrase "actual epitaph," the complete lack of verifiable information, the utter silence of online news archives, and the rather-too-pat coincidence of the surname Rich all lead us to classify this one as a made-up piece of Internet humor with a spurious name and location attached.

And it's not a good poem either!

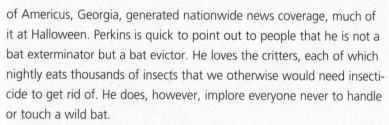

of Americus, Georgia, generated nationwide news coverage, much of it at Halloween. Perkins is quick to point out to people that he is not a bat exterminator but a bat evictor. He loves the critters, each of which nightly eats thousands of insects that we otherwise would need insecticide to get rid of. He does, however, implore everyone never to handle or touch a wild bat.

Batcave 1 is at 236 West Broad Street, Eufaula, a block west of U.S. Highway 82/431. Call (334) 687-7092.

Priester's Pecans

Fort Deposit

Priester's Pecans began in 1935, when L. C. Priester owned a Texaco station on the Mobile-Montgomery highway. He hired a man to knock pecans down from the trees with a stick and gather them in sacks for sale at the station.

The whole pecans sold so well that Priester soon hired a few women to crack and shell the pecans. They initially worked on the back porch of Priester's house, next door to the station. Eventually Priester gave up on the gasoline trade and devoted his whole business to pecans.

Today Priester's Pecans is a 6,000-square-foot store in the heart of Pecanland, at exit 142 from Interstate 65 South. It offers all-you-can-eat free samples of all Priester's goodies: pecan pralines, pecan logs, rum pecans, pecan clusters, pecan brittle, frosted pecans, honey-glazed pecans, pecan fudge, pecan divinity, butter-pecan crunch, pecans covered in milk chocolate, pecans covered in white chocolate. Customers also can buy online at www.priesters.com—without free samples, alas.

You'll find the store at 208 Old Fort Road East. It's open from 8:00 a.m. to 6:00 p.m., seven days a week. For more information call (800) 277-3226.

The Original Black Panthers

Fort Deposit

The African American militants of the 1960s and 1970s who called themselves the Black Panthers got their name from a much less well-known group of activists in Lowndes County, Alabama.

The county had seen a successful, if hard-won, voter registration drive in 1965–1966, but many of the newly registered voters quickly became disenchanted with the established political parties in the county and decided to start their own party to promote civil rights, on the order of the Mississippi Freedom Democratic Party. Thus was born the Lowndes County Freedom Organization.

At the time Alabama law required all registered political parties to have a logo that even illiterate voters could recognize. (There were many more illiterate Alabamians then.) The organizers of the new party decided to adopt the mascot of Clark College, a historically black Methodist school in Atlanta: a black panther.

The idea caught on, and other civil rights groups nationwide began calling themselves Black Panthers, too. In Oakland, California, in 1966, Huey P. Newton and Bobby Seale decided to call their anticapitalist militant group the Black Panther Party for Self-Defense, to distinguish it from those Black Panthers who weren't armed.

The Oakland group soon became so famous—or, many would say, infamous—that the less visible Black Panthers, including Alabama's, were forgotten. Besides Brown and Seale the ranks of the national Black Panthers included still-controversial figures such as H. Rap Brown, Stokely Carmichael, Eldridge Cleaver, and Angela Davis, but who can recite the names of Lowndes County's original Black Panthers? As Pulitzer Prize–winning historian Taylor Branch told Don Noble in the *Tuscaloosa News*, "It was a party of sharecroppers, mostly women in print dresses, risking their lives to vote for the first time." (For much more info see Branch's excellent book, *At Canaan's Edge: America in the King Years 1965-68*.)

The Lowndes County Freedom Organization is long gone, but the athletic teams at Clark College, now Clark Atlanta University, are still the Panthers. One wonders whether any alums ever think of Lowndes County—or, for that matter, of Oakland—while singing:

HAIL, ROARING PANTHERS
WE SING OUR PRAISE TO THEE.
YOU ARE OUR HEROES
AND WILL FOREVER BE.
RAH, RAH, RAH.
HONOR AND GLORY
YOU BRING TO OLD CC.
ALL HAIL TO THEE, O MIGHTY PANTHERS
ON TO VICTORY!

More Hank Williams Shrines
Georgiana

The legendary singer-songwriter Hank Williams was born September 17, 1923, in Mount Olive but grew up in nearby Georgiana, and Georgiana lets no one forget it.

On I-65, before a traveler even reaches exit 114, a sign commemorates the Hank Williams Memorial Lost Highway, an ominous sign to see late at night or in a thunderstorm.

Williams's modest boyhood home at 127 Rose Street is now the Hank Williams Museum, full of "bacoodles of stuff," in the words of Georgiana mayor Lynn Watson. Among the artifacts is a wooden headboard carved especially for Williams by a fan of the *Louisiana Hayride* radio show. A separate performance space at the museum is a replica of Thigpen's Log Cabin, a Georgiana honky-tonk where Hank used to perform.

The adjoining Hank Williams Music Park is the site of the annual Hank Williams Festival the first weekend of June. The musical lineup for the 2008 festival included country stars Aaron Tippin, Shenandoah, T. G. Sheppard, and Williams's daughter Jett Williams. Also on hand each year are the aging members of Williams's backup band, the Drifting Cowboys.

Georgiana is also the home base of the Hank Williams Fan Club (www.hankwilliamsinternationalfanclub.com), which charges members a nominal fee to "Keep on Hankin'." For more information on all this, call the museum at (334) 376-2396.

Alabama Re-Do's
Headland

Sculptor Doug Odom is a self-taught artist who built his first birdhouse at age nineteen. He became nationally known for his Alabama Re-Do's, whimsical wood-and-tin sculptures made of scavenged, vintage materials. Odom scrawled the history of the materials on the back or bottom of each work as a sort of historical record, and offered the pieces for sale with modest descriptions such as "Words cannot express

Doug Odom turned old barns and sheds into "re-did" artwork. NIKI SEPSAS

the beauty of this fish." While Odom still has a number of Re-Do's for sale, he's switched in recent years to painting—on canvases of primed roofing tar. For more information, call Doug or his wife, Anita, at (334) 693-5600.

An Epitaph as Common as Dirt
Jellico

When the author of the present volume was signing books at the Riverfest celebration in Wetumpka, Alabama, in 2005, a visitor recited from memory what she called "the famous epitaph from the cemetery in Auburn":

AS YOU ARE NOW

SO ONCE WAS I

AS I AM NOW

YOU SOON WILL BE

SO PREPARE FOR DEATH

AND FOLLOW ME.

To this, she went on to say, some wag once added graffiti:

I WOULD BE CONTENT

IF I BUT KNEW

WHICH WAY YOU WENT.

Some version of this epitaph (and, inevitably, some version of the graffiti) can be found in a lot of Alabama cemeteries. This is one of the most common epitaphs in the English-speaking world, found in cemeteries far and wide.

One documented occurrence in southeast Alabama, though not in Auburn, is the epitaph of Lonie A. Glover (1869–1962) in the Jellico Community Cemetery in Houston County, near Dothan. Judith Fowler records Glover's epitaph at the invaluable site www.interment.net, where you can browse thousands of cemetery records from around the world.

To reach the Jellico cemetery from Dothan, head west on U.S.

Highway 84 for 9 miles, then turn left on South County Road 9. About a quarter-mile along is the cemetery, across the road from Winslette Chapel Methodist Church.

Grancer the Dancer
Kinston

William "Grancer" Harrison (1789–1860) was a wealthy planter who loved to fiddle and to dance. His 2,500-acre Pea River plantation was known far and wide for its square dances and its specially built dance hall. According to family legend Harrison got his nickname from his slaves, who respectfully called him "Grand-sir."

Harrison designed his own tomb with the thoroughness of an Alabama pharaoh. His final requests were that he be buried in his dancing shoes, on the highest hill overlooking his plantation, within earshot of his dance hall.

The grave is in poor shape today because of a persistent, groundless legend that Harrison was buried with a hoard of gold. Treasure hunters have repeatedly desecrated Harrison's remains, most spectacularly in 1964, when they blew the tomb apart with dynamite.

One would expect Harrison to leave a vengeful ghost, but generations of passersby claim that late on Saturday nights, Grancer the Dancer can be heard fiddling and dancing around his grave, calling out the dances forevermore.

Many of Harrison's slaves are buried around him, but no trace remains of their markers, if indeed they ever had any. The grave of Grancer the Dancer is in the Harrison family cemetery on County Road 473 east of Kinston.

Eastern Airlines UFO
Letohatchee

One of the earliest and most celebrated UFO sightings, part of the U.S. Air Force's Project Blue Book investigation, occurred in the skies over Alabama at 2:45 a.m. on July 24, 1948.

John B. Whitted and Clarence S. Chiles were piloting an Eastern Air-lines DC-3 passenger flight from Houston to Boston, at an altitude of 5,000 feet, when they saw a cigar-shaped craft with lighted windows zoom past their right wing.

Chiles went aft to see whether the twenty passengers had seen the craft. Most were asleep, but Clarence McKelvie, an editor from an Ohio publishing house, said he had seen a "strange eerie streak."

The next day, the Whitted-Chiles sighting was page-one news nationwide, giving Americans further reason to be jittery a month into the Soviet blockade of Berlin. Gen. George C. Kenney, chief of the Strategic Air Command, told reporters his boys had no aircraft like the one described: "I sure wish we did." The *Atlanta Journal* headlines were typical: "'Sky Devil-Ship' Scares Pilots; Air Chief Wishes He Had One" and "Plane Makers Dubious about Alabama 'Thing.'"

The same object, whatever it was, had been reported flying south-ward over Robbins Field at Macon, Georgia, about an hour before the Eastern flight encountered it. The air force took the sightings seriously enough to determine the positions of every aircraft aloft in the South-east on the night of July 23–24, all 225 of them. The air force con-cluded that whatever Whitted and Chiles saw, it couldn't have been any of those.

A meteor shower was going on that night, and pioneering UFO researcher J. Allen Hynek—who later appeared in Steven Spielberg's movie *Close Encounters of the Third Kind*—concluded that the pilots had seen and misidentified a meteor, or "fireball." Many people remain skeptical. Researcher James E. McDonald later wrote: "A horizontally moving fireball under a cloud deck, at 5,000 feet, exhibiting two rows of lights construed by experienced pilots as ports, and finally executing a most nonballistic 90-degree sharp pull-up, is a strange fireball indeed."

Most of the UFO literature refers to this famous event as a Mont-gomery sighting, but as the plane was actually 20 miles southwest of Montgomery, it seems fairer to give credit to the town of Letohatchee, on Highway 97 just north of I-65 exit 151.

Don't Mess with Tecumseh

Milstead

At the Creek Nation town of Tukabachi on the Tallapoosa River, near what is now the town of Milstead, the great Shawnee warrior Tecumseh had an unsatisfying meeting with the Creek chief in October 1811.

Tecumseh hoped to enlist the Creeks in his uprising against the white man, but the Creeks showed no enthusiasm for the fight. According to Native American legend, the disgusted Tecumseh told the chief that when he got home to Detroit, he would stomp his foot on the ground and "shake down every house in Tukabachi."

On December 16 of that year, Tukabachi was indeed shaken to the ground—by the cataclysmic New Madrid earthquake, the largest North American quake in recorded history. Centered in the Mississippi Valley, it was felt across the eastern half of the continent, from Missouri to Washington, D.C.

Even More Hank Williams Shrines

Montgomery

Hank Williams frequently boasted in life that he could draw a bigger crowd dead than other country singers could draw alive. Thousands of people attended his January 4, 1953, funeral, and countless thousands have visited his grave in Oakwood Cemetery in the fifty years since.

From the Upper Wetumpka Road cemetery entrance, the grave is at the top of the hill on the right. The big marble monument is hard to miss. It includes Williams's boots and cowboy hat immortalized in stone, with LUKE THE DRIFTER inscribed beneath and a lyric from Williams's gospel song "I Saw the Light."

People leave flowers, money, bottles of whiskey. Alan Jackson had a 1991 country hit with "Midnight in Montgomery," a song about a nocturnal visit to the grave. A less reverent song by the Austin Lounge Lizards goes, "I want to ride in / The car Hank died in." The actual "death car," a blue 1952 Cadillac, is the grimmest and most popular

Alabama's favorite
son, Hank Williams,
will strum his guitar in
perpetuity in front of
a museum in his honor.
NIKI SEPSAS

★ ★

exhibit at Montgomery's Hank Williams Museum. It's on loan from Hank Williams Jr., who reportedly drove it to high school. Other items on display include the Gibson guitar that supposedly was Williams's first and a bottle of Hidalgo, the 12-percent-alcohol elixir he once hawked in a traveling medicine show.

Some people call the exhibit exploitative, but it's worth remembering that Williams actually charged admission to afternoon and evening performances of his wedding to his second wife, Billie Jean.

The museum is in the old Union Station downtown at 118 Commerce Street, across from the Civic Center. Hours are from 9:00 a.m. to 4:30 p.m., Monday through Friday, 10:00 a.m. to 4:00 p.m., Saturday, and 1:00 to 4:00 p.m., Sunday. Admission is charged. For more information about the museum, call (334) 262-3600 or log onto www.thehankwilliamsmuseum.com.

Did That Animal Just Wink at Me?

Montgomery

The Alabama Cattlemen's Association sponsors the MOOseum, "devoted to the history and preservation of the beef-cattle industry."

Opened in 1995 and aimed at kids, the MOOseum includes a miniature rodeo arena, exhibits about healthful beef eating and veterinary science, a Hoofprints through Alabama historical display, a play area called Slim's Buckaroo Cattle Club, and a "state-of-the-art" mannequin named Adam Bainbridge, who's full of beef information.

The MOOseum is at 201 South Bainbridge Street downtown, north of Interstate 85. Admission is free, but prospective visitors should contact the museum to schedule a tour. For MOOre information call (334) 265-1867 or visit www.bamabeef.org/NewMOOseum.htm.

Larger and more elaborate is the Mann Wildlife Learning Museum at the Montgomery Zoo—28,000 square feet of stuffed wild animals, a legacy of retired Alabama industrialist George P. Mann of Opelika. He made his fortune as owner of Opelika Metalfab, a welding and steel-fabrication company, but his lifelong passions are bow hunting

and wildlife photography. The Mann Museum, which opened in 2000, is Mann's dream project. He worked on it for twenty years at a cost of millions of dollars.

Most of the animals on display were hunted and killed by Mann, who also designed and arranged all the exhibits and wrote all the explanatory text. Only the taxidermy was left to others, mostly to Henry Inchumuk of Colorado, whose other clients include the Smithsonian Institution and the American Museum of Natural History in New York City.

The exhibits include everything from a 2,000-pound moose and a 14-foot polar bear to a porcupine that Mann killed with a rock. All the bear, deer, and skunk species of North America are represented in the museum.

Mann told the Columbus, Georgia, newspaper that his chief aim was education: "We're not looking to build a glorified trophy room."

The Mann Museum first opened in Mann's hometown of Opelika, but in 2003 it was moved to 325 Vandiver Boulevard in north Montgomery, next door to the Montgomery Zoo, where it is easier for tourists to find.

From I-65 take exit 173 to Lower Wetumpka Road, and then go left onto Vandiver. Hours are from 9:00 a.m. to 5:00 p.m. daily. Admission is charged. Call (334) 240-4900 for more details.

Centennial Hill

Montgomery

The historic Centennial Hill neighborhood, traditional center of African American Montgomery, is anchored on South Jackson Street north of I-85. It has a rich musical history, as Nat King Cole and Clarence Carter were both born and raised there, Ray Charles and Big Mama Thornton played clubs there, and Hank Williams's mentor, Rufus "Tee-Tot" Payne, was laid to rest there.

Born in 1884 on the Payne plantation in Lowndes County, Alabama, Payne got the nickname "Tee-Tot," short for teetotaler, while living in New Orleans. (The nickname was not apt.) Payne was a snappy dresser and a skilled musician with a large repertoire of songs and a vague but impressive New Orleans mystique when he showed up in Georgiana, Alabama, and dazzled a young Hank Williams. Soon Payne was teaching the boy songs. Later the two performed together, a black man and a white boy, on street corners and at private dances, at home and in Montgomery.

As an adult Williams often talked about Payne, on and off stage. He told an interviewer in 1951, "All the music training I ever had was from him."

Payne was buried in an unmarked pauper's grave in Centennial Hill's Lincoln Cemetery in 1939, when Williams was fifteen years old. No known photographs and no known recordings of Payne exist, and the whereabouts of his grave had been long forgotten when Hank Williams Jr. put blues historian Alice K. Harp on the trail in the 1990s. Thanks to their efforts, a historical marker honoring Payne now marks the entrance to Lincoln Cemetery, at Lincoln Road and Harrison Road, though the exact site of the grave inside the cemetery will never be known.

Another Centennial Hill resident honored with a historical marker, on Dericot Street south of the state capitol, is Georgia Gilmore. Gilmore (1920–1990) was never a household name like Rosa Parks and Martin Luther King Jr., but she was famous within the civil rights movement for doing what she did best: cooking. Among the political leaders she fed in her home were Robert F. Kennedy, Lyndon B. Johnson, and Martin Luther King Jr., who especially liked her pineapple upside-down cake. "I just served them and let them talk," she later said.

A cook at a downtown diner at the time of the Montgomery bus boycott, Gilmore organized sales of cakes, pies, and sandwiches to help fund the operation. She called her support organization the Club from Nowhere so that, if asked, boycotters could truthfully say their funding came from Nowhere. In the 1956 conspiracy trial of Martin Luther King Jr., Gilmore testified about ill treatment at the hands of racist bus drivers. "When they count the money," she told the court,

"they do not know Negro money from white money." She was promptly fired from her job.

Gilmore prepared thousands of meals for activists, organizers, and demonstrators through the years, and she was working in her kitchen right to the end. She died March 9, 1990, the day of the twenty-fifth anniversary of the Selma-to-Montgomery march. The fried chicken and mashed potatoes she made to serve the anniversary marchers instead were served to the mourners at her wake.

Fountain Creatures
Montgomery

The Flimp Fountain is part of the permanent collection of the Montgomery Museum of Fine Arts.

The fountain was created in 1937 by Geneva Mercer (1889–1984), a native of Jefferson, Alabama, who apprenticed under Giuseppe Moretti, creator of the giant iron Vulcan in Birmingham. Mercer said the whimsical creatures on the fountain were "flimps," or flower imps, responsible for making gardens bloom in springtime. So popular are the flimps with generations of Montgomery schoolchildren that the museum throws an annual Flimp Festival on the first Saturday in May. The fountain is at I-85 and the U.S. Highway 80 bypass.

The Carnival of the Waterbugs fountain is a few blocks south, outside the corporate offices of the KinderCare day-care chain, 2400 President's Drive, just off the US 80 bypass. This fountain is the creation of brothers Larry and Ronald Godwin of Art Wurks in Brundidge, Alabama.

The Beautiful and the Doomed
Montgomery

The F. Scott and Zelda Fitzgerald Museum in Zelda's hometown of Montgomery claims to be the only museum in the world devoted to the glamorous, doomed couple. It's an apartment in the house they rented—with their daughter, Scottie—from October 1931 to April 1932, while Scott worked on *Tender Is the Night* and Zelda on *Save Me the Waltz*.

They already had lived in New York City, the French Riviera, Rome, Capri, Paris, and Hollywood, and indeed Scott continued to commute to Hollywood, writing a Jean Harlow movie at MGM. Zelda was fresh out of a Swiss sanitarium and hoped that a return to her hometown would help her fragile mental state. But after her father, Judge Anthony Sayre, died, Zelda suffered another breakdown. In January 1932 she was admitted to the psychiatric clinic at Johns Hopkins in Baltimore.

Born Zelda Sayre on July 24, 1900, the daughter of an Alabama Supreme Court justice, Zelda was eighteen when she met Scott at a country-club dance. He was stationed at Camp Sheridan, an army base near Montgomery. She herself was a painter and a fiction writer, and she eventually had stories published in the *New Yorker*, *Scribner's*, and the *Saturday Evening Post*, but her career never rivaled her husband's. She was plagued with mental illness, eventually diagnosed as schizophrenia. (*Tender Is the Night* is about a psychiatrist whose wife is beautiful and insane.)

Scott died of a heart attack in his mistress's Hollywood apartment in 1940. Eight years later, Zelda died in a fire at an Asheville, North Carolina, mental hospital. Neither lived to age fifty.

The museum includes photos and letters, paintings by Zelda, and furniture from Zelda's long-gone childhood home. A gift shop sells Scott and Zelda clocks, shirts, mugs, tote bags, caps, mouse pads, and barbecue aprons. A $25-per-person fund-raising gala at the museum each January includes a Scott and Zelda look-alike contest. The historical marker outside the house quotes Zelda's 1929 story "Southern Girl."

The museum is at 919 Felder Avenue, Apartment B. Admission is free. Hours are from 10:00 a.m. to 2:00 p.m. Wednesday through Friday, and from 1:00 to 5:00 p.m. Saturday and Sunday. For more details call (334) 264-4222.

Rattlesnake Rodeo
Opp

The Rattlesnake Rodeo, held the first weekend in April at Channell-Lee Football Stadium in Opp, is devoted to the eastern diamondback rattlesnake. Thirty thousand people show up to watch rattlesnake milking, rattlesnake handling, and rattlesnake races, in which snakes are poured from a garbage can into a circle on the ground so that spectators can cheer whichever snake slithers out of the circle first.

Another highlight of the event is the crowning of a Miss Rattlesnake, who gets not a mink stole but a live you-know-what draped across her shoulders in victory.

All this has gone on since 1959, despite the growing qualms of animal rights activists. The Humane Society of the United States opposes all rattlesnake rodeos on principle, arguing that it's cruel to round up wild rattlers and play with them, even if they're released afterward. The group also argues that far more people are bitten each year than rodeo organizers claim.

Some years rain has driven the Rattlesnake Rodeo indoors, to the Covington County Arena in nearby Andalusia. For more information, call the Opp Chamber of Commerce at (334) 493-3070 or log on to www.opprattlesnakerodeo.com.

The Former "Wickedest City in America"
Phenix City

As early as the nineteenth century, the west bank of the Chattahoochee had an unsavory reputation as a lawless haven for fugitives of all stripes. In the mid-twentieth century, Phenix City became known as an AWOL paradise of prostitution, drug dealing, and gambling, all preying on off-duty soldiers who crossed the river from Fort Benning, Georgia.

Disgusted by the town's bad influence, Henry L. Stimson, U.S. secretary of war, called it "the wickedest city in America," and George S.

★ ★

Patton threatened to send tanks across the bridges to "mash Phenix City flat."

Phenix City's underworld figures had colorful names out of a Dick Tracy strip: the brothers Hoyt and Snooks Shepherd, Head Revel, Arch Ferrell, Fate Leeburn, "Ma" Beachie Howard. It is said the clatter of illegal slot machines was audible from the courthouse steps, but nothing was done because the gangsters had powerful friends not only in Phenix City but in Montgomery as well. Bombings, beatings, and crooked elections kept reformers at bay.

In 1954 fed-up lawyer Albert Patterson ran for state attorney general, vowing to rid his hometown of corruption. He received the Democratic nomination, in a day when that was as good as election in Alabama. On June 18 he was assassinated on a downtown street moments after leaving his Coulter Building law office. (The building still stands at Fifth Avenue and Fourteenth Street, just 2 blocks west of the river.)

This brazen slaying marked the beginning of the end of Phenix City's crime syndicate. The governor declared martial law and sent national guardsmen to the city to maintain order. The county's chief deputy was convicted of the murder; other persons indicted included the local solicitor and the state attorney general, who promptly checked himself into a Texas mental hospital.

The *Columbus (Georgia) Ledger* won a Pulitzer Prize for its coverage of all this. Patterson's son John, a Korean War veteran, carried on his father's crusade, was elected attorney general in his father's place, and in 1958 was elected governor—defeating another young idealist, George Wallace.

To capitalize on the headlines, Hollywood rushed into production *The Phenix City Story* (1955), a violent drive-in movie starring John McIntire and Richard Kiley as Patterson father and son, respectively. Filmed in Phenix City with locals as extras, the movie has a cult following, Martin Scorsese being one of its champions. (Its director, Phil Karlson, later made another hit movie about a corrupt southern town, *Walking Tall*, starring Joe Don Baker and also supposedly based on real events.)

Recent books about the episode include *The Tragedy and the Triumph of Phenix City, Alabama* by Margaret Anne Barnes; *When Good Men Do Nothing: The Assassination of Albert Patterson* by Alan Grady; and the novel *Wicked City* by Ace Atkins.

Bi-City Christmas Parade
Phenix City

Snicker all you like; the name of this parade implies only that it's half in one city, half in another. It parades both ways.

Traditionally held on the second Saturday in December, the parade starts in Phenix City, Alabama, and then crosses the Chattahoochee River into Columbus, Georgia. For more information call the Phenix City–Russell County Chamber of Commerce at (800) 892-2248.

The Mayor's Office
Pittsview

"Mayor" Frank Turner's title in this crossroads community, which Turner calls a "wide place in the road," is proudly honorary, and the only business done in the Mayor's Office on US 431 is the business of art.

Once a junk shop, the Mayor's Office is now a gallery devoted to the work of three nationally known local self-taught folk or "outsider" artists: Butch Anthony, James A. "Buddy" Snipes, and John Henry "Mustache Jesus" Toney, all of whom made their first sales there.

Snipes, born in 1943, lives in a three-room house with no running water and makes sculptures from roots, limbs, vines, scrap lumber, tobacco cans—anything, really. He also paints on scrap lumber and sheets of roofing tin. Toney, born in 1928, lives on the edge of a swamp in a trailer with no running water, and he paints on plywood, posterboard, and any scrap wood he can find, including old doors. Butch's place, meanwhile, is a tourist attraction all its own (see "Alabama Museum of Wonder, Seale"). These artists do striking work with equally striking titles: *Toten the Load* (Anthony), *Camp Meeting Mullet* (Snipes), and *Miss "It" and a Boar Hog* (Toney).

As for the store itself, Turner says the Mayor's Office is open "by chance or appointment." Call for directions and to be sure he's there: (334) 855-3568.

Alabama Museum of Wonder and Annual Doo-Nanny
Seale

When outsider artist Butch Anthony, whose never-used first name is Bishop, isn't hanging out at the Mayor's Office in Pittsview or traveling to art festivals in the wackily decorated hearse he calls the Alabama Mamma Jamma Superintertwangleistic Car, its grille-mounted manne-quin's head grinning into other people's rearview mirrors, he does busi-ness out of his home studio/office/gallery, which he calls the Alabama Museum of Wonder. And rightly so. It looks like something Picasso

Who could resist the chance to see Sparky the "Electrocuted" Chicken, with or without quota-tion marks? BUTCH ANTHONY

★ ★

would have come up with if he had ever toured the Southeast with a combination sideshow and tent revival.

Once a year, when the mood strikes, Butch cooks a pig and invites a dozen visiting artists—such as Suzie Ham of Andalusia, Libby Benton of Eufaula, and Trey Williams of Seale—for an art and music festival called the Alabama Doo-Nanny.

The Alabama Museum of Wonder is at 41 Poorhouse Road, which connects US 431 and Highway 169. Anthony welcomes visitors (admission is charged) but suggests they e-mail him for directions: butchanthony63@yahoo.com or visit www.museumofwonder.com.

That Dog Won't Hunt
Union Springs

In downtown Union Springs a life-size bronze bird dog stands in perpetual point atop an 8-foot granite pillar. On the pillar are engraved the names of eleven Bullock County citizens in the Bird Dog Field Trial Hall of Fame.

A field trial is a bird dog competition in which the dogs run along designated courses as spectators follow on foot or on horseback.

Church of the Seven Sisters

Fitzpatrick United Methodist Church, off Highway 110 northwest of Union Springs, is nicknamed the "Church of the Seven Sisters" because it was founded, in 1858, by seven pioneer women: three Methodists, two Baptists, one Presbyterian, and one Episcopalian. The Methodists had the plurality, so it's a Methodist church to this day.

Field trials have been a big deal in Bullock County since the 1930s, when washing-machine magnate L. B. Maytag, indulging a wintertime hobby, developed the 14,000-acre private hunting preserve known as Sedgefield Plantation. The largest field trial in the United States, the charmingly named National Amateur Free-for-All, draws hundreds of contestants to Sedgefield each February, and nearby Union Springs calls itself the Bird Dog Field Trial Capital of the World.

Unveiled in 1996, the bronze bird dog replaced a Civil War monument that once stood on the spot at the corner of Hardaway Avenue and Prairie Street. Each December, the bird dog is decorated with a Christmas wreath around its neck. For more information, visit www.unionspringsalabama.com/birddogmonument.html.

Hanging Demonstrations
Union Springs

This is where condemned prisoners took their last step in Union Springs' 1897 jail building, the oldest still standing in Alabama. You may find yourself reaching for your throat as the trapdoor slams.

The three-story redbrick Victorian Gothic structure, complete with turrets and spiked "witches hats," is known as the Pauly Jail because it was built by the Pauly Jail Building Company of St. Louis, still in business. Its jails now cost considerably more than the $7,250 spent on the Union Springs building.

The Pauly Jail is behind the 200 block of Prairie Avenue downtown. To schedule a tour call (334) 738-8687 or e-mail tourbc@ustconline.net. For more information visit www.unionspringsalabama.com/pauly jail.html.

A Hawaiian Troubadour Who Wasn't Don Ho
Wing

Country-music pioneer "Pappy" Neal McCormick, an innovator of the electric steel guitar, was born October 3, 1909, in this town on the

Florida border. A Creek Indian who never made it to Hawaii, McCormick named his band the Hawaiian Troubadours because the steel guitar was associated, at the time, only with Hawaiian music.

He helped change all that, becoming the first musician to play an electric instrument on Nashville radio station WSM, home of the Grand Ole Opry. He lived most of his life in Walton County, Florida, playing local gigs such as the Pensacola Barn Dance.

He also was active in politics. When he ran for sheriff, he picked up a celebrity endorsement from none other than country-music great Hank Williams, who got his start as a member of McCormick's band. Much later, President Jimmy Carter recognized McCormick as principal chief of the Eastern Creek Nation.

McCormick died in 1998 and is commemorated in the Alabama Music Hall of Fame. His daughter, Juanealya McCormick Sutton, wrote a book titled *The Man behind the Scenes: "Pappy" Neal McCormick and Hank Williams*.

Wing is at the intersection of County Road 4 and Highway 137, just north of the Florida line. Nearby DeFuniak Springs, Florida, has a Pappy Neal McCormick Day and Bluegrass Festival on the last Saturday in May.

4

North

The hill country *of north Alabama has a lot of interesting stuff that seems misplaced—or, to put it more charitably, exists in an unexpected location. Intrepid visitors can find a Saturn rocket in an interstate rest area, a river that courses along a mountaintop, and a film festival named for George Lindsey, who played Goober on* **The Andy Griffith Show***, while Cook's Pest Control has a bug museum, and the Quick Stop Muffler Shop has a sculpture exhibit. Some of north Alabama's unique places have a certain poignancy: the Coon Dog Cemetery, the Unclaimed Baggage Center, the out-of-the-way churches where ecstatic parishioners dance with rattlesnakes. The nineteenth-century genocide of the area's native peoples is commemorated not only in a hand-built stone wall that may be the largest monument to a woman in the United States, but in a Trail of Tears Motorcycle Ride. Other annual events in the area include the Maple Hill Cemetery Stroll, the UFO Days festival, and the World's Largest Yard Sale. Famous north Alabamians include Helen Keller, Tallulah Bankhead, and Pat Buttram, who played Mr. Haney on* **Green Acres***. Other local artists include mule-driving potter Jerry Brown, the monk who built the Ave Maria Grotto, second- (or third-) generation soul men the Alabama Brothers, and whoever got the idea for the pickle-cicles at the Gu-Win Drive-In. North Alabama also can claim the first 911 call and the last Rick Nelson concert, as well as the Jazz Man, the Tinfoil Alien, the White Thang, and the Downey Booger. And if none of that interests you, go to Buck's Pocket with the rest of the losers.*

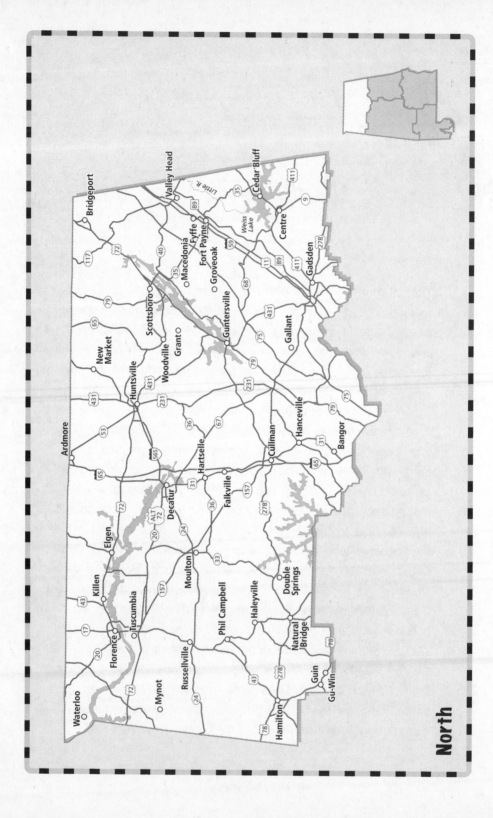

North

Rest Area Rocket

Ardmore

The Interstate 65 rest area just inside the Alabama line has its very own Saturn 1B rocket, a reminder to travelers that nearby Huntsville was the center of NASA's Apollo rocket-building program, led by the German-born engineer Wernher von Braun.

Though many visitors, after they leave the restrooms, snap photos of the "moon rocket," the Saturn 1B actually was used to launch

The Saturn 1B rocket is the second thing people visit at this rest area. NIKI SEPSAS

astronauts into Earth's orbit but no farther. *Apollo I*, *Apollo VII*, the *Apollo-Soyuz* rendezvous, and the three Skylab missions, for example, all were launched with a Saturn 1B like this one.

For moon missions, which required the extra weight of a lunar landing module, NASA used the massive Saturn V rockets, also built in Huntsville. Each was taller than the Statue of Liberty and expended the blastoff energy generated by eighty-five Hoover Dams.

Only three complete Saturn V rockets survive: one at the Kennedy Space Center in Florida, one at the Johnson Space Center in Texas, and one at the U.S. Space and Rocket Center in Huntsville, one of Alabama's top tourist attractions. But all are in bad shape, and a "Save the Saturn V" campaign is under way. Information is available at www.spacecamp.com.

The State Line between Drunk and Sober
Ardmore

Half the town of Ardmore is in Tennessee, half in Alabama. The two Ardmores share police, water, and sewer departments, but each has its own elected officials.

You can buy liquor and lottery tickets in Ardmore, Tennessee, but not in Ardmore, Alabama. Tennessee has a state lottery, unlike Alabama; and Limestone County, Alabama, is a dry county, unlike Giles County, Tennessee.

The more sober-sided Ardmore is on Highway 53, just east of I-65 at exit 1.

An Underground Nightspot (Literally)
Bangor

Today it's off limits to the public, but Bangor Cave once was a jumping joint, a man-made underground restaurant and nightclub with roulette wheels, a live orchestra, tuxedo-clad waiters, the works. Still reportedly there, covered in graffiti, are the stone bar where drinks were served and the stone benches where revelers sat.

Pam Jones reports in the summer 2006 issue of *Alabama Heritage* magazine that, like many other "social caves" nationwide, Bangor Cave already had been the site of political rallies, concerts, and July Fourth celebrations in the late nineteenth century, decades before owner J. Breck Musgrove and a group of investors set about turning the place into a Depression-era nightspot. "The pioneers in this unique development," the *Birmingham News* reported, "have outmaneuvered nature to convert the recesses of Bangor Cave into a place of comfort, charm, and beauty." The largest room, 350 feet long by 57 feet wide, included a fieldstone bar, a green-and-red-tiled dance floor, and a stone orchestra pit that could seat thirty musicians.

Local legend has it that the club was an illegal speakeasy during Prohibition, but the club didn't open until 1937, four years after Prohibition was repealed nationwide. The club did, however, offer an illegal casino and, it was whispered, more sensual illegal entertainments as well. Governor Bibb Graves called the underground club a "notorious dive" and had it raided repeatedly.

"The club's doors were finally padlocked permanently in January 1939, its owners were arrested, and within the year a mysterious fire destroyed the cave's interior," Jones writes. "But during its heyday, the club reportedly took in more than a million dollars and provided thousands of Alabamians with a taste of glamour and excitement often in short supply during the dark days of the Depression."

Bangor Cave is in the Bangor community of Blount County, off I-65 about 30 miles north of Birmingham. The cave entrance is on private property and not open to the public, but you can get very near it via Bangor Cave Road, a dead end that parallels the old Louisville & Nashville Railroad tracks, now owned by CSX. (The L&N built a spur to deliver well-heeled patrons directly to the cave entrance.) Turn off U.S. Highway 31 onto Eldon Lane, between Garden City and Blount Springs, and Bangor Cave Road is about 500 feet ahead on the left.

10,000 Years of Garbage
Bridgeport

If you were looking for a nice cave to live in, you couldn't do better than Russell Cave. It's roomy with fresh running water inside and a mouth that faces the morning sun. That's why Russell Cave is believed to have been inhabited continually by Native Americans over the course of more than 10,000 years.

Sometimes it was a hunting camp or winter quarters, sometimes a permanent dwelling, though it never held more than thirty people at a time. We know this because ceiling erosion and silt deposits through the millennia kept raising the cave floor, bit by bit, so that archaeologists now have about 30 feet of old campfires and debris to sort through—the layered leavings of successive generations.

First excavated by the Tennessee Archaeological Society in 1953 and by the Smithsonian in 1956–1958, Russell Cave was designated a national monument by President John F. Kennedy in 1961. It's 5 miles west of U.S. Highway 72, via County Roads 75 and 98, and is open daily except Thanksgiving, Christmas, and New Year's Day. Admission is free. For more information call (256) 495-2672 or visit www.nps.gov/ruca.

All's Fair in War
Cedar Bluff

Cedar Bluff on the Coosa River was the site of one of the most famous battlefield ruses of the Civil War.

For several days and nights in late April and early May 1863, a Confederate force chased a Federal force eastward across northern Alabama. The Federals, led by Gen. Abel Streight, were determined to destroy the railroad at Rome, Georgia, a vital supply line for Atlanta. The Confederates, led by Gen. Nathan Bedford Forrest, were just as determined to stop them.

The two forces fought six battles, but the Federals—who included at least six Alabamians in their ranks—kept forging ahead. Streight's men were riding braying mules, not horses, so they were easy to follow even at night. Locals referred to them as the Jackass Cavalry.

Forrest, a dashing figure, received some help along the way from teenage girls. At Royal the young sisters Celia and Winnie Mae Murphree took three marauding Federals prisoner and marched them to Forrest's camp. At Black Creek sixteen-year-old Emma Sansom climbed onto the back of Forrest's horse and led Forrest to a cattle ford where his men could safely cross. A statue of her pointing the way was erected in 1907 in Gadsden; you can see it at the Coosa River bridge on Broad Street. (To date the statue's pointing index finger has been broken off by vandals or souvenir hunters—and replaced—five times.)

Another local hero was Gadsden resident John Wisdom, the Paul Revere of the South, who rode 70 miles in eight and a half hours, changing mounts six times, to warn Rome that the Yankees were coming. Alabamians point out that he rode both farther and faster than Revere. Today, signs along his route commemorate the John Wisdom Trail.

By the time the opposing forces reached Cedar Bluff on May 3, Forrest had only 600 men in his command, compared to Streight's 1,500. Rather than attack again, Forrest decided he'd try to trick Streight into surrendering. Forrest had his men march the same two cannons around and around a hilltop that he knew was visible to Streight. Each time they passed into view, the cannons bore different regimental colors. Streight looked on in horror, convinced that Forrest had somehow obtained reinforcements—many regiments, much artillery. Streight surrendered.

When he found out the truth, Streight was not a good sport. He raged and complained and demanded his weapons back. According to legend Forrest replied, "All's fair in love and war," leading Forrest disciples to claim that he invented this cliché (in fact, it appears in *Frank Fairleigh*, an 1850 novel by the British writer Francis Edward Smedley).

Streight may have got the last laugh, anyway. Though he didn't make it to Rome, his Jackass Cavalry had accomplished a larger

"Blues Siblings" Just Didn't Cut It

In the crowded field of Blues Brothers imitators, it's important to be somehow distinctive—to be women, like the Blues Broads, or Danish, like the Copenhagen Blues Brothers, or creatively misspelled, like the Blooze Brothers, the Bluz Brothers, or the Blues Brothers Banned.

Justin and Jamey Crisler of Town Creek, a.k.a. the Alabama Brothers ("We're on a mission of fun"), have a distinction that's hard to beat. Unlike the Bavarian Blues Brothers and the Illinois Blues Brothers and Jake & Elwood's Blues Revue, unlike Briefcase Full of Blues and Out of the Blue and the Soulmen and Son of John, the Alabama Brothers are actual brothers. Not even the Blues Brothers themselves could make that claim!

Justin, who plays the Elwood-like harmonica player, has an associate degree in criminal justice and runs the act full-time. Jamey, eight years older, does the Jake-like lead vocals; he's a psychiatric nurse at Decatur General Hospital. They drive to gigs in a restored 1974 Dodge Monaco "Bluesmobile" that's an exact replica of the one in the movie. They're backed by a veteran session musician, saxophonist Jim Nelson, and his band, Soul Society.

The Alabama Brothers have a lengthy resumé of more than 600 performances, having appeared in Nashville at the Opryland Hotel and the Hard Rock Cafe, in Memphis at the Peabody Hotel, in Orange Beach, Alabama, at the swank Perdido Beach Resort, and at many southeastern street festivals, including, of course, the Courtland, Alabama, Christmas parade. They've performed with Patty Loveless, the Georgia Satellites, Gary Lewis and the Playboys, Mark Lindsay (formerly of Paul Revere and the Raiders), and even Sonny West, "Elvis Presley's bodyguard and friend."

The Alabama Brothers' Web site used to include several legal disclaimers: "The brothers are not to be confused with Belushi and Aykroyd! (even though they look just like them)." "'Blues Brothers' is a registered trademark of Daniel E. Aykroyd and Judith Jaclyn Pisano [Belushi's widow]." And most elaborately, "They [the Alabama Brothers] sing Blues music and choose of their own free will in this great nation to dress in beatnik, '50s-style black suits and black hats to disguise themselves as businessmen from the rest of the world seeking to 'harass' musicians. ANY similarities to the below referenced 'Blues Brothers' are strictly and purely coincidental."

The disclaimers aren't there anymore, and the messages were always mixed, because the Alabama Brothers' Web site is www.thealabama bluesbrothers.com, and their e-mail address is thebluesbrothers@aol .com. Aykroyd and Pisano's lawyers must be busy with all those other Blues Brothers bands, or maybe they've just chilled a bit upon remembering that the Blues Brothers was a cover band in the first place.

Unlike Jake and Elwood, the original Blues Brothers played by Dan Aykroyd and John Belushi, Jamey and Justin are really brothers. Really.

aim—keeping Forrest away from Grant's landing at Vicksburg. To add insult to injury, Streight soon escaped from Confederate custody.

After the war Forrest, a lifelong Tennessean, helped found the Ku Klux Klan, which did nothing to enhance his twentieth-century reputation.

Since the Coosa was dammed in the twentieth century, the town of Cedar Bluff now overlooks the man-made reservoir of Weiss Lake on Highway 68. A book-length account of Streight's raid and Forrest's pursuit is *The Lightning Mule Brigade* by Robert L. Willett (1999).

If Only He Had Lived to See Liquid Paper

Centre

Locals say John Pratt invented the typewriter, not a typewriter, but the history is more complicated than that, as history usually is.

A lawyer and newspaperman who lived in Centre until 1864, Pratt moved to England and there patented his pterotype, which used piano keys and a rotating ball to put type onto paper. It was notable enough to be written up in *Scientific American* that July, but it was only one of dozens of such machines being worked on at the time, by dozens of inventors.

The first such machine to be mass-produced was introduced in 1873 by Carlos Glidden and Christopher Latham Sholes of Milwaukee. They made a deal with the Remington gun-making company to manufacture their machine, which they called a "Type-Writer"—the name that stuck. But Pratt continued to patent improvements to his pterotype as late as 1894.

Pratt's grave is in John Pratt Memorial Park on old U.S. Highway 411 in Centre. For much more information on typewriter history than you really want to know, visit the wonderful Virtual Typewriter Museum at www.typewritermuseum.org.

Ave Maria Grotto
Cullman

The Ave Maria Grotto was a labor of love by a gentle, hunchbacked monk named Brother Joseph. This self-taught artist, using concrete, stone, and found materials, created more than a hundred intricately detailed miniature buildings, most of them replicas of holy sites such as St. Peter's Basilica and the Shrine of Lourdes.

All the structures are on display in a four-acre park on the grounds of St. Bernard Abbey in Cullman, the Benedictine monastery where Brother Joseph lived most of his life. Strictly speaking, the Ave Maria Grotto is the arched artificial cave that houses many of the structures, but most people call the whole park by that name.

Born Michael Zoettl in Bavaria in 1878, Brother Joseph lived at St. Bernard Abbey from age fourteen. He was deformed in a serious accident at age sixteen while hoisting a several-hundred-pound bell, but his physical troubles didn't inhibit his creativity. He worked without sketches or even a ruler, guided only by photos in books and his mind's eye. Word of the beautiful miniatures made by the little monk in Cullman began to spread, and his abbot eventually okayed the construction of a permanent display area for Brother Joseph's creations in an abandoned quarry that had provided building stones for the abbey in the nineteenth century.

At the grotto's formal opening on May 10, 1934, the shy Brother Joseph hid in the crowd. For years thereafter if he happened to encounter a visitor, he wouldn't identify himself, saying only that he worked in the gardens. Toward the end he had to be carried down the hill to visit his creations. His funeral Mass in 1961 was sung in the grotto to which he had devoted so much of his life.

The Ave Maria Grotto is at 1600 St. Bernard Drive Southeast. From I-65 go east on U.S. Highway 278 and follow the signs. Hours are 8:00 a.m. to 6:00 p.m. April through September, and 8:00 a.m. to 5:00 p.m. the rest of the year. Admission is charged; group rates are available. For more information call (256) 734-4110 or log onto www.avemariagrotto.com.

★ ★

Cook's Pest Control Museum
Decatur

Years ago, Decatur exterminator John R. Cook started collecting the different bugs killed on the job so that he could train his employees to know their enemy.

Once you start collecting things, it's hard to stop, so now the Cook's Pest Control collection is housed at Cook's Natural Science Museum: mounted birds, mammals, minerals, seashells, coral, and, of course, 2,000 mounted bugs. Visitors are welcome to—yikes!—touch all of them.

Known to Decatur schoolchildren as the "bug museum," Cook's is at 412 Thirteenth Street Southeast. Admission is free. Hours are 9:00 a.m. to 5:00 p.m. Monday through Saturday (except for the noon hour), and 2:00 to 5:00 p.m. Sunday. If you have questions, call (256) 350-9347 or visit www.cookspest.com/museum.html.

Muffler-Shop Art
Decatur

"Keeping the Tennessee Valley quiet since 1967," the Quick Stop Muffler Shop in Decatur sells, repairs, and installs mufflers. More recently it has developed a profitable sideline: muffler art.

The Quick Stop sells whimsical creatures made of mufflers. These include Spotz and Blackie, the muffler dogs ($30); Felix and Callie, the muffler cats ($35); Pinky and Ellie, the muffler pigs ($30); Rudy, the muffler deer ($55 to $75); Stinky, the muffler skunk ($25); Bama, the muffler elephant ($35); Allie, the muffler space alien ($75); and a not-yet-named muffler giraffe ($40 and up).

The shop is at 1303 Sixth Avenue Southeast, but all the muffler creatures also are sold online at www.quickstopmuffler.com. Call (256) 355-0131 for more information.

The Jazz Man

Most local ghost stories, alas, aren't really local at all. The same basic ghost stories are told and retold ad infinitum all over the country. Hundreds of towns claim, for example, to have a "crybaby lane," where ghostly children are heard weeping, or a decapitated train employee or construction worker or soldier who searches for his head, or a college student who keeps committing suicide in her dorm room for all eternity.

Without a doubt the most clichéd ghost story in the United States is the one that folklorist Jan Harold Brunvand dubbed "The Vanishing Hitchhiker." Calling it "one of the oldest and most widely told of all urban legends," Brunvand explains that its basic element is a hitchhiker who disappears from the car before the destination is reached; often the hitchhiker is identified as a teenage girl (or teenage boy or old man or small child) who died on that very date years earlier.

That so many towns claim this generic story as their own without variation is somewhat disappointing, a sort of collective failure of imagination. Elgin, then, deserves credit for coming up with a more interesting vanishing hitchhiker.

Many years ago, Elgin was the home of an eccentric street musician who roamed the town in a white zoot suit, tooting his trumpet. He was called the Jazz Man. One day, walking along the Second Street Bridge on his way to Florence, he was hit by a speeding car and killed. Now, night after night after night, a white-suited figure carrying a trumpet paces the Second Street Bridge, flags down cars, and cadges rides into Florence—but when the car arrives, the Jazz Man is always gone.

The Muscle Shoals area has a rich musical history, so it's appropriate that a local vanishing hitchhiker be identified as a trumpet-toting musician. But as Muscle Shoals and Sheffield have famous recording studios, why is the Jazz Man so determined to get to Florence?

The Free State of Winston
Double Springs

The state of Alabama seceded from the Union in January 1861, but many Alabamians thought this was a serious mistake. Pro-Union sentiment was especially strong in the hardscrabble hill country of northern Alabama, far from the wealthy plantations of the lowlands.

About 3,000 pro-Union citizens gathered on July 4, 1861, at Looney's Tavern in Winston County to discuss their options. Some advocated seceding from Alabama, just as Alabama had seceded from the Union, and declaring what one attendee jokingly called "the Free State of Winston." Others proposed joining similarly minded counties in Alabama and Tennessee to form a larger pro-Union state; someone suggested this state be named Nicajack, after a Cherokee tribe.

Neither of those fantasies came to pass, but hundreds of Alabamians headed north to enlist in the U.S. Army, and many more who stayed behind harassed and bedeviled the Confederates in a pro-Union resistance movement.

The owner of Looney's Tavern, Bill Looney, became a particularly daring outlaw, leading raids to free Unionists from Confederate jails and personally escorting many Alabamians to safety behind Federal lines. No one quite knows what became of Bill Looney—he drops from the historical record after being granted a federal pension in 1870—but he remains a legendary figure in Winston County.

Tinfoil Alien
Falkville

October 1973 brought a rash of UFO sightings and "close encounter" reports across the Southeast, none more interesting than the story told by the police chief of Falkville.

The night of October 17, Chief Jeff Greenhaw got a phone call from a hysterical woman who claimed to have seen a "spaceship" land in a pasture west of town. He drove out to investigate, taking along a Polaroid camera just in case. What he found was no spaceship but a shiny humanoid figure, 6-foot-5 or taller, with an antenna on its head, walking mechanically along the side of the road.

"He was real bright, something like mercury on nickel, but just as smooth as glass," Greenhaw said later. He added, "I don't believe it was aluminum foil," thus ensuring that his sighting would be known as the "tinfoil alien" forevermore.

With no preparation the chief ad-libbed the best imaginable first-contact line: "Howdy, stranger." The figure, startled by Greenhaw's headlights, took off running. Greenhaw gave chase in his truck across a field, but the figure outran him, "running faster than any human I ever saw," and disappeared into the woods—but not before Greenhaw snapped four Polaroid photos of the thing.

All four were published in the *Decatur Daily*, alongside Greenhaw's breathless account of his adventure. What is now known as a "media frenzy" ensued, and most of Greenhaw's neighbors did not appreciate the attention being paid to their town and to their police chief. A month after Greenhaw made his claims public, he was out of a job.

Interestingly, two space aliens in silvery suits were reported in Athens, Georgia, an hour before Greenhaw's alleged encounter. But the tinfoil alien was never seen again in Falkville, and the ridiculed police chief who reported it eventually dropped from sight.

Falkville is on US 31 about 19 miles south of Decatur, just off I-65 in Morgan County.

Over Budget and There's No Spa Tub

Florence

The only Frank Lloyd Wright building in Alabama is this house that the legendary architect built for newlyweds Stanley and Mildred Rosenbaum on a two-acre lot in 1939.

It was one of Wright's first "Usonian houses"—"Us" as in "U.S." The Usonian house was Wright's idea of a humble, inexpensive, comfortable dwelling that could be reproduced everywhere and made affordable for the average American. He described it this way: "A

★ ★

Unlike most Frank Lloyd Wright houses, this one stayed in one family's hands. NIKI SEPSAS

modest house, this Usonian house, a dwelling place that has no feeling at all for the 'grand' except as the house extends itself in the flat parallel to the ground. It will be a companion to the horizon."

The Rosenbaum House is a near-perfect example of the Usonian design: a single story on a concrete slab with two angled wings, a "public" wing (with the living room and dining room) and a "private" wing (with the bedrooms). At the junction of the two wings are the kitchen, bath, and hearth, which Wright viewed as the heart of any house.

Wright was notorious for going over budget on his projects, and the Rosenbaum House was no exception. Wright claimed the Usonian houses would cost $5,000 apiece, but all of them—sixty total—wound up costing twice that (still a bargain, compared to home prices today!).

The Rosenbaum House is actually a modified Usonian, as Wright returned in 1948—by which time the Rosenbaums had four growing boys—to design an addition, including a children's dormitory, that nearly doubled the square footage of the house. The house stayed in the Rosenbaum family for sixty years; they sold it to the city of Florence in 1999. Now it's a museum.

The Rosenbaum House is at 601 Riverview Drive. Hours are 10:00 a.m. to 4:00 p.m. Tuesday through Saturday, and 1:00 p.m. to 4 p.m. Sunday. Admission is charged. For more information call (256) 740-8899 or visit www.wrightinalabama.com.

Alabama's Version of Cannes

Florence

The George Lindsey Film Festival, held each spring at the University of North Alabama, honors one of the school's most famous alumni, actor and comedian George Lindsey, who played Goober on *The Andy Griffith Show* (1964–1968) and its spin-off, *Mayberry R.F.D.* (1968–1971) and then spent twenty years in the cast of *Hee Haw* (1972–1992).

Lindsey went to UNA and then Florence State Teachers College, on a football scholarship alongside Harlon Hill, who later played for the Chicago Bears. Lindsey says their team had only one play: "Harlon, go long." Lindsey got his first taste of showbiz in Florence, appearing in a Little Theatre production of *Oklahoma!* and winning a campus talent show with his imitation of Franklin Roosevelt. (On *The Andy Griffith Show*, Goober was known for his lame celebrity imitations.)

The film festival includes juried competitions, screenings, workshops, and lectures by visiting artists. Past guests include Oscar-winning actor-writer-director Billy Bob Thornton, Oscar-winning actor Ernest Borgnine, comic singer-songwriter Ray Stevens, *Seinfeld* director Tom Cherones, *Welcome Back, Kotter* writer-director George Yanok, and songwriter and soundtrack producer Mike Curb, formerly of the Mike Curb Congregation. For more details call (256) 765-4592 or log onto www.lindseyfilmfest.com.

★ ★

Te-lah-nay's Wall
Florence

On his land along the old Natchez Trace in Lauderdale County, in the northwest corner of the state, Tom Hendrix has been building, for more than fifteen years, an unmortared stone wall to honor his great-great-grandmother, Te-lah-nay, a Yuchi tribeswoman who survived the nineteenth-century genocide known as the "Trail of Tears."

At its highest points the irregular wall is 4 feet high; at its widest points, it's 10 feet wide. At 2.5 miles long it may be the largest monument to a woman in the United States. Hendrix told the *Florence Times Daily* in 2003 that the wall contains stones from every U.S. state and 126 stones from foreign lands.

After her family was killed by U.S. troops, Te-lah-nay selected stones from the riverbank and placed them around the burial mounds to honor her ancestors. And so Hendrix continues to place stones today, to honor the brave woman who walked home from Oklahoma, determined to live in her own land and not on a reservation.

"She did not make an ordinary journey," Hendrix told the *Times Daily*. "I did not build an ordinary wall."

The wall is in Lauderdale County at 13890 County Road 8, near the intersection of the Natchez Trace Parkway, just off Highway 20 near Florence. Hendrix's book about Te-lah-nay is titled *If the Legends Fade*. His Web site, which includes a photo of the wall and contact information, is www.ifthelegendsfade.com.

Sock Capital of the World
Fort Payne

Fort Payne once called itself the Sock Capital of the World. DeKalb County, of which Fort Payne is the county seat, once had more than 150 sock factories, producing twelve million pairs of socks a week. According to the National Association of Hosiery Manufacturers, if you were an American, and you put on socks in the morning, the odds were one in eight that they were made in DeKalb County, Alabama.

But in recent years two-thirds of the sock factories have closed, driven out of business by cheaper imported socks from China. Happily, a number of new industries have moved in to replace them, often with higher-paying jobs than sock making.

The W. B. Davis Hosiery Mill was the first sock factory in DeKalb County, opening in 1907. That first mill building, known as the "Big Mill," still stands, but it's an antiques mall now. It's located at 151 Eighth Street Northeast, near the eastern end of Eighth Street downtown. Hours are 10:00 a.m. to 4:00 p.m. Monday through Saturday, and 1:00 to 4:00 p.m. on Sunday. Call (256) 845-3380 for more information. The whole town has an annual Hosiery Week celebration in August.

Joe's Truck Stop

Fort Payne

As it comes into Fort Payne from the east, Highway 35 drops steeply down the Lookout Mountain plateau until it's stopped by a T intersection at Fifth Street—at Joe Faulkner's house.

A lot of brakes fail coming down Highway 35, and the runaway vehicles all used to wind up in Faulkner's yard. Thirteen big trucks wiped out there in 1950 alone. Some of those trucks or their loads actually hit his house. Finally, Faulkner got fed up and built a 4-foot-thick wall on his property line, a wall he reinforced with wire, pipe, and the chassis of two Dodge trucks. Now the runaway trucks hit the wall and go no farther, which is why locals call the wall "Joe's Truck Stop."

Joe's Truck Stop is at 600 Fifth Street Northeast, 4 blocks east of U.S. Highway 11, the main north-south route through town.

Watch for "Black Helicopters"

The incident reports began October 20, 1992, and continued for months, in Marshall and DeKalb Counties. Dozens of cattle were found dead in their pastures with various organs missing. Witnesses described charred, bloodless, surgically precise incisions. There were no tire tracks or footprints around the carcasses. Wild stories spread of mysterious "black helicopters" skimming the treetops, and locals stocked up on high-powered rifles and ammo.

A celebrated April 7, 1993, press conference featured Fyffe's police chief and Fyffe's mayor backing up Ted Oliphant, a Fyffe Police Department patrolman who was the town's chief investigator into the claims. "To date," said the police department's official statement, "no police agency has established a suspect or motive for these incidents of phantom surgery perpetrated on area livestock."

These claims brought Fyffe much publicity and much ridicule. That Fyffe was a homonym for Fife, as in Mayberry deputy Barney Fife, was widely noted. But Fyffe was actually behind the curve in cattle-mutilation folklore. Claims that livestock have been found mutilated by forces unknown to society or science, perhaps extraterrestrial in origin, have been eagerly discussed by UFO buffs since 1967, though they became widespread only in the 1980s, thanks to spooky documentaries such as *Strange Harvest*, by Philadelphia UFO enthusiast Linda Moulton Howe, who contends that space aliens are harvesting genetic material with the collusion of the U.S. government.

By the time of the Fyffe hysteria, the whole cattle-mutilation phenomenon had been pretty thoroughly debunked to the satisfaction of all but true believers. Two extensive investigations in the 1970s, one by the State of Colorado and one by the State of New Mexico, each of which studied hundreds of case reports, concluded that 99 percent of the so-called mutilations were the work of coyotes, vultures, and other commonplace predators and scavengers. The remaining 1 percent, the reports concluded, were outright hoaxes. The 1983 book *Mute Evidence*, by Daniel Kagan and Ian Summers, argued that only media hype keeps this non-story going year after year.

Ken Rommel, the twenty-eight-year FBI veteran who wrote New Mexico's report—available in its entirety at www.parascope.com/articles/0597/romindex.htm—placed much of the blame on small-town law-enforcement officers, ignorant of animal pathology, who call in the wrong "experts" and accept their wild theories without question. "You've got Sheriff Num-nutz up in some place where he can't even find his own police car, saying, 'It looks like laser surgery,' and the reporters love quotes like that, so they repeat it. Now, if I were a reporter, I would ask, 'Sheriff, how much do you know about laser surgery?'"

Patrolman Oliphant of Fyffe moved to California, where he is now a freelance UFO documentarian and a believer in a massive government cover-up to hide the truth of cattle mutilations. "We've got two choices," he wrote on one Web site. "It's either the aliens or your tax dollars at work. Take your pick."

Fyffe, meanwhile, has decided to take advantage of its cult notoriety with an annual UFO Days festival, a hot-air-ballooning event held each August. For more information visit www.fyffecity limits.com.

★ ★

Noccalula Falls Memorials
Gadsden

Overlooking the lovely 90-foot drop of Noccalula Falls, a.k.a. Black Creek Falls, is a statue of an Indian princess in the act of diving off the bluff. According to local legend the beautiful maiden Noccalula hurled herself into the falls centuries ago rather than marry a man she didn't love.

The same story is told about dozens of other waterfalls and precipices all over North America, most famously Niagara Falls, where the *Maid of the Mist* tour boat is named for the tragic princess. Other places where she supposedly leaped include Lovers Leap in Indiana, Slave Falls in Manitoba, Bash Bish Falls in Massachusetts, Stony Brook Glen in New York, Multnomah Falls in Oregon, Indian Rock in

The statue depicts the tragic princess about to give her life for tourism. NIKI SEPSAS

Un-Reconstructed

Based in Gallant, Un-Reconstructed is a five-person acoustic band that plays Irish and Scottish folk music and music of the period 1861–1865. Many people would call this time the Civil War, but many Southerners view that phrase as fighting words. The band prefers to call it the War between the States or the War for Southern Independence.

Un-Reconstructed's busy tour schedule includes battle reenactments, Sons of Confederate Veterans dances, and cemetery dedications. Band members include Dave Edwards on guitar, lead vocals, pennywhistle, and harmonica; Susie Stephenson on hammered dulcimer, jaw harp, bodhran, and tambourine; Chris Dempsey on fiddle and mandolin; Heather Dempsey on tambourine and vocals; and Doug Carson on fiddle and bass.

The band's repertoire includes "Wayfaring Stranger," "Shady Grove," "Sally Good'en," "Goober Peas," "I Wonder As I Wander," "Soldier's Joy," and, inevitably, "Ashokan Farewell," a 1982 tune by Jay Ungar that became permanently associated with 1861–1865 when Ken Burns used it extensively (fifty-nine minutes and eleven seconds total) in his TV documentary *The Civil War*.

For bookings, a tour schedule, and copies of the band's CDs, including *Cotton Bales and Barley, Christmas 1864*, and *We Dare Sing Dixie*, visit www.un-reconstructed.com.

Pennsylvania, Lake Jocassee in South Carolina, and Maiden Rock in Wisconsin. In North Carolina the same story is told in at least three different places: Blowing Rock, Jump Off Rock, and Lovers Leap. In the legend of Issaqueena Falls in South Carolina, the princess only pretended to jump

and then eloped with her lover. The Noccalula Falls legend isn't unique even in Alabama; Clear Creek Falls in Winston County has its own jumping princess.

Another Noccalula Falls memorial, however, is perhaps one of a kind. It's the grave of Big Pedo, a tame deer in the Noccalula Falls Park petting zoo. While grazing, Big Pedo was shot and killed by a poacher. The epitaph on the tombstone reads: BIG PEDO, 1957–1978. BELOVED PET OF THE CHILDREN OF GADSDEN. DEDICATED BY CLARK MEMORIALS TO THOSE WHO LOVE GOD'S GENTLE CREATURES.

Noccalula Falls Park is on Highway 211, south of exit 188 off Interstate 59. It's open year-round from 9:00 a.m. to dusk. Admission is charged. For more information call the park at (256) 549-4663.

World's Longest Yard Sale

Gadsden

The World's Longest Yard Sale was begun in 1987 by the Chamber of Commerce of Fentress County, Tennessee. Today it's officially 630 miles long, from Noccalula Falls in Gadsden, Alabama, north to Defiance, Ohio, and it lasts for four days each August. The event's slogan: "I drove, I stopped, I shopped till I dropped!"

More than 1,000 yard sales line the 93-mile Alabama section, which calls itself "America's Most Scenic Shopping Mall" because it follows the Lookout Mountain Parkway—Highway 176 to DeKalb Country Road 89 to Highway 117. For information contact the DeKalb County Tourist Association at (888) 805-4740 or visit its Web site, www .tourdekalb.com/yardsale.htm.

A similar event each May is the 502-mile Antique Alley Yard Sale, along US 11 from Meridian, Mississippi, through Alabama and Tennessee to Bristol, Virginia.

Buck's Pocket
Groveoak

Modern Alabama folklore has it that Buck's Pocket (www.alapark
.com/buckspocket), now a state park on County Road 174 northeast
of Guntersville, is the place where politicians who lose elections go to
"lick their wounds"—or, according to the more bloodthirsty versions of
the story, to jump off the bluff and end it all.

Newspaper columnists and TV pundits routinely mystify outsiders
by speculating about which candidates are the most likely to be sent
to Buck's Pocket. Even the sign at the park entrance identifies it as a
"Haven for Defeated Politicians," although no one can remember any
politician actually beating a retreat there.

Most observers say the legend began with colorful Alabama governor
"Big" Jim Folsom (the one who preceded the all-too-colorful George
Wallace), who during his many campaigns frequently threatened to
send his opponents to Buck's Pocket, or to go there himself—perhaps
because Buck's Pocket was, in the 1940s and 1950s, about as remote as
a self-exiled Alabamian could get without leaving the state altogether.

Reasons to go to Buck's Pocket include campsites, picnic areas, hiking trails, and gorgeous mountain scenery, even if you edged out your
challenger last November. Call the park office at (256) 659-2000 for
more information.

All News Is Local
Guntersville

The best-known small-town newspaper in Alabama, and one of the
most eccentric small-town newspapers anywhere, is the *Advertiser-
Gleam* in Guntersville. Among its distinctions are the following:

- It refuses to run any news, however compelling, that isn't local. If it
  happened outside Marshall County, Alabama, and involves no one
  from Marshall County, Alabama, you won't read about it in the
  Advertiser-Gleam.

- It refuses to run any headline wider than a single column of type. No story is worth a shout in the *Advertiser-Gleam*.

- The *Advertiser-Gleam* seems to have shunned every newspaper design innovation of the past fifty years. It has no color, no big photos (in fact, few photos of any kind), no computer graphics—just column after column of tiny type and those demure, one-column headlines. The cumulative effect is wonderfully calming.

- Everyone in Guntersville who dies gets a lengthy, well-written, thoroughly reported obituary in the paper, like celebrities in the *New York Times*. The *Advertiser-Gleam* assumes that everyone in Guntersville is interesting, and this turns out, week after week, to be true, as obits note, for example, that a woman was born into a family of ten children and subsequently had ten children of her own, or that a man was the last person to deliver mail on a bicycle in Parches Cove.

- While the meat and potatoes of the *Advertiser-Gleam* is the small-town news that no one outside town would print—for example, the complete list of winners of the Girl Scout Grand Prix soapbox derby at the Guntersville Rec Center—the newspaper also has an abiding fascination for weirdness. Nearly every issue includes something startling: a confused killdeer that is trying to hatch a pecan, a family that keeps finding 6-foot snake skins in the attic, a man who grows green beans in the shape of teepees, a rumor that a duck hunter on Lake Guntersville shot down an angel. These stories are all the more startling because, remember, they're all local.

The *Advertiser-Gleam* was founded in 1941 by Porter Harvey, who already had fifteen years of reporting experience at the *New York Post*, the *Nashville Tennessean*, and the *Birmingham Post-Herald*. His dream was to found the ultimate small-town newspaper. He named it for the gleam of the light on the surface of Lake Guntersville, a couple of blocks downhill from the newspaper office, and his initial delivery vehicle was a little red wagon that he pulled from door to door.

Porter Harvey was in all the newspapers, not just the *Advertiser-*

Gleam, when he celebrated his ninetieth birthday with a bungee jump, but his finest hour—perhaps one of the great moments of the American press—was the day he wrote a front-page story about the long column of ants in the bank parking lot across the street. You can't teach those instincts in journalism school.

Porter Harvey died in 1995, at age ninety-one. Since then, the paper has been ably run by his son, Sam. The *Advertiser-Gleam* is published Wednesday and Saturday. Copies are for sale all over town and at the newspaper office itself, 2222 Taylor Street, at the U.S. Highway 431 intersection downtown. People outside Marshall County can subscribe to it for only $48 a year. It's worth every penny. You can read some sample articles online at www.advertisergleam.com. Also highly recommended is Sam Harvey's book *High Adventure: Porter Harvey and the* Advertiser-Gleam.

Rick Nelson's Final Number

Guntersville

Rick Nelson's final rock 'n' roll show, though no one realized it at the time, was December 30, 1985, at P.J.'s Alley in Guntersville, a converted tire store. Nelson's three-night gig was a favor to an old friend and former bandmate, Alabama native Pat Upton, who owned the club. Nelson's last number, ominous only in hindsight, was a Buddy Holly hit, "Rave On."

The next day Nelson climbed into a chartered plane with his fiancée and his band members and headed toward Dallas for a New Year's Eve show. Like Buddy Holly they never made it. The plane made an emergency landing in DeKalb, Texas, just west of Texarkana, and erupted in flames on the ground, killing everyone aboard.

Nelson had grown up in America's living rooms, playing himself for seventeen years in the long-running family sitcom *The Adventures of Ozzie & Harriet*, first on radio and later on ABC television. The show costarred his brother, David, and his parents, bandleader Ozzie Nelson and singer Harriet Nelson.

★ ★

When young Rick picked up a guitar in 1956, he became a teen sensation, with hits including "Poor Little Fool," "Hello Mary Lou," and "It's Late." In 1987 Nelson was posthumously inducted into the Rock and Roll Hall of Fame, then in its second year of existence.

P.J.'s Alley is long gone, but the Holiday Inn where Nelson stayed that last night is still there, at 2140 Gunter Avenue, on the shore of Lake Guntersville. The hotel has put a plaque on the door of Room 106, where Nelson stayed, and a Rick Nelson display in the lobby.

Gu-Win and the Blue Moon Drive-In

Guin and Gu-Win

The neighboring Marion County towns of Guin and Gu-Win on U.S. Highway 78 were not founded, as folklore has it, by rival factions who disagreed bitterly on whether *Guin* was pronounced "gwen" or "gu-win" (rhymes with "to win").

Guin, named for a local family, is the much older town, incorporated in 1893. Guin grew, and by the 1950s it threatened to annex the neighboring community of Ear Gap. To prevent this, the citizens of Ear Gap incorporated their town in 1956, but they changed its name in the process.

A leader of the incorporation campaign was George Thornton, owner of the town's most prominent business, the new Gu-Win Drive-In movie theater, so named because it lay halfway between the towns of Guin (the "Gu") and Winfield (the "Win"). When Ear Gap was incorporated, it became Gu-Win, too. Locals claim Thornton pushed the name change because he didn't want to buy a new sign for his theater.

For years the drive-in was closed and used as a junkyard, but new owner David Curtis has reopened it as the Blue Moon Drive-In. Stadium seating, the latest rage at mall multiplexes, has been standard at this drive-in for years, as the cars park on a terraced hillside facing the giant screen at the foot of the hill. The projection booth and snack bar are behind the cars at the top of the hill. The movies broadcast on 91.1

FM on the theory that 911 was easy for patrons to remember. The snack bar sells standard drive-in fare but also a local delicacy, "pickle-cicles"—frozen pickle juice on a stick. If you want to know more, call (205) 468-8046 or write Blue Moon Drive-In, 4609 Highway 43, Guin, AL 35563.

Besides its name and its drive-in, Gu-Win's other claim to fame in Alabama is that every December since 1997, its town government has given each of its 200-odd citizens a $15 grocery certificate as a sort of Christmas bonus for being good neighbors all year.

Mr. Haney's Grave
Haleyville

His name was Pat Buttram, but to millions of *Green Acres* fans, he'll always be Mr. Haney.

The surreal sitcom *Green Acres*, which aired on CBS from 1965 to 1971, starred Eddie Albert and Eva Gabor as transplanted New Yorkers in the lunatic rural enclave of Hooterville. Their hopeless farm had been sold to them by a local con artist named Mr. Haney, a walleyed sharpie with a cracked voice who showed up in every episode with a truck full of dubious merchandise, on an eternal mission to talk the Douglases out of yet more money.

Mr. Haney was played by the veteran country comedian Pat Buttram (1915–1994), who in the 1940s and 1950s played Gene Autry's side-kick in Western movies, radio, and television. Before his Autry gig Buttram spent thirteen years as a regular on the *National Barn Dance* on Chicago radio station WLS, as the "Winston County Flash," working alongside such country stars as Patsy Montana, Red Foley, and "Lonesome" George Gobel.

Buttram had planned to go into the ministry like his father and studied to that end at Birmingham Southern College, but a trip to the 1933 Chicago World's Fair sealed the young Alabamian's fate. The *National Barn Dance* emcee picked Buttram out of the live audience at random to interview on the air. His ad-libbed jokes and unforgettable voice—which he once described as "a handful of gravel thrown in a Mix-Master"—brought the house down, and he was hired as a regular on the spot.

"Pat" was a nickname; his actual first name was Maxwell, after his mother's family. Buttram is buried at Maxwell Chapel United Methodist Church, which his grandparents founded and where his father was pastor for more than fifty years. Buttram's epitaph reads: A MAN DESERVES PARADISE WHO CAN MAKE HIS COMPANIONS LAUGH. The church is on County Road 93 less than a mile from Highway 195, north of Haleyville.

Coincidentally, Haleyville was the birthplace of another country radio comedian, Lloyd "Lonzo" George (1924–1991), who with Rollin "Oscar" Sullivan created the Grand Ole Opry comedy team of Lonzo and Oscar. In the 1940s they recorded such numbers as "I'm My Own Grandpa," "You Blacked My Blue Eyes Once Too Often," "Who Pulled the Plug from the Jug," and "If Texas Told What Arkan-saw Then What Did Tennes-see?" George left the act in 1950 and had a solo career as a country crooner, using the stage name Ken Marvin.

Number One in 911

Haleyville

In 1967 a presidential commission recommended a uniform emergency number throughout the United States, similar to the 999 number that Britain had instituted thirty years before. AT&T, then the national phone company, decided in January 1968 the number should be 911, in keeping with its new numbers for Directory Assistance (411) and Repair Service (611).

That decision was not binding on any of the smaller phone companies that provided local service independent of the Bell system, but reading about 911 in the *Wall Street Journal* inspired Bob Gallagher, president of the Alabama Telephone Company, to set up his own 911 service before AT&T could. One of his top technicians, Robert Fitzgerald, recommended Haleyville as a good place to start, and he set about designing the system.

Interesting Alabama Place Names

Big Coon Creek (Jackson County)

Big Nance Creek (Lawrence County):
Named for a legendary Indian chief.

Blubber Creek (Pickens County)

Bughall Creek (Bullock County)

Cold Fire Creek (Fayette County): Settlers fording the creek in winter found it "cold as fire."

Hells Creek (Fayette County): A corruption of Herald's Creek, after the Herald family.

Murder Creek (Conecuh County): Site of the murder of a party of settlers in 1788. The three murderers were a white man, a black man, and a Native American.

Peckerwood Creek (Coosa County)

Penitentiary Mountain (Lawrence County): The eighteenth-century stagecoach stop here also was a jail for prisoners being hauled to Tuscaloosa.

Pickwick Lake (Lauderdale County): Named for Dickens's *The Pickwick Papers*.

Point A Lake (Covington County): There is no Point B Lake.

Polecat Creek (Perry County)

Poor Creek (Henry County)

Puss Cuss Creek (Choctaw County): From the Choctaw *puskus*, meaning "child."

Rattlesnake Mountain (Cleburne County)

Shades Mountain (Jefferson County): The Chickasaws called its valley the Shades of Death.

Splunge Creek (Winston County)

Straight Mountain (Etowah County): Named for Abel Streight, the Union commander who made the celebrated raid through here in 1863.

Tight Eye Creek (Coffee County)

Turkey Heaven Mountain (Cleburne County)

On February 16, 1968, only a month after AT&T's announcement, the ceremonial first 911 call was placed from Mayor James Whitt's phone by Rankin Fite, speaker of the Alabama House. It was answered at the Haleyville police station by Congressman Tom Bevill as the chairman of the state Public Service Commission looked on. That chairman, enjoying the first statewide elected office of his political career, was the infamous Eugene "Bull" Connor, who as Birmingham's public safety commissioner had used dogs and fire hoses against civil rights marchers five years before.

The red "hotline" phone used to place that first 911 call is now in a display case at the Haleyville Police Department, 1901 Eleventh Avenue. For more details call the Haleyville Area Chamber of Commerce at (205) 486-5074. *Dispatch Monthly Magazine* has a fine, detailed history of Haleyville's accomplishment online at www.911dispatch .com/911/history/index.html.

Mule-Powered Pottery
Hamilton

Ninth-generation potter Jerry Brown does almost everything the old-fashioned way. He digs his own clay from a 110-year-old pit, grinds it in what may be the last mule-driven clay mill in the United States, and then hand-turns each piece before firing it in a brick kiln. He also favors traditional glazes and designs, including grotesque and comical "face jugs" like those made by slaves, for obscure reasons, 200 years ago.

Thoroughly up to date, however, is www.jerrybrownpottery.com, where online shoppers can buy everything from face jugs ($125 to $250 and up) to rooster-shaped teakettles ($110 to $200) and large popcorn bowls ($45) with "Ain't no more" scrawled on the inside bottom.

The online experience is no substitute for a visit with Brown at his showroom and studio, where the former Alabama Folk Artist of the Year welcomes visitors and does demonstrations. With advance notice he might even hook up old Blue, the mule. Jerry Brown Pottery is at 1414 County Road 81, between US 78 and downtown Hamilton. For more information call (800) 341-4919.

Above, Jerry Brown denies that any of his "face jugs" are self-portraits. Below, mules don't always cooperate with photographers—or with anyone else, for that matter.
NIKI SEPSAS

No Yankee Dogs Will Be Inducted
Hartselle

Inductees in the Alabama Animal Hall of Fame, sponsored by the Alabama Veterinary Medical Association, include Pioneer, a therapy horse at the Alabama Institute for Deaf and Blind in Talladega; Red Dog, a bloodhound at the St. Clair County Correctional Facility in St. Clair Springs; Paxton, a service dog who saved his master's life by knocking him out of the path of a pickup truck; and Fred, the adopted town dog of Rockford.

A building too house the Animal Hall of Fame will take years of fund-raising by the Alabama Veterinary Medical Foundation. In the meantime tickets for the $100-a-plate black-tie induction dinner, held annually in January, are available from Animal Hall of Fame chair Dr. Jan Strother, North Alabama Cat and Bird Clinic, 809 Highway 36 East, Hartselle, AL 35640-4725 or call (256) 773-0844. For more information, including a complete list of inductees by year, visit www.alvma.com.

Gimme Shelta
Huntsville

Shelta Cave is directly beneath the headquarters of the National Speleological Society, which represents more than 2,000 cave enthusiasts organized into 200 chapters, or "grottos." Access to Shelta Cave, which the society owns, is one of the many perks of membership.

Shelta Cave has two sinkhole entrances, is 2,500 feet long, and contains a seven-acre lake. In the nineteenth century it was a commercial cave with an underground dance hall. The cave used to abound in underground wildlife, including gray bats, beetles, and crustaceans, and was the only known habitat of the cave crayfish, an unhurried creature with a life expectancy of one hundred years. Alas, the bats flew away years ago, and the smaller creatures that fed on their leavings have all but disappeared.

The National Speleological Society is at 2813 Cave Avenue in Huntsville. For more information call (256) 852-1300 or visit www.caves.org.

Tallulah Hallelujah!

Huntsville

Her grandfather and uncle were U.S. senators and her father a congressman and speaker of the house. Her family stamped their name all over Alabama—the Bankhead National Forest, the Bankhead Endowment at the University of Alabama. But more famous than all the respectable Bankheads put together is the flamboyant actress Tallulah Bankhead (1902–1968), who did her best to ruin the family name and, in the process, earned the ongoing admiration of millions.

The historical marker in front of the Schiffman Building, where Tallulah was born January 31, 1902, is an inadequate tribute to her rich and shameless life. Much better is the excellent Web site created by fan Phillip Oliver of Florence, Alabama: "Tallulah: A Passionate Life." The home page proclaims, "Welcome Dahlings!" The address is http://home.hiwaay.net/~oliver/bankhead.html.

Tallulah was a fifteen-year-old beauty when she won a photo contest sponsored by *Picture Play* magazine. It was reason enough to move to New York City and seek Broadway stardom. She checked into the Algonquin Hotel and proceeded to drive her chaperone, her aunt Louise, to despair. As Tallulah famously put it, "My father warned me about men and booze, but he never said anything about women and cocaine." When Tallulah turned eighteen, Aunt Louise washed her hands, moved to Paris, and joined the International Red Cross.

Tallulah eventually became a star of the London stage, mobbed nightly by hundreds of female groupies who chanted, "Tallulah Hallelujah!" The great Augustus John painted her portrait in 1929. Later came Broadway smashes such as Lillian Hellman's *The Little Foxes* (1939) and Thornton Wilder's *The Skin of Our Teeth* (1942), as well as a classic Alfred Hitchcock movie, *Lifeboat* (1944). But Tallulah was never as famous for her acting as she was for her private life, if "private" is quite the word.

She had hundreds of affairs with men and women and loudly discussed all of them, smoked a hundred cigarettes a day, drank Cossacks under the table, lived out of a suitcase full of drugs, shed her clothes at parties as others shed their coats, and sashayed grandly past every setback—bad movies and flop plays, a brief and disastrous marriage, a near-fatal bout of gonorrhea, losing the role of Scarlett O'Hara to some nobody Limey strumpet. Tallulah may have been the first Hollywood star to have breast-implant surgery and then brag about it, showing the results to everyone who asked and many who didn't. In an era when Lucy and Desi officially slept in twin beds, Tallulah announced that she was on a quest to try every known sexual position in hopes of finding one that was actually comfortable and didn't make her sore afterward.

At the end she played the Black Widow on the *Batman* TV show and starred in a horror movie titled *Die, Die, My Darling*. She said she looked "older than God's wet nurse." She died December 12, 1968, and was buried in Maryland. On her deathbed the last intelligible word she spoke was "bourbon." They don't put that sort of thing on historical markers, but they should.

The historical marker noting Tallulah's birthplace is in front of the Schiffman Building, 231 Eastside Square, which means it's downtown on the east side of the Courthouse square. From Interstate 565, take exit 19C onto southbound Jefferson Street, which leads to the square. Follow the traffic around the square to the left. The Schiffman Building is on the left, and there's a metered parking lot behind it.

On a similar note, the long-vacant Tallulah Hotel in downtown Cordova, a Walker County town southeast of Jasper, is thought by some residents to have been Tallulah Bankhead's namesake or vice versa, but in fact Bankhead was named for her grandmother (who in turn had been named after the town of Tallulah Falls, Georgia), and the hotel was named after its founder's wife. Yet, when the famous actress visited the place, she was duly impressed by the inlaid floor tiles that spelled out *Tallulah*.

Those Wacky Raelians

Most Alabamians consider themselves religious, but very few consider themselves Raelian. Followers of a Frenchman named Rael (formerly named Claude Vorilhon), Raelians believe humans were created by space aliens. They also believe cloning holds the key to immortality. Rael says he learned all this when he was visited by peace-loving aliens in 1973.

The movement's Web site, www.rael.org, calls it "the world's largest Atheist, nonprofit UFO related organization . . . working towards the first embassy to welcome people from space . . . destroying the myth of god." Rael urges his followers to "fully get involved in the technologies of the future and become pioneers in order to rid society of all the Judeo-Christian taboos that slow down progress." On the other hand, Rael considers Raelism a branch of Judaism, since Moses, too, was a prophet visited by space aliens, and Jerusalem will be where the aliens reveal themselves to humanity.

Raelians became suddenly famous in December 2002, when a Raelian biotech company, Clonaid, claimed to have cloned a human. No evidence was produced, and most scientists dismissed the claim. But several Raelians in the scientifically minded, high-tech Huntsville area were interviewed a lot, most notably Hortense Dodo, an Alabama A&M microbiologist trying to clone an allergy-free peanut. "I know it [Raelism] sounds far-fetched," she told the *Huntsville Times*, "but everything that is normal to us now seemed far-fetched once upon a time."

★ ★

Maple Hill Cemetery
Huntsville

Maple Hill Cemetery, about a mile northwest of downtown, has been
a final resting place for Huntsville residents since 1818. Today, the
Huntsville Times reports, it has 80,000 permanent occupants, more
than most Alabama towns. The most famous of them is probably
Mary Chambers Bibb (1816–1835), who according to legend poisoned
herself by accident shortly after her wedding, perhaps in an attempt to
lighten her complexion (!). She supposedly was buried not only wearing her wedding dress, but sitting upright in her favorite rocking chair.
Teens have scared themselves witless for generations by putting their
ears against the cold marble of the crypt and convincing themselves
they hear Mary Bibb inside rocking . . . rocking . . . rocking. (Hers was
the first mausoleum in Huntsville, reason enough for locals to have
been fascinated by it at the time.)

Mary's father-in-law is the focus of another Maple Hill ghost story.
According to legend a spectral horse-drawn carriage can be seen in the
cemetery at night, carrying Governor Thomas Bibb home to his beloved
mansion, Belle Mina.

Colorful characters buried at Maple Hill include

- Cobweb artist Annie Bradshaw Clopton (1878–1956), a longtime
  Huntsville schoolteacher of infinite patience who stretched spider-
  webs across picture frames and then painted them with oils. (Some
  of her cobweb paintings are in the collection of Huntsville's Burritt on
  the Mountain museum, www.burrittonthemountain.com.)
- Palm reader Lena Mitchell (1906–1959), whose funeral was attended
  by hundreds of gypsies, and who since her death has been nicknamed "the Gypsy Queen."
- Samuel B. Moore, whose Jersey cow Lily Flagg won a blue ribbon for
  cream production at the 1893 Chicago World's Fair, and who threw
  a lavish celebratory party in Lily's honor.
- Mollie Teal (1852–1899), the town's most celebrated madam, who
  upon her death willed to the city her brothel, near the intersection

of what are now Whitesburg and Governors Drives. Her house of ill repute thus became a godsend: the original Huntsville Hospital.

Keeping the memory of all these folks alive is the Huntsville Pilgrimage Association, which stages a Cemetery Stroll each spring. At each famous grave site—more than sixty-five of them—a costumed reenactor tells the story of that notable, including poor Mary Bibb. Donations go to preserve and maintain the cemetery. For more information visit www.huntsvillepilgrimage.org.

Science Fiction Tax
Huntsville

Michael Williams of Huntsville, then a twenty-eight-year-old supermarket bagger, became briefly famous in 2002 when he proposed to tax science fiction.

At the time Williams was running for the Republican nomination in Alabama's Fifth Congressional District. He was unsuccessful; the incumbent, Bud Cramer, had that nomination sewed up. But Williams's proposal created quite a (negative) buzz on the Internet and in the ranks of the Science Fiction and Fantasy Writers of America.

Williams argued that just as highways are funded by gasoline taxes, so NASA could be funded by a science fiction tax—specifically, a 1 percent federal sales tax on science fiction books, comics, toys, movie tickets, and so on. "Taxing the science fiction," he told *Wired* magazine, "you're actually taxing the interest group of space."

Among the many objections quickly raised were the following:

- No one agrees on what is science fiction and what isn't, not even science fiction writers.
- Much science fiction, perhaps most, isn't about space at all. (Three Hollywood franchises come to mind: *Jurassic Park, The Matrix, X-Men.*)
- In order to fund NASA's $15 billion annual budget, the science fiction industry would have to gross $1.5 trillion a year, more than

twice as much as the computer industry. In short, science fiction editor Patrick Nielsen Hayden told *Wired* magazine, "This is like asking people who like murder mysteries to subsidize the jury system."

Williams's other proposals included a global assembly to ensure all Earthlings the rights granted in the U.S. Constitution and a mandatory constitutional convention whenever the human population of the Moon, Mars, and so on reaches 30,000.

Robbin' and Killen
Killen

People think of famed nineteenth-century outlaws Frank and Jesse James as Old West figures, but most of their robberies—after their Civil War stint as Confederate guerrillas—were committed in the Midwest and Southeast. One of their last exploits happened in the vicinity of Killen, north of the Tennessee River and the old Muscle Shoals Canal.

The canal was under construction by U.S. Army engineers, so paymaster Alexander G. Smith routinely carried the payroll from the bank in Florence to the Bluewater Creek work camp east of town, along the towpath. On March 11, 1881, he was held up by three armed men who took $5,000 in cash and gold, plus $200 of Smith's own money. They left him $21, his watch, and his overcoat. The robbers soon were identified as the James brothers and their new sidekick, the hapless William "Whiskey Head" Ryan, who was swiftly in custody.

Jesse died a year later in St. Joseph, Missouri, shot in the back of the head by gang member Robert Ford to claim a $10,000 reward. Frank turned himself in lest he meet the same fate.

In 1884 Frank finally was tried in Huntsville for the payroll robbery. Though positively identified by seven witnesses, he was acquitted—an unsurprising verdict, since the victim was a Yankee soldier, the jurors were all Confederate veterans, and the defense attorney was none other than Huntsville's favorite son, Gen. LeRoy Pope Walker, former Confederate secretary of war.

Frank was tried only three times in his life and was acquitted each time. He died of old age in 1915. Whiskey Head was killed when he was knocked off his horse by an overhanging tree limb in 1889.

Visit the Pettus Museum on US 72 in Killen to see a James Gang display or to purchase Ronald Pettus's book *The History of Killen, Alabama, Once Known as Masonville*, which includes a chapter on the payroll robbery. Call (256) 757-3624 or visit www.pettusmuseum.net for more information.

The "White Thang" and the "Downey Booger"

America's woods and lonely places are disappearing, and few people travel on foot or by horseback anymore, so reports of mysterious wild creatures encountered on backroads aren't as frequent as they used to be.

The Lynn area, on Highway 5 south of Natural Bridge and US 278, was the home of two such beasts, both reported by numerous people in earlier times but neither seen in many years.

In the 1930s people reported seeing a creature with long white hair that ran on all fours. It became known as simply the "White Thang." Much earlier, in the late nineteenth century, a hairy Bigfoot-like creature that walked on two legs like a man scared a number of travelers. It became known as the "Downey Booger" after John and Joe Downey, the first people to report it.

Whatever these things were, they seem to be long gone—but you might keep your camera handy as you drive through, just in case.

★ ★

No Cameras or Mice, Please

Macedonia

The snake-handling congregations of Appalachia, which use poisonous rattlesnakes, copperheads, and cottonmouths in their worship services, get their inspiration from Mark 16:15–18, in which Jesus appears to his disciples after the Crucifixion and instructs them:

> Go ye into all the world, and preach the gospel to every creature. He that believeth and is baptized shall be saved; but he that believeth not shall be damned. And these signs shall follow them that believe; In my name shall they cast out devils; they shall speak with new tongues; They shall take up serpents; and if they drink any deadly thing, it shall not hurt them; they shall lay hands on the sick, and they shall recover.

These worshipers view the snakes as symbols of Satan. By removing the snakes from their boxes during the worship service and holding them aloft, passing them back and forth, and wrapping them around their necks and arms, they demonstrate that they do not fear Satan, that Satan has no power over them.

Old Rock House Holiness Church in Macedonia, one of the oldest snake-handling congregations anywhere, was founded in 1916, only a few years after the movement began in the coalfields of eastern Tennessee. One of the most prominent snake-handling preachers, John Wayne "Punkin" Brown Jr. of Parrottsville, Tennessee, died of snakebite in 1998 during a service at Old Rock House Holiness.

In the past century dozens of snake handlers around Appalachia have died of snakebite. Some states have outlawed the practice, but Alabama isn't one of them, and the services at Old Rock House Holiness continue.

Macedonia is located between Scottsboro and Fyffe, on Sand Mountain just south of Section. The church is at the end of a gravel road leading from the intersection of Jackson County Roads 43 and 415. Services are on Wednesday and Sunday nights. There is no phone number, and the church services are open to all, though the worshipers are leery of anything resembling a camera, note pad, tape recorder, or superior attitude. Sit in the back with a clear path to the door, just to be safe.

Coon-Dog Cemetery
Mynot

On Labor Day 1937 Key Underwood buried his beloved coon dog, Troop, in the Colbert County woods, at a peaceful spot that both man and dog knew well. The glade long had been a gathering place for

Poodle owners need not apply to this happy hunting ground.
NIKI SEPSAS

coon hunters, and it seemed fitting to lay Troop to rest in a place that held such happy memories for him. Locals call the area Freedom Hills, and what better afterlife could one imagine for a coon dog?

Underwood's hunter friends, moved by his gesture, began to ask his permission to bury their own coon dogs there—not just any dogs, but the ones that were especially skilled, noble, brave, loving, and so on. Underwood said that was fine with him.

The Legend of Aunt Jenny Brooks Johnson

Many legends of violence and lawlessness linger in the hills of northern Alabama, none more so than the story of Aunt Jenny Brooks Johnson.

Aunt Jenny (1826–1924) was a half-white, half-Cherokee mountain woman raising a passel of kids in what is now the Bankhead National Forest. She and her first husband, Willis Brooks, ran a tavern on the old Byler Road connecting the Tennessee River valley to the north with Tuscaloosa to the south. And one day in 1864, her husband and her oldest son, John, were murdered.

How they were murdered, and for what reason, is unclear. In her old age Aunt Jenny maintained that marauding Yankee soldiers killed them. Others held that the Brookses, already feuding, were killed by a rival family. The best-known and most-oft-repeated story, however, says Willis and John, like most north Alabamians, were anti-Confederate and pro-Union, which is why they were tortured and murdered by the Confederate Home Guard—just the sort of backcountry misery depicted in Charles Frazier's Civil War novel *Cold Mountain*.

All versions of the story agree, however, on Aunt Jenny's reaction.

Today there are more than 185 coon-dog graves, some virtually unmarked, but many others with elaborate tombstones and monuments with epitaphs for Old Blue, Preacher, Bean Blossom Bomma, Hunter's Famous Amos, Doctor Doom. One epitaph reads: HE WAS GOOD AS THE BEST AND BETTER THAN THE REST. The most poignant says: HE WASN'T THE BEST, BUT HE WAS THE BEST I EVER HAD.

She gathered all the kids—from the teens down to the newborn baby—and made everyone, especially the four surviving sons, swear vengeance on the killers. Her clan made good on that pledge. Through the years, the story goes, seven men involved in the 1864 incident were murdered by members of Aunt Jenny's family—two of them by Aunt Jenny herself.

This came at a cost, of course. One of Aunt Jenny's boys, Gainum, was killed in a shootout in 1884. The other two Brooks boys, Willis Jr. and Henry, fled to Texas with their brother-in-law, Sam Baker, where they all became known as gunfighters. Willis Jr. and his son, Clifton, died in an Oklahoma shootout in 1902. Henry lasted the longest. After Baker was shot dead in 1911, Henry came home to Alabama, minus a leg that had been shot off somewhere along the way. He settled in, taking care of his mama and making moonshine. He was shot dead at his still by a sheriff's posse in 1920.

Aunt Jenny herself died four years later, at age ninety-eight, proud that all her boys "died like men, with their boots on."

The inn run by Aunt Jenny and her husband was on what is now Lawrence County Road 23, in the Bankhead National Forest south of Mount Hope. Be wary—her ghost is said to walk the road.

★ ★

The sign at the entrance says: ONLY GRAVEYARD OF ITS KIND IN THE WORLD. ONLY COON HOUNDS ARE ALLOWED TO BE BURIED.

The mood at the cemetery turns festive every Labor Day, when coon hunters, their friends, and, of course, their dogs gather for barbecue, music, dancing, and a liar's contest.

The cemetery is on Coon Dog Cemetery Road, 5 miles west of Highway 247, south of Cherokee and southwest of Tuscumbia. The Colbert County Tourism and Convention Bureau is used to giving directions: (800) 344-0783. For more information visit www.coondogcemetery.com.

So Who Collects the Tolls?
Natural Bridge

Virginia may have the more famous Natural Bridge, but Alabama is very proud of this sandstone and iron span, 60 feet high and 148 feet long. It's the longest natural bridge east of the Rockies.

It's the namesake of the neighboring community, which according to the U.S. Census Bureau is Alabama's smallest inhabited municipality, population twenty-eight. The townsfolk say it's closer to forty-nine. What are they counting?

The man-made landmark in Natural Bridge the town is the Natural Bridge Restaurant at US 278 and Highway 13. Natural Bridge, the rock formation, is on US 278 in the privately owned Natural Bridge Park, open daily from 8:00 a.m. to dusk. Admission is charged. Call (205) 486-5330 for more details.

Watercress Capital of the World
New Market

The neighboring city of Huntsville also calls itself the "Watercress Capital of the World," but the title more properly goes to tiny New Market, where much of the actual harvest has taken place since the nineteenth century.

The British eat watercress sandwiches at teatime, but in the United States it's used more commonly as a salad green, a garnish, and a soup ingredient. Watercress is the oldest green vegetable known to man. Ancient Persians and Romans alike ate it to get strong, as Popeye eats spinach, and the ancient Greeks believed it cured insanity.

The world's leading watercress company, Florida-based B&W, has an operation in New Market and an informative Web site at the easy-to-remember www.watercress.com.

Dismals Canyon and the Dismalites

Phil Campbell

In the nineteenth century Dismals Canyon, known to locals simply as "the Dismals," was viewed mainly as a sinister place, a hideout for fugitives who took advantage of its narrow, twisting rock corridors, its dozens of sandstone grottos, its 16-inch-wide crevice of an entrance. Today it's better known for its natural beauty and a unique ecosystem, the result of odd geography and remoteness from the outside world.

Dismals Canyon is a privately owned eighty-five-acre preserve that contains one of the few remaining primeval forests east of the Mississippi. The Discovery Channel special *When Dinosaurs Roamed America* was filmed there because it suggests the landscape of the Earth one hundred million years ago. The state trees of thirty states grow naturally in the Dismals. Its 138-foot Canadian hemlock, isolated hundreds of miles south of its normal habitat, may be the largest in the world.

The most celebrated creatures living in the Dismals are the "Dismalites," which are glowworms—specifically, the larvae of the fungus gnat. Millions of eerily glowing Dismalites cling to the cliffs of Witches Cavern, eating any mosquitoes and flies attracted to the light. (The Dismals may be the only place in Alabama where one can take a mosquito-free hike.) Even weirder is the fact that when the fungus gnats finally mature, they have no mouths and cannot eat. Fungus gnats therefore live only a couple of days as adults, long enough to mate and produce more Dismalites.

Dismals Canyon is off U.S. Highway 43 west of Phil Campbell. The canyon is open daily in summer, but only weekends in spring and

Remlap and Palmerdale

Remlap is the backward spelling of *Palmer*, which is what Palmerdale once was called. There are several stories about how Remlap and Palmer, 5 miles apart on Highway 75, got their names in the nineteenth century.

One story says both towns wanted to name themselves Palmer after the founding family of the area. The rival town leaders flipped a coin. The winner named his town Palmer; the loser named his town Remlap out of spite.

A better story is endorsed by Alex Sartwell of Tuscaloosa, retired from the Geological Survey of Alabama and an expert on Alabama place names. Sartwell says Palmer was founded first, by Perry Palmer. Perry and his brother James had a falling out. James stormed out of town, started his own rival town tauntingly near his brother's, and named it Remlap because of his determination to reverse everything he disliked about Palmer.

Remlap has another claim to fame. Many years ago, the story goes, it was the site of an ostrich farm. The owner went bankrupt and released his stock into the wild. The free-range ostriches supposedly roamed the area for years.

fall. Cabin and canoe rentals and group tours are offered year-round. Guided night tours to see the Dismalites begin at approximately 8:30 p.m. on Friday and Saturday. Admission is charged. For more information call (205) 993-4559 or log onto www.dismalscanyon.com.

★ ★

Oops! Mistake Carved in Stone
Russellville

The World War II memorial at the Franklin County Courthouse in Russellville includes the names of all the locals who died in that war—and the name of one local who didn't.

Dalton Hutchins of Russellville was a radio operator aboard a B-17 bomber that was shot down over Germany in 1943. His family was notified of his death in action, but, in fact, Hutchins and eight other crewmen had parachuted out of the plummeting bomber. Immediately captured by German troops upon landing, Hutchins spent the rest of the war in Germany's infamous POW camp, Stalag 17. He returned home to a shocked but ecstatic welcome in Russellville and lived in the area for another sixty-two years, until his actual death on October 13, 2007.

Nevertheless, no one ever changed the memorial's brass plaque, which for all these years continued to list Dalton Hutchins among the honored dead.

The memorial can be found at 410 North Jackson Avenue, at the intersection of Jackson and Madison Streets downtown, west of US 43.

The Bad News Is, They Found Your Luggage
Scottsboro

"Lost treasures from around the world" are on sale daily at the Unclaimed Baggage Center, a 50,000-square-foot store that unloads, cheap, the belongings left behind on airplanes and never picked up by their owners.

Doyle and Sue Owens opened the store in 1970 with a borrowed truck, a rented house, and a $300 loan. Today their son Bryan runs an operation that brings in 7,000 new items every day and draws a million shoppers a year. Clothes are 60 percent of the business, but the store also does a brisk trade in jewelry, cameras, electronics, sporting goods, books, and of course, luggage.

It's amazing what people will leave behind: designer clothes (Hermès, Versace, Burberry, Christian Dior), a tennis bracelet valued at

$28,000, a six-carat diamond, a forty-one-carat emerald. Rummaging through unclaimed luggage, store employees also have found a shrunken head, a suit of armor, a 3,000-year-old mummified falcon, a Barbie doll stuffed with $500, a live rattlesnake, a Muppet used in the movie *Labyrinth*, a NASA camera designed for the space shuttle, the guidance system for an F-16 fighter jet—and a carefully packed, unopened, presumably unneeded parachute.

The store assures air travelers that airlines make every effort to return items to their rightful owners before giving up and hocking them in Scottsboro. "Only .005% of all checked baggage is permanently lost," says the store's Web site, www.unclaimedbaggage.com.

The Web site also offers an irresistible "Peek in the Bag" feature. Visitors click on an actual sales receipt, showing what "treasures" an actual Unclaimed Baggage Center shopper found and what she paid for them. For example, one customer scored an Eddie Bauer sweater, $10; a Liz Claiborne dress, $18; an Isaac Mizrahi silk top, $7.50; a pair of Donna Karan suede pumps, $20; and, weeping with delight, a 50-cent box of Kleenex.

The Unclaimed Baggage Center is at 509 West Willow Street. Hours are 9:00 a.m. to 6:00 p.m. Monday through Friday and 8:00 a.m. to 6:00 p.m. Saturday. For more details call (256) 259-1525.

Ironically, a Lot to See and Hear at Ivy Green

Tuscumbia

William Gibson's play *The Miracle Worker*, about the conflicts and triumphs of young Helen Keller (1880–1968) and her teacher, Anne Sullivan (1866–1936), has had success in many forms—as a TV play, a Broadway play, an Oscar-winning movie. But Tuscumbia's annual stage production beats them all in one crucial respect: It's performed on location.

The production is at Ivy Green, the home where Helen Keller was born and raised and where the events depicted in the play actually took place. Built in 1820 by Keller's grandparents, Ivy Green has been maintained just as Keller knew it, right down to the famous well pump where seven-year-old Helen realized what *W-A-T-E-R* meant.

The veneration of Keller's childhood tends to obscure her more controversial adulthood. After illness rendered her blind and deaf at nineteen months of age, Keller—thanks to Sullivan and to her own determination and brilliance—evolved from a feral child into an internationally known advocate for socialism and for the rights of minorities, women, and the disabled. She was a founder of the American Civil Liberties Union.

"So long as I confine my activities to social service and the blind," she wrote to a friend, "they compliment me extravagantly, calling me 'archpriestess of the sightless,' 'wonder woman,' and 'a modern miracle.' But when it comes to a discussion of poverty, and I maintain that it is the result of wrong economics—that the industrial system under which we live is at the root of much of the physical deafness and blindness in the world—that is a different matter!"

The Miracle Worker is performed at Ivy Green only in June and July, premiering the weekend of Tuscumbia's annual Helen Keller Festival, but the house and grounds are open year-round, 8:30 a.m. to 4:00 p.m. Monday through Saturday, and 1:00 to 4:00 p.m. Sunday. The last tour starts at 3:45 p.m. daily. Admission is charged for the play and house tour. Ivy Green is at 300 West North Commons Street, 2 miles east of the intersection of US 72 and US 43. For more information call (256) 383-4066 or visit www.helenkellerbirthplace.org and www.helenkellerfestival.com.

Mountaintop River
Valley Head

Little River is the most curious river in the United States in one respect: It forms and flows for most of its length on top of a mountain.

Its 30-mile length is almost entirely atop Lookout Mountain, a somewhat misnamed 200-acre sandstone plateau. The famous bluff overlooking Chattanooga, Tennessee, which most people think of as

Lookout Mountain, is only the northeast edge of the plateau.

Through millions of years, Little River has cut deep into the Lookout Mountain sandstone, creating a 12-mile-long canyon, one of the longest and deepest in the United States. At some points the gorge is 600 feet deep—or the cliffs are 600 feet high, depending on your perspective. Because it's so sheltered and, until recently, inaccessible, the gorge is the home of several rare plants and animals, including Kral's water plantain, which is found nowhere else in the world.

Little River Canyon is a national preserve and a tourist attraction. But one of the canyon's most interesting features is no longer open to the public. DeSoto Falls Fortress is the ruin of a centuries-old rock-hewn hideaway in the cliffs high above the river, accessible only by a narrow footpath. Early travelers noted that a handful of men could hold off an army from that redoubt.

Native American tradition goes that the fort had been built by white men. It was long assumed to have been the work of Spaniards under Hernando de Soto, hence its name, but historians now doubt that de Soto's men ever were so far north. Some therefore believe it was built by a band of Welsh explorers under the legendary Prince Madoc, slowly making their way north from Mobile Bay centuries before Columbus.

The main road across the canyon, with a great view of Little River Falls at the bridge, is Highway 35 between Fort Payne and Watson. It intersects the scenic drive, Highway 176, a.k.a. Canyon Rim Road. The rangers' office is at 2141 Gault Avenue North in Fort Payne. Call them at (256) 845-9605 for more information. Located within the acreage of the national preserve is DeSoto State Park on DeKalb County Road 89, off Highway 35 on Lookout Mountain. Its Web site, www.desotostatepark.com, includes a good summary of the legend of Prince Madoc and the Welsh Caves—click "Legends on the Lookout."

Trail of Tears Motorcycle Ride
Waterloo

In the 1830s the U.S. government performed an infamous act of ethnic cleansing (officially referred to as "relocation") on its native peoples. Thousands of men, women, and children—mostly Cherokee, Choctaw, Chickasaw, Creek, and Seminole—were forced to march from their southeastern homelands to Oklahoma. Thousands died on the roadside along the "Trail of Tears" or as a consequence of the move to a harsh and unfamiliar environment. Today the Trail of Tears is an official National Historic Trail, recognized by the National Park Service and commemorated with a number of signs and maps (see www.nps.gov/trte/).

Alabama's share of that long-ago atrocity is memorialized in an unusual way. On the third Saturday of September, thousands of motorcyclists ride east to west from the vicinity of Chattanooga, Tennessee, to northern Alabama near the Mississippi line. The first ride, in 1994, started with eight motorcycles and finished with a hundred. By 2002 the number of bikers was 95,000. In 2003 it was 150,000—a police-escorted biker motorcade 51 miles long, taking more than an hour to pass any given point.

Two of the ride's early organizers since have parted ways, meaning there are now two separate Trail of Tears rides the third Saturday of September. The Alabama Indian Affairs Commission has endorsed the route of the Trail of Tears Commemorative Motorcycle Ride, an all-Alabama route from Bridgeport in the east to Waterloo in the west. Its website is www.al-tn-trailoftears.net. The Trail of Tears Remembrance Motorcycle Ride, on the other hand, ran mostly through Tennessee in 2008 from Chattanooga in the east to Florence, Alabama, in the west. Its website is www.trailoftears-remembrance.org.

All bikers are welcome on both rides, neither of which require registration or fees. Spectators are welcome to cheer from the roadside. Sales of T-shirts and other merchandise go to Native American scholarships, museums, and cultural centers, as well as the purchase of additional historical markers.

★ ★

Crappie Capital of the World
Weiss Lake

Locals call Weiss Lake, a 30,000-acre reservoir on the Coosa River, the Crappie Capital of the World, which sounds much better than Crappiest Lake in the World.

The crappie here can top two pounds, and anglers come from all over to test their luck against them. More out-of-state fishing licenses are issued at Weiss Lake than anywhere else in Alabama. Even the Kentucky Open Crappie Tournament, which draws hundreds of Kentuckians annually, is held not in Kentucky but on Weiss Lake in Alabama. There's also a two-month annual Crappie Rodeo, a fishing tournament that benefits the Weiss Lake Improvement Association.

Other lakes that claim to be the Crappie Capital of the World include Grand Lake in Oklahoma and Kentucky Lake in, of all places, Kentucky, which may be angling for the Kentucky Open.

For visitor information contact the Cherokee County Chamber of Commerce, P.O. Box 86, 110 Northwood Drive, Centre, AL 35960 or call (256) 927-8455.

One Man's Dream, Underground
Woodville

Cathedral Caverns was the life's work of Jay Gurley, a Redstone Arsenal missile worker who discovered the cave in 1952. He scraped together the $400 needed to buy the cave (and the 160 acres of land above it), then almost single-handedly cleared an access road, tunneled a passageway through 250 feet of rock, cleared out tons of rubble, and installed 40 miles of electrical wiring.

For years Gurley ran Cathedral Caverns as a privately owned tourist attraction, but it was bought in 1987 by the State of Alabama, which finally reopened it as a state park in 2000.

Tour guides say the formation called Goliath, 60 feet tall and 243 feet in diameter, may be the world's largest stalagmite, but caves in

Brazil, China, Cuba, France, Italy, and Slovakia make that claim, too. Cathedral Caverns also claims the world's largest cave opening at 25 feet high and 128 feet wide.

More bizarre are a stalagmite 45 feet tall but only 3 inches wide and a closed-to-the-public Crystal Room full of calcite formations that could be shattered by a human voice.

Cathedral Caverns is at 637 Cave Road. From US 72 east of Huntsville, take Jackson County Road 63 toward Grant and follow the signs. The aboveground park is open daily 9:00 a.m. to 5:00 p.m. year-round; tours of the cave are hourly in summertime and less frequent the rest of the year. Admission is charged. For more information, call (256) 728-8193 or visit www.alapark.com/CathedralCaverns.

5

West

The Gee's Bend *quilts that recently took the art world by storm are only the start of the amazing indigenous art scene in west Alabama. Centered around the annual Kentuck Festival, they're characterized by visionary creativity, Depression-era thrift, and an outsider's cussedness. Jimmie Lee Sudduth painted not with paint but with mud; Sybil Gibson painted not on canvases but on paper bags. The sculptors use everything* **except** *marble: industrial sand, scrap metal, scrap tires, haystacks. The students of Auburn's Rural Studio build churches, houses, and day-care centers out of anything that isn't nailed down. (They'll probably ask whether you brought any spare tin, glass, or rubber with you.) Ma'Cille's Museum of Miscellanea is, alas, long gone, but if you hurry, you still can admire Joe Minter's African Village in America and W. C. Rice's Cross Garden—not to mention Pettus Randall's Miniature Museum of American History, the neon sign outside the Moon Winx Lodge, and a fine cypress-log front-yard Jesus.*

Art aside, there's a haunted radio station and a haunted journalism school, a ghostly face in a courthouse window and a heavenly face on a hospital door, while the Virgin Mary (so the pilgrims say) visits Sterrett regularly. Legendary inhabitants of west Alabama include William Rufus King, U.S. vice president and gay icon; gangster's moll Virginia Hill; psychic Edgar Cayce; Hazel Farris's mummy; the elusive "skunk apes" of Clanton; and—just possibly—John Henry, the steel-drivin' man. And true connoisseurs of hard luck must visit Smith Hall at the University of Alabama, which houses the only meteorite ever to land on somebody.

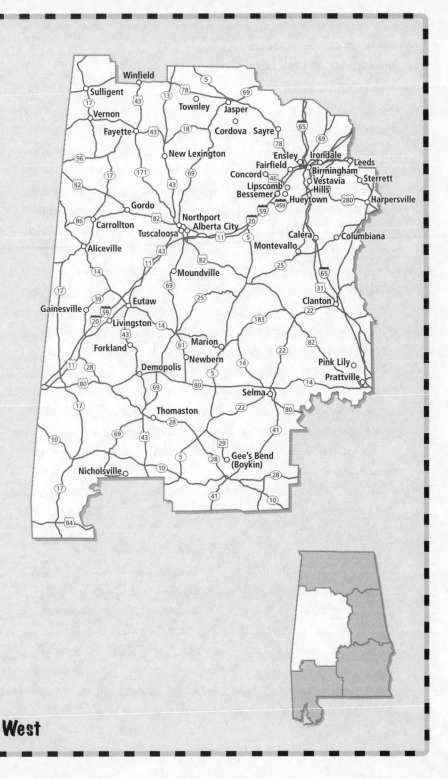

West

★ ★

No Vacancy at the "Fritz Ritz"
Aliceville

During World War II hundreds of POW camps in the United States held 425,000 Axis troops, mostly Germans. Most of these camps were in the South, where the climate was more favorable to Geneva Convention standards for the treatment of prisoners.

One of the largest camps was in Aliceville, where 1,000 U.S. troops guarded 6,000 inmates, four times the population of the town. Hundreds of locals gathered at the railroad station June 2, 1943, to watch the arrival of the first German soldiers, all of them captured in North Africa, who stepped off the train in gray uniforms dusted with white delousing powder.

Most of the inmates were officers and therefore not required to work, though some volunteered to pick peanuts and stack sawmill lumber. The others spent their time painting, staging variety shows, brewing beer, and playing soccer. They created an orchestra with borrowed musical instruments. In the prison shop inmates made red wagons and other toys for Aliceville children. They followed the war news from Europe with a large map studded with stickpins.

There was one escape attempt, a man shot while scaling a barbed wire fence. Another inmate was killed in a fight with a U.S. soldier, and illness claimed another eight. In general the Germans considered themselves well treated. Nationwide, 5,000 of the former POWs became U.S. citizens after the war.

Some Aliceville residents mightily resented the Germans' leisure and the fact that the Germans' daily meat allotment exceeded that allowed U.S. citizens in that time of strict grocery rationing. Things seemed mighty cushy at the "Fritz Ritz." But the enlisted men's club for U.S. soldiers was very popular, especially among the young men and women of Aliceville, because it served legal alcohol in an otherwise dry county.

The camp was closed July 11, 1945. The Aliceville barracks were used as chicken coops, the enlisted men's club for a VFW hall, and

S'pose they were in a hurry to check out? The Aliceville Museum contains many artifacts left behind by the German POWs. NIKI SEPSAS

★ ★

other buildings were dismantled and recycled all over town. Today the site of the camp is Sue Stabler Park, but the only structure that remains is a single stone chimney, part of the enlisted men's club.

The Aliceville POW Museum and Cultural Center, downtown at 104 Broad Street, has many camp items on display: prisoner artwork, equipment, uniforms, photographs, swastika armbands, a Luger pistol. Admission is charged. Museum hours are from 10:00 a.m. to 4:00 p.m., Monday through Friday (except for the noon hour), and 10:00 a.m. to 1:00 p.m. on Saturday. Call (205) 373-2365 or visit www.city ofaliceville.com/MuseumMain.htm for more details.

Many of the tickets to the museum are sold to aged former POWs, brought by their children and grandchildren. Every two years a camp reunion is held during the Aliceville Dogwood Festival. The number of potential attendees, sadly, gets smaller every year.

Since the local textile mill closed, Aliceville's civic leaders have been wooing the federal government, specifically the Department of Homeland Security. They'd like to jump-start the local economy—with a brand-new prison.

Did Hitler Hunt and Peck or Touch Type?
Bessemer

At the close of World War II, American GIs brought home from Europe all manner of Nazi souvenirs, smuggled into thousands of duffel bags and footlockers. In the 1980s one such souvenir was discovered in the basement of Bessemer's old railroad station, now a history museum: a typewriter scavenged from Wolf's Lair, Hitler's Eastern Front headquarters in occupied Poland.

Now "Hitler's typewriter" is, of course, the most popular exhibit at the museum. Whether the typewriter was actually used by Hitler is unknown. Wolf's Lair was a headquarters complex of eighty buildings with 2,000 soldiers and employees—and any number of typewriters.

The Hall of History is at 1905 Alabama Avenue, in downtown Bessemer east of US 11. Hours are from 9:00 a.m. to 4:00 p.m., Tuesday

Hitler probably had people do his typing for him. NIKI SEPSAS

through Saturday (except for the noon hour), and admission is free. Call (205) 426-1633 or visit www.bessemerhallofhistory.com for more information.

That Little Richard Is Such a Square

Bessemer

Alabama has been the home of many great singers and musicians, but in a class all his own is R&B singer Andre Williams, a Bessemer native who as a youth idolized both Hank Williams ("Hank was my god") and the dapper Harlem bandleader Cab Calloway (he says he once vowed, "I'm a-gonna dress like that man till the day I die!").

Williams began his recording career in Detroit in the 1960s. His singles for Fortune Records included "Bacon Fat," "Please Pass the Biscuits," and "The Greasy Chicken," but audiences knew Williams actually had one thing on his menu and one thing only, baby. That one

★ ★

thing is more overt in such Williams classics as "Shake a Tailfeather," "The Stroke," "Humpin', Bumpin' and Thumpin,'" and the infamous "Jailbait." One critic said he made Little Richard sound like Pat Boone.

Williams worked for Berry Gordy at Motown, produced records by Stevie Wonder, the Contours, and Ike and Tina Turner, and wrote songs for George Clinton, but by the 1980s he had become a homeless crack addict. Back from the abyss, Williams began recording and performing again in 1996.

Recent recordings include "Lapdance," "You Got It and I Want It," "Weapon of Mass Destruction," "My Sister Stole My Woman," "Pardon Me (I've Got Someone to Kill)," and "Sling It Bang It and Give It Cab Fare Home."

On the 2003 live album *Holland Shuffle*, Williams chats with the audience about current events: "If I go into Afghanistan, everybody would have been having sex. There would not be no guns."

Dirt-Dyed Clothing—No, Really

Bessemer

Years ago, Joy "Dirt Woman" Maples of Alabama met Martin "Dirt Man" Ledvina of the Czech Republic. Romance ensued—and, eventually, a business. Red clay is unknown in Ledvina's homeland, so he was fascinated by this stuff underfoot that left permanent stains on Maples's mountain-biking wardrobe.

After a lot of experimentation, Dirt Man and Dirt Woman founded Earth Creations, maker of "dirt-dyed" clothing sold at environmentally conscious stores nationwide, as well as online at www.earthcreations.net.

All the clothes are made in the United States from natural fibers (hemp, organic cotton, flax) and colored with natural clays—no manufactured dyes, no bleaching. Maples and Ledvina collect clays everywhere they go, in buckets. A company slogan: "Red dirt runs through our veins."

Earth Creations is at 3056 Mountainview Way. For more information call (800) 792-9868.

Heaviest Corner on Earth

Birmingham

Birmingham boosters were proud of their downtown building boom in the early years of the twentieth century. Between 1902 and 1912 four skyscrapers were built at the intersection of Twentieth Street North and First Avenue North, one on each corner. The city proclaimed the site the Heaviest Corner on Earth.

The four buildings are still there, still hives of activity, both business and residential. They are the ten-story Woodward Building at 1927 First Avenue North (built 1902), the sixteen-floor Brown Marx Building at 2000 First Avenue North (built 1906), the sixteen-floor Empire Building at 1928 First Avenue North (built 1909), and the twenty-floor John Hand Building at 17 Twentieth Street North (built 1912).

The Woodward Building is the lightest on the heaviest corner.

Hazel, Is That You?

The paying customers were told this story: Hazel Farris of Louisville, Kentucky, shot and killed her husband on August 6, 1905, when he objected to her new hat. For good measure she then shot and killed three policemen and a deputy sheriff, getting her own right ring finger shot off in the process. Then she fled to Bessemer, Alabama, became a prostitute, and had the bad judgment to have an affair with a police officer, who ratted on her when he learned she was a fugitive murderess. Before the cops could beat down her door, a drunken Hazel Farris killed herself with a gut full of arsenic.

But just as in a comic-book origin story, the combination of the alcohol and the arsenic in Hazel Farris's system had unexpected side effects: Her body, rather than decaying, naturally mummified. This was noticed by the owner of the Bessemer furniture store where Hazel's unclaimed body lay in storage. (In those days furniture stores built and sold caskets and therefore often had one or more corpses on the premises.) Deciding to turn lemons into lemonade, the store owner put Hazel's mummy on exhibit, admission 10 cents a head.

In 1907 O. C. Brooks of Nashville, Tennessee, bought Hazel Farris's body for $25 and took her on the road. She toured sideshows, carnivals, and fairs for more than fifty years all over the United States. Brooks estimated he made $2 million lugging Hazel around. He willed her to his nephew Luther, stipulating that she must never be buried—she had sinned too horribly, Brooks maintained, to deserve that—but that further exhibitions should be only for charity. Luther complied. In the 1970s she did a return engagement back home in Bessemer, as a fund-raiser for the Hall of History museum; and five Tennessee churches were built with money raised by Hazel Farris's corpse.

Eventually, the Brooks family decided to get rid of its grisly heirloom and give poor Hazel a proper burial. But she had one more performance, before a worldwide TV audience of millions. For the cameras of the National Geographic Channel's *Mummy Road Show*, a team of experts examined and autopsied the body in hopes of finding out whether the side-show pitch told about Hazel all those years was true.

The examination confirmed a few facts about the dead woman. She was full of arsenic, yes, but that was how people were embalmed back then. She died in her twenties, she had borne a child, she had bad teeth and gum disease, and she had lost a finger, probably to surgery, before her death, which prob-ably was caused by pneumonia. All this was consistent with a sad and squalid life but was no evidence at all of her having murdered five men or being the one-woman Thelma and Louise of 1905.

After the televised autopsy Hazel Far-ris's remains were finally cremated and entombed in Madison, Tennessee. Hit-ler's typewriter is now the big attrac-tion at Bessemer's Hall of History. And Heather Pringle's 2001 book, *The Mummy Congress,* is required reading for mummy enthusiasts. Bodies crum-ble, but stories live on.

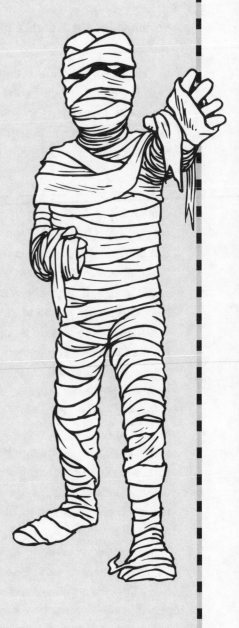

Birmingham, the Florence of Alabama

Birmingham

Vulcan, god of the forge, is the largest cast-iron sculpture in the world. Visible all over Birmingham, the 55-foot, sixty-ton behemoth stands atop a 124-foot pedestal in Vulcan Park, atop Red Mountain. Thousands of visitors trek to the park just to ascertain that Vulcan is indeed naked under that apron and to get a closer look at his mighty bronzed butt.

Proud of their iron and steel industry, Birmingham civic boosters commissioned Vulcan from New York sculptor Giuseppe Moretti for their exhibit at the 1904 World's Fair in St. Louis, an extravaganza that also gave the world the ice-cream cone.

Back home in Birmingham, Vulcan stood for thirty years at the state fairgrounds, where he was rented out as advertising space. In the 1930s he was moved to Vulcan Park. In the 1940s a neon beacon was added to the spear in his upraised right hand; its green glow was switched to red whenever there was a traffic fatality in Birmingham.

The park was closed in 1999, and the statue was dismantled for expensive repair and recasting. Alabama's U.S. senators got federal money for the project, leading future presidential candidate John McCain of Arizona to denounce the Vulcan millions—and pork-barrel spending in general—on the floor of the U.S. Senate. Noting with tongue in cheek that federal donations to a Roman god may violate the separation of church and state, McCain urged, "Not one more federal dollar to promote tributes to pagans." The U.S. Senate cast McCain's objections into the furnace eighty-seven to twelve.

Vulcan Park reopened in 2004 in time to celebrate the statue's centennial. No longer a traffic beacon, the restored Vulcan is back in business as the town's oddest and most beloved tourist attraction. Vulcan Park is at Twenty-first Street South and Valley Avenue just west of U.S. Highway 280. Admission is charged. For more information call (205) 933-1409 or visit www.vulcanpark.org.

Vulcan may be the largest sculpture, but he's not the only game in

The glass elevator affords a good view of Vulcan's vast rear.

town. Birmingham teens scare one another with wild tales about *The Storyteller*, a fountain at the intersection of Twentieth Street South and Eleventh Avenue in the bohemian Five Points neighborhood. A man with a ram's head reads from an open book while holding a 9-foot staff in his right hand. An owl perches atop the staff as other animals gather around. Sculpted by Alabama artist Frank Fleming and dedicated in 1991, the piece was commissioned by the Birmingham Art Association, which added an explanatory plaque: STORYTELLING IS A DEEPLY ROOTED SOUTHERN HERITAGE. THE ANIMALS ARE LISTENING TO A STORY INTENDED TO CONVEY THE IDEA OF A PEACEABLE KINGDOM.

People love to pose for photos with the "ram-man," put hats on his head, and stick rolled-up magazines in his back trouser pocket. Yet he strikes some as creepy, and baseless rumors swirl about late-night satanic rituals in the fountain. Conspiracy buffs claim, for example, that the five frogs are arranged to form a pentagram. All this is invention, but it's appropriate that a statue devoted to storytelling would inspire stories of its own.

Electra is a slim, nude, golden goddess perched frustratingly high atop the old Alabama Power building downtown. She clutches two fistfuls of lightning bolts. Designed by Edward Field Sanford Jr. and installed in 1926, she had no official name until newspapers started referring to her as "Miss Electra." She bears little resemblance to the Electra of Greek myth, the vengeful and murderous daughter of Agamemnon.

Cleaned and regilded for her seventieth birthday in 1996, Electra looks great. Locals long have joked that she and Vulcan might be an "item," but clearly there's still some distance between them.

Birmingham claims the world's largest miniature Statue of Liberty, a one-fifth-size replica cast in France in 1956. It's 23 feet tall and weighs 4,000 pounds, and the natural-gas flame in its torch burns continuously. Commissioned by Frank Paul Samford, founder of Liberty National Life Insurance, it used to sit atop the Liberty National building downtown. In 1989 it was moved to the Boy Scout headquarters

The world's largest miniature Statue of Liberty, top, is inspirational; *Police Dog Attack*, bottom, is terrifying.
NIKI SEPSAS

The Storyteller, dedicated in 1991, acquired an urban legend with admirable speed.

on Liberty Parkway, where it's a familiar sight to the huddled masses yearning to breathe free of rush-hour traffic on Interstate 459.

Locals call it the "Hellhounds," but *Police Dog Attack* is the official name of James Drake's 1992 statue in Kelly Ingram Park, scene of the infamous attacks on civil rights protesters with dogs and water cannons in May 1963. Visitors walk between the leaping, snarling bronze and steel dogs, trying to imagine what that must have been like. Other stark sculptures in the park depict the water cannons and the children who were arrested and sent to jail for marching.

An 18-foot-tall Muffler Man, locally nicknamed "Stan," has stood atop a Birmingham tire company, in several locations under several owners, since 1954. For years he was a landmark on Interstate 65 downtown. High winds broke him in half in 1998, but a small group of well-wishers soon repaired and restored him with all the love, a fraction of the money, and none of the publicity that was poured into the restoration of Vulcan. Today he stands in front of the GCR Tire Center (3340 Vanderbilt Road), near the Tallapoosa Road exit from Interstate 20/59.

They're Running Post Patterns in Heaven
Birmingham

More than twenty years after his death, the cult of Paul "Bear" Bryant in Alabama only grows. His aphorisms are quoted by executives in board meetings, by preachers in pulpits, and by politicians on the stump. Framed photographs, paintings, and sketches of his scowling, houndstooth-hatted face are in homes, offices, businesses, restaurants, and bars. At every home football game in Tuscaloosa, students who weren't even alive when Bryant stalked the sidelines deal harshly and swiftly with infidels who don't stand in reverent silence while tribute is paid to the great man on the scoreboard screen.

And at the sprawling Elmwood Cemetery in Birmingham, attendants finally gave up and painted a red line—no, a crimson line, as in Crimson Tide—from the cemetery entrance to Bryant's grave in Block 30. It saves both attendants and pilgrims a lot of time.

For those people who need reminding, Bryant was head football coach at the University of Alabama, his alma mater, for twenty-five years. His record there was 242 wins, 46 losses, 9 ties, and 6 national championships. He got his nickname (which he disliked) when he was a teenager, by wrestling a bear at the Fordyce Theatre in his Arkansas hometown. He retired in December 1982 and died of a heart attack a month later. Tens of thousands of mourners lined the funeral route.

The Elmwood Cemetery is at 600 Martin Luther King Jr. Drive, at the Sixth Avenue intersection. From I-65, take exit 259A onto Sixth Street, and drive south 1½ miles.

Tuscaloosa, home of the Crimson Tide, can't claim Bryant's grave, but it does have the Paul W. Bryant Museum, where the exhibits include a reconstruction of Bryant's office, with all the original furniture, and a reproduction of Bryant's houndstooth hat in Waterford crystal. The museum is on Paul W. Bryant Drive on the University of Alabama campus. Hours are from 9:00 a.m. to 4:00 p.m. daily. Admission is charged. For more information call (205) 348-4668 or visit bryant.ua.edu.

Yard Art Seeks to Recycle Pride
Birmingham

Joe Minter's yard contains a lush, quarter-acre garden of roses, marigolds, zinnias—and homemade sculptures. Everywhere there are assemblages of tin, wood, and found objects (chains, dolls, boots, auto parts) and hand-lettered placards with quotes from the Bible and the civil rights movement. The artwork long ago outgrew the garden. Now it surrounds Minter's house as well as the house across the street.

Minter, a construction worker and self-taught artist, began work on his African Village in America in 1989. "The whole idea handed down to me by God," he once said, "is to use that which has been discarded, just as we as a people have been discarded, made invisible."

Minter's yard overlooks two historically black Birmingham cemeteries, Grace Hill and Shadow Lawn, and the garden, too, is

Whereas others have mere yards, Joe Minter has a statement. NIKI SEPSAS

commemorative. There are replicas of African huts, African warriors (with old hair dryers for heads), and a slave ship. Four empty folding chairs honor the children killed in the Ku Klux Klan bombing of a Birmingham church. Most striking is a replica of Martin Luther King's cell in the Birmingham jail, adorned with chains, work gloves, and boots. Its most prominent furnishing is a toilet, because King wrote his famous jail-cell letter on toilet paper.

Joe Minter's yard is located at 931 Nassau Avenue Southwest. There is no charge, and the yard is open in the daytime whenever Mr. Minter happens to be home. Courteous visitors are welcome.

Blind Golfer Preferred Playing at Night
Birmingham

The nation's most famous blind golfer, Charles A. "Charley" Boswell (1916–1995) of Birmingham, played football and baseball at the University of Alabama and enlisted in the U.S. Army in spring 1941. He was wounded and permanently blinded November 30, 1944, at the Battle of the Bulge and took up golf while recuperating at a rehab hospital.

Caddies would tell him the lay of the ball and the distance, and he would do the rest. He once shot an eighty-two at Highland Park Golf Course in Birmingham. He was a seventeen-time national blind golf champion and a winner of the Ben Hogan Trophy from the Golf Writers Association.

At a tournament Boswell once said, "That was the worst swing I ever heard." He supposedly once challenged Bob Hope to a match—at midnight. A native and lifelong resident of Birmingham, Boswell founded an annual charity golf tournament that raised more than $1 million for that city's Eye Foundation Hospital. And President Eisenhower once sent him a congratulatory telegram: "I have read with great interest the story of Mr. Charles Boswell. It is a superb testimony to the unconquerable spirit of a brave man and a strong encouragement to everyone who has tried to become proficient in the game of golf."

Boswell is one of the heroes enshrined in the Alabama Sports Hall of

Fame, 2150 Richard Arrington Jr. Boulevard North in downtown Birmingham. For more information call (205) 323-6665 or visit www.ashof.org.

Hardwood Floors, Eat-In Kitchen, and Turret Access
Birmingham

Quinlan Castle is a 1927 apartment complex built to look like a medieval fortress, complete with turrets at each corner.

In the 1920s any apartment house full of unmarried men and women was considered scandalous in the Deep South, and Quinlan Castle's lordly exterior must have made it especially suspect. For years tongue-waggers spread rumors about orgies, opium dens, spy rings,

This fanciful apartment building may be someone's dream house.

and witches' covens, all supposedly operating out of Quinlan Castle. The rumors were stoked by a 1940 police raid on the apartment of a local Communist Party official.

More recently, Gothic novelist Caitlín Kiernan, an Alabama native, set her 2007 thriller *Threshold* partially in a crumbling Quinlan Castle, "abandoned to the homeless people who have broken in through first-floor windows and torn up the carpet for their smoky, toxic fires."

What the director of the Birmingham Historical Society called "a crazy, quirky, wonderful piece of architecture" was nearly razed in the 1990s but got a reprieve, thanks to a public outcry. There were many proposals through the years for renovating Quinlan Castle's seventy-two efficiency and one-bedroom apartments. The place has been on the Alabama Trust for Historic Preservation's "Places in Peril" list since 1998. In 2008, the city of Birmingham sold it to the neighboring Southern Research Institute, which plans to preserve the building's distinctive façade, at least.

Quinlan Castle is at the corner of Ninth Avenue South and Twenty-first Street South, in the Five Points neighborhood.

Quinlan Castle may be the oldest and best-known castle in Alabama, but it's not the only one.

- In the twenty-first-century, Richard and Anna Moxley have built themselves a 7,000-square-foot castle in Autauga County, near Montgomery. It's loaded with faux-medieval trappings: fleurs-de-lis, suits of armor, turrets, stone archways, stuffed boars' heads, and banquet tables. The Moxleys plan to add a moat and threaten to stock it with bass and bream.
- Near Fort Payne is Excalibur Castle, a four-turret edifice originally built by Jeff Cook of the country-music group Alabama.
- Open to the public since its official blessing in 2001 is Castle San Miguel in Hanceville, built by Catholic TV host Mother Angelica, founder of the Eternal Word Television Network. Among other things this castle houses the gift shop of the Our Lady of the Angels Monastery (www.olamshrine.com).

- On land 15 miles southeast of Talladega, a group of investors hopes to build Tirion Castle, named for an Elvish city in J. R. R. Tolkien's *The Silmarillion*. The plan—in the works for more than ten years—is to run a bed-and-breakfast at the castle, plus rent it out to Renaissance fairs, weddings, Society for Creative Anachronism events, and so on.

His Jazz Is Really Far Out, Man

Birmingham

Jazz innovator Sun Ra (1914–1993), born Herman Poole "Sonny" Blount in Birmingham, claimed the robed figures from the planet Jupiter first took him into their spaceship in the 1930s, when he was studying music education at Alabama A&M in Huntsville.

Blount had a fairly straightforward jazz career as a pianist, composer, arranger, and bandleader in the 1930s and 1940s, first in Alabama and then in Chicago, but he had a reputation as an eccentric even then. He wore tunics and sandals decades before they were commonplace, went to jail for refusing his draft service in World War II, and earned the nickname "Moon Man" for his spacey utterances.

Eventually he adopted a sort of science-fictional black Egyptian nationalism. In 1952 he announced that he was not a human being, but an angelic being, a citizen of the planet Saturn, a designated Cosmic Communicator. He legally changed his name to Le Sony'r Ra, or Sun Ra for short.

The Sonny Blount Orchestra became Sun Ra's Intergalactic Arkestra, and its concerts became increasingly elaborate, with wild costumes, light shows, dancers, acrobats, performance poetry, New Orleans–style processionals, and windup toy robots released into the audience. The presiding elder himself, wearing a robe and headdress, often delivered what Sun Ra scholar Robert Campbell calls "sermons to benighted Earthlings." Notable Sun Ra quotes include the following gems:

- "There's five billion people on this planet, all out of tune."
- "To save the planet, I had to go to the worst spot on Earth, and that is Philadelphia, which is death's headquarters."

* "Light and all that, someone made that. It's written that they did. But nobody made the darkness."
* "I'm not a part of history. I'm a part of mystery."
* "I teach my musicians not to know things, and that's a totally different thing. They don't teach that in schools."
* "My music is about dark tradition. Dark tradition means a lot more than black tradition. There is a lot of division in what they call black. I'm not into division."
* "I want several solar systems and quite a few galaxies. I like that! That would give me something to do, you see."

More traditionally Sun Ra insisted that he was not playing "free jazz," but carefully composed orchestrations, like the 1930s big bands he loved. His demands for around-the-clock rehearsals forced his musicians into a sort of communal existence, a musical and mystical boot camp.

Sun Ra made hundreds of self-published recordings and toured for decades, especially in Europe, but remained, unsurprisingly, a cult figure. Only late in life, when he appeared on *Saturday Night Live* and was hailed by a new generation of rappers, performance artists, and alternative rockers did he start getting anything approaching mainstream recognition. At the end when a stroke sent him to the hospital in Birmingham, he listed his place of residence as Saturn.

Besides the hundred-plus LPs, many of them now on CD, Sun Ra resources include two movies now on DVD: Robert Mugge's 1980 documentary *Sun Ra: A Joyful Noise* and Sun Ra's own 1974 science-fiction musical *Space Is the Place*, in which Sun Ra and his music-powered spaceship free the black race from a dying Earth (it's *Yellow Submarine* meets *Superfly*). John F. Szwed's fine biography is *Space Is the Place: The Lives and Times of Sun Ra*. Joe Moudry's Sun Ra fan site includes a link to Robert Campbell's funny and fascinating 1995 Sun Ra presentation for the Alabama Jazz Hall of Fame, as well as links for the Sun Ra Arkestra, which continues to tour under the leadership of longtime member Marshall Allen: www.dpo.uab.edu/~moudry.

Alabama Poet, Hero of . . . Japan!?!

Birmingham

More popular among Japanese tourists than American ones is the restored home of Samuel Ullman (1840–1924), a turn-of-the-century Birmingham business and civic leader.

Ullman is the author of the oft-reprinted, 250-word prose poem "Youth," which begins: "Youth is not a time of life; it is a state of mind." Its most quoted passage: "You are as young as your faith, as old as your doubt; as young as your self-confidence, as old as your fear; as young as your hope, as old as your despair."

Long a favorite of newspaper advice columnists, the poem also was loved by Gen. Douglas MacArthur, who kept a framed copy of it on the wall of his many offices and who quoted it all over Japan during his years as supreme commander of the Allied occupation forces, 1945–1951. A generation of Japanese leaders found inspiration in the

To Japanese tourists, poet Samuel Ullman's house is worth a visit.

★ ★

poem, and its author, though obscure in the United States, remains a hero to millions of Japanese.

The Samuel Ullman Museum is at 2150 Fifteenth Avenue South, just west of US 280 between Five Points and Vulcan Park. Operated by the University of Alabama at Birmingham, it's open by appointment. Call (205) 934-3328 or visit http://main.uab.edu/Sites/UllmanMuseum.

Alabamians Invade Cuba at the Bay of Pigs

Birmingham

For many years the corpse of an Alabamian named Pete Ray was on display in a Havana morgue, the most bizarre trophy in Fidel Castro's collection.

Today, Ray's body rests in his hometown of Birmingham, in Forest Hills Cemetery overlooking the airport. An Alabama Air National Guard pilot, Ray was shot down by Cuban forces on April 19, 1961, during the disastrous CIA-backed invasion of Cuba at the Bahia de Cochinos—the Bay of Pigs.

Ray was one of sixty Alabama guardsmen, both pilots and technicians, sent to Guatemala and Nicaragua by the CIA to train the Cuban exiles who were to carry out the invasion. Why Alabama? Because the Alabama Air Guard was the last military unit in the country still flying the obsolete B-26, which the Cuban Air Force also flew. Sending in B-26s to provide air support during the invasion was intended as a psychological tactic; the CIA wanted to make the Cubans think their own air force had turned against them. The Alabamians were supposed to be strictly support personnel, staying behind at the base in Nicaragua while Cuban exiles piloted the planes. But the invasion bogged down, and the Cuban pilots exhausted themselves flying back and forth between base and battlefield. Eight Alabamians eventually volunteered to fly the planes themselves—knowing that if they were killed or captured, the U.S. government would deny any knowledge of their existence.

Of the eight, only four survived. One who didn't was Pete Ray; his plane was shot down, and though he survived the crash, he was executed by Fidel Castro's troops. Ray's body was kept on ice in Havana for eighteen years, as Castro's prime evidence that U.S. troops were indeed involved in the botched invasion. Dignitaries were trooped in to admire Ray's body and make sport of it. Not until 1977 did the CIA admit the Alabamians' involvement and award posthumous medals to the four dead men. Not until 1979 did Castro return Ray's body to the United States for burial.

Many of the Alabamians who were part of the Bay of Pigs invasion are still alive. They may be the state's least known, least honored, and, in some circles, most controversial veterans.

Their story is well told by Warren Trest and Donald Dodd in the winter 2005 issue of *Alabama Heritage* magazine and in their book *Wings of Denial: The Alabama Air National Guard's Covert Role at the Bay of Pigs* (NewSouth Books, 2001).

Eastwood Texaco Sues OPEC

Birmingham

Eastwood Texaco, at the intersection of Montclair Road and Oporto Madrid Boulevard in Birmingham, south of I-20 near Irondale, is no ordinary gas station. Its owners took OPEC to court.

Carl and Debbie Prewitt sued the Organization of Petroleum Exporting Countries in April 2000, charging in federal court that OPEC indulges in illegal price-fixing. The name of the case was *Prewitt Enterprises Inc. et al. v. OPEC.*

Now, everyone agrees that the international oil cartel does engage in price-fixing; OPEC happily admits that on its own Web site. Moreover, everyone agrees that OPEC price-fixing, if done in the United States, would be illegal under federal antitrust law. After all, Standard Oil, the behemoth founded by John D. Rockefeller, was dismantled by the federal government for just such infractions.

But does the United States have any jurisdiction over OPEC? Though the cartel's actions have an incalculable impact on the American

economy, OPEC is based not in the United States but in Austria—so any price-fixing, like any other OPEC action, presumably takes place far from U.S. soil.

The Prewitts' hardworking lawyer argued, with plenty of recent examples, that U.S. law enforcement extends all over the world, wherever criminals working against U.S. interests are to be found. In the 1990s, he pointed out, the U.S. Justice Department went after various international cartels, including a vitamin cartel, on behalf of wronged U.S. companies. Companies paid hundreds of millions of dollars in fines, and executives went to prison. The U.S. Justice Department ought to go after OPEC the same way, the Prewitts argued.

In rebuttal, OPEC argued that being served with court papers at its Austrian offices was illegal according to Austrian law. That's true. Believe it or not, Austrian law specifically says no one can serve OPEC with papers without OPEC's consent. Clearly, OPEC has good lobbyists in Vienna. But should Austrian law trump U.S. law in a U.S. courtroom?

The Prewitts enjoyed an early victory in April 2001, when U.S. District Judge Charles R. Weiner ordered OPEC to stop all price-fixing activities. That injunction quickly was thrown out, however, and the case began anew before another judge, who ultimately agreed with OPEC, ruling there was no possible way to serve OPEC with court papers. The Prewitts' suit was thrown out in March 2003. The Prewitts appealed twice but got nowhere, and the case ended in October 2004, when the U.S. Supreme Court dismissed it without comment.

There was very little news coverage of the case, but Timothy Noah's "Chatterbox" column in *Slate* provided good, snarky commentary as the case dragged on. Go to www.slate.com and search for "Suing OPEC." Noah was on the Prewitts' side, but let's face it: What fun would OPEC's side be? Eastwood Texaco's phone number is (205) 956-9676.

Tire Failure, Art Success

Birmingham

Sculptor Randy Gachet of the Alabama School of Fine Arts scavenges rubber "gators" from the roadside—the discarded treads of failed tires—and makes art of them, such as the cyclical "Ouroboros" or a thicket of "Carbon Spires," tall, totemlike poles built around rebar. Frequently seen at the Kentuck Festival in Northport, his works also are on display in many collections around Alabama, including the Southern Environmental Center at Birmingham-Southern College (www.bsc.edu/sec).

Randy Gachet's scrap-rubber "Ouroboros" is inspired by the ancient symbol of a serpent eating its tail.
RANDY GATCHET

It Sounded Good to Him!

The mayor of Calera, George Roy, signed a proclamation making May 2004 Dianetics Month, urging all citizens to follow the example of the late L. Ron Hubbard "and strive to improve the lives of each other by working together and assisting each other to attain a brighter future."

The mayor was unaware at the time that dianetics is the foundation belief of the controversial Church of Scientology, founded by the late science fiction writer L. Ron Hubbard, author of *Battlefield Earth.* The mayor's office had received the text of the proclamation as a form request, with the name of the city to be filled in; presumably, many other municipalities got one, too.

When this was pointed out, the mayor hastily rescinded the proclamation, but not before Joseph Bryant's *Birmingham News* story about the gaffe had been reprinted all over the world.

The Face in the Courthouse Window
Carrollton

The tourist draw at the old Pickens County Courthouse, built in 1877, is a single window, the attic window on the north side of the building. The lower right-hand pane supposedly contains a "lightning portrait" of a terrified human face.

According to legend the image belongs to Henry Wells, a black man wrongly arrested in 1878 on a charge of burning down the previous courthouse. The officers of the new courthouse stashed their prisoner in the attic to protect him from a lynch mob. Wells was in that window, staring down in horror at the gathering crowd, when BOOM! Lightning struck the courthouse square—or, according to some versions of the story, the courthouse itself.

Had this been the storyline of a 1960s Marvel comic book, the lightning blast would have left Henry Wells with superpowers, self-esteem issues, and a duty to fight crime. But we'll have to be satisfied with something much more mundane. The story told in Carrollton is that the

The "face" is on the bottom right-hand pane of the topmost attic window. (A telescope helps.) NIKI SEPSAS

lightning burned a photographic image of Henry Wells's face into the windowpane, preserving his moment of terror for all time.

The legend pretty much ends there, and we're left to wonder how the lynch mob reacted to a lightning bolt in their midst. (Seems a strong hint to go back home!) Skeptics point out that the current windowpane is unlikely to be the same one installed in 1877. The legend has two answers to this: One, that it is the original pane, that it survived even the big hailstorm of 1928 that smashed every other courthouse window; two, that the pane has been repeatedly changed, but the face magically appears in each successive one.

Writer John Carmichael, a contributor to the University of Alabama's Dateline Pickens Web site, verified the least fantastic parts of the story. The 1876 burning of the old courthouse was considered deliberate, and two years later, a black man named Henry Wells was arrested for the crime. Shot twice while fleeing capture, Wells died of his wounds. No historical evidence exists for the lynch mob, or the lightning strike, and when the legend of the face in the window actually got started is unclear.

Visitors aren't allowed into the attic to study the window up close. Heretics have accused the civic boosters of Carrollton of "touching up" the face from time to time, lest the faces of tourists fade away as well. But even with the help of the big arrow on the exterior wall and the coin-operated telescope across the square, many people are hard pressed to see anything in the window but a set of blobs that suggest a smiley face with the grin reversed.

The best view of the face may be on the $8 souvenir mugs sold by the Pickens County Courthouse Preservation Committee. The mug is decorated with a drawing of the famous window. Pour hot coffee into it, and voilà! The face of Henry Wells appears. The mugs are sold at the courthouse and at West Alabama Bank & Trust across the square. For more information, call Dora Johnson of the preservation committee at (205) 367-8286.

★ ★

But What Do You Do with the Pit?

Clanton

The biggest peach in Chilton County is the 120-foot-tall, peach-shaped water tower on I-65 at exit 212, between Birmingham and Montgomery. It was built in 1992 by the Chicago Bridge and Iron Company, which had also built a giant peach in Gaffney, South Carolina, eleven years earlier.

A much smaller giant peach is located at Peach Park, a roadside fruit market. This peach has a funny shape and from certain angles looks

This water tower is a peachy keen symbol for the town of Clanton. NIKI SEPSAS

like an eggplant—but the market also sells ice cream and pastries, so who can complain? Peach Park Gardens is a few miles south of the biggest peach on I-65, exit 205 at U.S. Highway 31. It's open April through November. For more details call (205) 755-2065 or log onto www.peachpk.com.

You may have guessed by now that the Clanton area is proud of its peaches. The Chilton County Peach Festival, held each June since 1947, features a Peach Parade, a Peach Auction, a Peach Art Show, and, of course, a Peach Pageant that crowns Miss Peach, Junior Miss Peach, Young Miss Peach, and Little Miss Peach. For more information contact the Chilton County Chamber of Commerce at (205) 755-2400 or on the Web at www.chiltoncountychamber.com.

Alabama's Not-So-Big Bigfoot
Clanton

Bigfoot stories are as common in Alabama as they are in other rural states. Here's one example of many.

In fall 1960 several people reported seeing apelike creatures in the woods around Clanton. Most of the sightings were in the Walnut Creek area, where I-65 and US 31 intersect south of town.

According to a July 8, 2004, article in the *Clanton Advertiser*, Clanton County Sheriff T. J. Lockhart had made a concrete mold of some alleged footprints in the 1960s, "about the size of a person's foot but looking more like a hand." The sheriff's office kept the mold around for decades but eventually—alas for science—threw it away.

Cryptozoologist Loren Coleman believes the Clanton sightings were of Bigfoot's smaller southeastern cousins, often called "swamp apes" or "skunk apes" or "monkey men" or "the little red men of the woods" or, most vividly, "boogers": chimpanzee-like creatures that have been spotted fitfully for 250 years but never (yet) proven to exist.

James M. Smith's *Bigfoot Sightings of East Central Alabama* details fourteen sightings in only four counties: Chambers, Lee, Randolph, and Tallapoosa. (To order Smith's book, send $10 to James M. Smith, P.O. Box 6, Wadley, Alabama, 36276-0006.)

Other books on the subject include *Sasquatch: Alabama Bigfoot Sightings*, again by James M. Smith, and *UFO and Bigfoot Sightings in Alabama* by Wyatt Cox, the second available on Amazon.

The Web site of the Alabama Bigfoot Seekers Research Group—alas again for science—seems to be defunct, but the Gulf Coast Bigfoot Research Organization has picked up the torch at www.gcbro .com/index.htm.

Peaches, Possums, and a Handy Generator

The late Jerry Clower (1926–1998) spent eighteen years as a fertilizer salesman in Yazoo City, Mississippi, before becoming a celebrated Grand Ole Opry comedian. Most of his many albums were recorded live. What turned out to be the final one was recorded in the high school gymnasium in Clanton, during a power outage.

The show went on as scheduled, thanks to flashlights, candles, and a generator that kept the recording equipment going. "This is probably the only album in the history of MCA Records to be recorded with makeshift, generated power," Clower said.

The album that resulted, in October 1998, was titled *Peaches & Possums,* from Clower's opening remarks to the audience: "When you speak of Clanton, Alabama, you gotta think of peaches and possums." It was a posthumous release. Clower had died that August after heart surgery at age seventy-one.

Washington Didn't Sleep Here
Columbiana

The only thing curious about the Karl C. Harrison Museum of George Washington is the town in which it's located. Wasn't the first U.S. president a Virginian?

Yes, he was, but Charlotte Smith Weaver of Shelby County, Alabama, a descendant of First Lady Martha Washington by an earlier marriage, inherited more than a thousand of the family heirlooms. These form the nucleus of the Karl C. Harrison Museum of George Washington, founded in 1982 and named for the local banker, legislator, and philanthropist who made it happen.

On exhibit are tools from George's surveyor case, Martha's prayer book, the handwritten will of her first husband's grandfather (dated 1710), and the original 1787 sketch of the landscaping at Mount Vernon. The museum also sells copies of Harrison's book *Every Man's Shakespeare*.

The museum is in the Mildred B. Harrison Regional Library at 50 Lester Street, 1 block west of Main Street (a.k.a. Highway 47). Hours are 10:00 a.m. to 3:00 p.m., Monday through Friday. For more information call (205) 669-8767 or visit www.washingtonmuseum.com.

Guardian Angel of Lilly Lane
Concord

One of the more reassuring ghost stories told in Alabama is told about Lilly Lane, a dead end that intersects Jefferson County Road 46 (a.k.a. Warrior River Road) just west of Concord. The story goes that a ghostly old man in a white T-shirt and blue jeans has walked Lilly Lane, by day and by night, for many years. Locals believe the apparition is looking out for them, as a sort of ectoplasmic neighborhood-watch program.

Rooster Bridge Rollover

Demopolis

On April 28, 1979, during record high water on the Tombigbee River, amateur photographer Charles Barger was standing on the Rooster Bridge waiting for the drawbridge to lower, when he snapped a series of photographs of a remarkable event: A towboat, caught crosswise in the current, capsized, rolled beneath the bridge, and emerged, right side up, on the other side, its engine still running, its dazed skipper still at the wheel.

The photographs were published in the weekly newspaper in Linden, the *Democrat-Reporter*, but the incident was soon forgotten except among hardcore rivermen. Not until 2001–2002, when the series of photographs bobbed to the surface of the Internet, did the Rooster Bridge rollover become internationally famous.

The photographs appear on countless Web sites, accompanied by various texts that are humorous, suspenseful, or inspirational, depending on the mood of the poster. (One poster summarized the event thus: "Tug, tug, tug, tug, blub! blub! blub! tug, tug, tug.") Lately, the photos are being cast in a patriotic light, since Old Glory is still flying when the boat reappears. Hundreds of thousands of people have had the links or the photographs e-mailed to them and have forwarded them in turn to others. One site reported 13,000 hits to look at the photos in a single day.

Warrior and Gulf Navigation of Chickasaw, Alabama, the company that owned the towboat at the time, has been inundated with phone calls. "It's generated more interest now than back when it happened," *Democrat-Reporter* owner and publisher Goodloe Sutton Sr. told *Professional Mariner* magazine in 2002.

Both the photographer and the skipper are dead now, but the handful of people who were there, or who knew the parties involved, have been asked to tell the story over and over again. The towboat was the *Cahaba*, skippered by Capt. Jimmy Wilkerson, who stayed at the controls during the whole nightmarish roll beneath the surface. As

★ ★

he went under, he cried into his loudspeaker, "All right, y'all, this ain't no fire drill. Get off the damn bridge!" The awful sound of the boat scraping beneath the bridge was clearly audible to the people standing on it, and the photos clearly show water pouring from the wheelhouse door after the boat rights itself.

Wilkerson was unhurt but, as one could imagine, badly rattled. A friend, Capt. Michael L. Smith, said that a month later Wilkerson's hands were still shaking so badly that he didn't need an ashtray. The rivermen say the boat never would have righted itself if Wilkerson hadn't topped off the fuel tanks a few miles upriver. Had the tank been half full, the fuel would have shifted during the roll, and the shift would have sent it to the bottom.

The big mystery, of great interest to river workers, Internet wonks, and folklorists alike, is who originally posted the photos online. Ray Fagan of Pascagoula, Mississippi, has come forward to say he scanned the photos and posted them in 2001 because he thought folks might be interested, but he can't be sure whether he was the first person to do so.

The *Cahaba* is still in service on West Virginia's Kanawha River, with a new owner and a new name, the *Capt. Ed Harris*. The Rooster Bridge was demolished years ago, but its location was just downstream from the new U.S. Highway 80 bridge.

Online, the photos most reliably can be found on Barbara and David Mikkelson's invaluable Urban Legends Reference Pages at www .snopes.com, one-stop shopping for Internet skeptics curious about whether something really happened. The specific link is www.snopes .com/photos/towboat.asp. Pennsylvania Web designer Rio Akasaka also has a good site, with links, at www.rioleo.org/mv-cahaba.php. *Professional Mariner* magazine did an extensive article on the incident and its strange online afterlife in its June/July 2002 issue.

Wilkerson didn't own a computer, but before he died, someone printed the rollover photos off the Internet and showed them to him. His response was not recorded.

The Great Rooster Auction
Demopolis

The lack of a Tombigbee River bridge at Demopolis was a major impediment to the World War I–era Dixie Overland Highway project, a 2,700-mile paved road from Savannah, Georgia, to San Diego, California. To raise money for the bridge, Demopolis civic leaders turned to a local auctioneer and showman, Frank Derby. He proposed a celebrity rooster auction. His slogan? "Bridge the Bigbee with Cocks."

President Woodrow Wilson and the leaders of the Allied nations at Versailles all donated roosters, in a ceremony that made the front page of the *New York Times*. Roosters also were donated by movie stars Fatty Arbuckle and Mary Pickford, as well as by Helen Keller and Gen. John J. Pershing.

Becky Willis tells the story of the great rooster auction in the winter 2003 issue of *Alabama Heritage* magazine. The two-day auction in August 1919 drew tens of thousands of people to Liberty Park in downtown Demopolis. Besides the auction, festivities included an air show, a barbecue, a jazz dance, and, alas, a number of cockfights. The top bid of $55,000 went to the president's bird, "Woodrow," but that bidder, like many others, failed to pay up afterward. Although paper bids surpassed $200,000, only $65,000 was collected, which after expenses left only $45,000 for the bridge, $30,000 short of the goal.

Eventually built mostly with federal money, the bridge finally opened with no fanfare in 1925. It was officially named Memorial Bridge, but in 1959, to commemorate Frank Derby's seventy-fifth birthday, the Alabama Legislature finally named it what locals had called it all along: Rooster Bridge.

The old bridge was dynamited in 1980, a year after it was the site of the belatedly famous rollover of the towboat *Cahaba*. The new US 80 bridge, just upstream, is also named Rooster Bridge. The old 1959 bridge marker, which lists all the illustrious rooster donors, is now in Liberty Park, actual site of the great rooster auction. Since renamed Confederate Park, it's bounded by Main, Capitol, Walnut, and Washington Streets in downtown Demopolis.

★ ★

Napoleon's Man in Alabama

Demopolis

A group of French aristocrats, about 150 of them, showed up in the Alabama wilderness in 1817. All supporters of the disgraced and defeated Napoleon, they had been banished from France by Louis XVIII, and Congress granted them some Choctaw land in Alabama, the Choctaws having been forced out shortly before.

The French called their settlement Aigleville (Eagletown), the eagle being symbolic of Napoleon. A mile from present-day Demopolis, one of the first log cabins they built was a shrine to the great man, centered around a bust of Napoleon on a pedestal that they had carried across the Atlantic.

The most famous settler in Aigleville was the great cavalry commander Charles Lefebvre-Desnouettes, who had been Napoleon's aide-de-camp when he defeated the Austrians at Marengo. From Alabama, Lefebvre-Desnouettes wrote fevered letters to Napoleon, plotting improbable escapes from St. Helena.

The plan was to grow olives and grapes, but the aristocrats didn't know much about farming, and the other settlers made fun of them. According to legend the men farmed in tricornered hats and crimson capes, the women in brocaded gowns and satin slippers. Most of the settlers went back to France when the new king, Louis-Philippe, granted them amnesty. Napoleon died and left Lefebvre-Desnouettes 150,000 francs. When he left Alabama to claim the money, his ship was lost at sea off the coast of England.

Aigleville is long gone, but a few olive trees still grow in Marengo County, which was named for Napoleon's great victory.

The colony's memory is kept alive, to some extent, by the 1949 John Wayne movie *The Fighting Kentuckian*, in which frontiersman Wayne helps the French settlers keep their land out of the hands of some no-good thieving Alabamians, in the process romancing a French colonel's sexy daughter, played by Vera Hruba Ralston. (She actually was Czech, but being the studio head's girlfriend made her perfect for the part.) Perhaps more memorably, Wayne's coonskin-hatted comic sidekick is played by Stan Laurel's derby-hatted comic sidekick, Oliver Hardy.

Tuxedo Junction
Ensley

Though now considered part of Birmingham, Ensley was for many years a thriving town all its own, known in the 1920s and 1930s as the center of African American nightlife for miles around. The hub of the action was the intersection of Twentieth Street and Ensley Avenue, a.k.a. Tuxedo Junction.

According to legend, at this intersection people would step off the streetcar in their work clothes and then rent tuxedos at the clothing store on the corner. After a night of clubbing, they would drag back into the clothing store to change into their drab daytime clothes again. The second-floor dance hall in the Nixon Building was a notable hot spot, but there were many others.

The neighborhood was immortalized in song by a Birmingham native, trumpet player and bandleader Erskine Hawkins (1914–1993), a star of New York's Roseland and Savoy ballrooms in the 1930s and 1940s. (The young vocalist Della Reese was one of his protégés.) Hawkins wrote and recorded the big band standard "Tuxedo Junction" (1939), a favorite of GIs during World War II.

The lyrics to the song are etched into the windows of the Alabama Jazz Hall of Fame in Birmingham's historic Carver Theatre, 1631 Fourth Avenue North (205-254-2731; www.jazzhall.com), which isn't near the actual intersection.

Today the Ensley neighborhood landmark is Holy Family Catholic Church at 1910 Nineteenth Street West (205-780-3440). It was founded in 1938 to minister to the fun-loving souls of Tuxedo Junction.

★ ★

This Gives a Whole New Meaning to "Finish" Line
Eutaw

Joe Dump's grave is at the finish line of the old greyhound racetrack in Eutaw, a spot he knew well in life. At that spot on May 15, 1979, Joe Dump set a world record by winning his twenty-eighth consecutive race. He won three more races before his streak ended at thirty-one. The current record for consecutive wins in greyhound racing is thirty-seven, set by JJ Doc Richard in Mobile in 1995.

During his winning streak at Greenetrack, Joe Dump was so heavily favored in each race that bettors found it almost impossible to make money on him. Yet the seasoned gamblers bet on him anyway, pocketing 10 cents' profit on each $2.00 ticket, because they loved him so. They said Joe Dump knew when to hold back and when to come from behind just as if he had a jockey aboard. Hard-boiled touts wept when he finally lost.

Joe Dump died in 1989 and was buried in a private ceremony at the finish line, where a marker stands today. Sportswriter Tommy Deas retold the story of Joe Dump in the January 18, 2004, issue of the *Tuscaloosa News*, a newspaper that had published a mock interview with the dog twenty-five years before. Live racing at Greenetrack ended in 1997, though bingo, gambling machines, and simulcast races still draw fans. The track is on Union Road at exit 45 from I-20/59. Call (800) 633-5942 or visit www.greenetrackpaysyoumoney.com for more details.

Lloyd "Not Lloyd Nolan" Noland
Fairfield

According to the Internet Movie Database, the late actor Lloyd Nolan, who often played doctors (in the movie *Peyton Place* and the TV sitcom *Julia*, for example), bore a strong resemblance to an actual Alabama doctor named Lloyd Noland, causing confusion through the years.

In fact, Lloyd Noland didn't look much like Lloyd Nolan, although his name frequently was misspelled as "Nolan" through the years, even in legal documents—just as Nolan's name frequently was misspelled "Noland" through the years, even in movie reference books. But Lloyd Noland's story is fascinating in its own right.

An iron and coal company brought Noland to Jefferson County in 1917. He had been chief surgeon of a 600-bed hospital in Panama, working under William Crawford Gorgas during the Panama Canal project, and upon arrival in Alabama, he set to work ridding Birmingham of the same endemic diseases the public health pioneers had been fighting in Panama: smallpox, typhoid, dysentery, and malaria.

The persuasive Noland talked his employers into building a $750,000 hospital—a remarkable achievement, considering that the sum was larger than the entire public health budget of the State of Alabama. He also was a pioneer in establishing an anesthesiology program and a residency program for the training of young doctors.

For many years Lloyd Noland Hospital in Fairfield, a southwest Birmingham suburb, was the leading hospital in Jefferson County. For decades it served thousands of elderly and low-income people.

In the 1990s the aging hospital, since closed, was bought first by Tenet and then by HealthSouth, which renamed it HealthSouth Metro West. Lloyd Noland Parkway, the street leading to the hospital, was renamed Richard M. Scrushy Parkway, after HealthSouth's flamboyant founder and CEO.

Soon after, HealthSouth became mired in a colossal corporate scandal. Fifteen executives, including every finance chief in HealthSouth's twenty-year history, pleaded guilty in a $2.7 billion accounting fraud. Scrushy himself was controversially acquitted, only to be indicted shortly thereafter in a bribery case involving former Alabama governor Don Siegelman. At press time Scrushy was in federal prison serving a six-year sentence, and Siegelman was appealing his own conviction.

For far too long, exit signs on I-20/59, near Miles College, continued to beckon travelers onto Richard M. Scrushy Parkway, while the name of the man who rid Birmingham of its Third World plagues less than a century ago remained mostly forgotten. Public indignation eventually won out, however, and today the street is called Lloyd Noland Parkway once again.

Noland's name also lives on via the nonprofit Noland Health Services, based in Fairfield, which operates long-term hospitals and retirement communities across the state.

Mud + Paper Bags + Gourds = Fine Art
Fayette

Other than the late Howard Finster of Georgia, no self-taught Southern artist gained more renown late in life than Jimmie Lee Sudduth, an old man in overalls who became internationally famous for painting in mud with his fingers.

Asked why he didn't use a brush, Sudduth once raised his hand and said, "That brush don't wear out. When I die, the brush dies." Well into his nineties, Sudduth continued to show up early every year on the Saturday morning of the Kentuck Festival of the Arts in Northport. Sudduth slowly lowered himself into a folding chair just inside the front gate and watched his more able-bodied relatives unceremoniously stack several dozen of his new plywood paintings against a pine tree. A hundred avid art collectors gathered around, breathing heavily.

The asking price for each plywood sheet—each containing a vivid, childlike scrawl of a dog, a house, a school bus, a city skyline—was hundreds of dollars; the larger ones, thousands. Sudduth chatted with each purchaser, cackled at his own jokes, and autographed each plywood sheet on the back with a felt-tip marker. Sometimes he doodled something impromptu, like a house, then turned to the crowd and exclaimed: "Look at that! I made a house out of nothing." By lunchtime Sudduth would be out of inventory, and he and his family would be on the road back home to Fayette. Sudduth died September 2, 2007, at age ninety-seven.

A 1982 exhibit at the Corcoran Gallery of Art in Washington, D.C., made him famous, but Sudduth started painting full-time in the

1960s, after a lifetime of other work with his hands. Born in 1910, he had been a gardener, a farm laborer, and a sawmill hand. He initially painted only in mud, having developed a personal palette of thirty-six different shades of Fayette County clay, to which he added anything that was handy—berry juice, crushed leaves, flour, charcoal, molasses, even the "pot liquor" from a batch of turnip greens.

As he grew more frail, Sudduth remained prolific but switched to the much easier medium of house paint. The many paintings that earned him the nickname "Mud Man" now are sought-after collectors' items.

Excellent examples are on display in Sudduth's hometown, among the 3,500 folk-art pieces in the permanent collection of the remarkable Fayette Art Museum. Two other celebrated west Alabama folk artists are also well represented:

- "Brother" Benjamin Perkins (1904–1993), a U.S. Marine turned preacher, began to paint on patriotic and religious themes after his twenty-year marriage broke up. The Fayette County native painted in acrylics on canvases, boards, and dried gourds. He lived near Bankston in a red, white, and blue house that was a mecca for enthusiasts of "art environments"; sadly, his family had it burned to the ground upon his death.

- Sybil Gibson (1908–1995), an elementary-school teacher in the neighboring Walker County town of Cordova, painted animals, portraits, and children on guitar cases, mirrors, and, most often, brown paper bags. Her art career began on Thanksgiving Day 1963, when she set about making some homemade wrapping paper for Christmas presents. See www.sybilgibson.com.

The Fayette Art Museum is inside the Fayette Civic Center, a renovated 1930 school building, at 530 North Temple Avenue. Call (205) 932-8727 or visit www.fayette.net/chamber/locart.htm for more information.

An Artistic Career Stacked on Hay
Forkland

Retired farmer Jim Bird has used his pasture mostly to amuse passersby (and himself) since 1993, when he found himself with a surplus of hay and decided to make art with it.

Like any self-taught haystack artist, he started with the obvious subjects: a caterpillar, a spider. Then he tried the less obvious: a horse, a rabbit, a tank, a pirate ship, Betty Boop.

A 1950 engineering graduate of Auburn University, Bird accessorizes the hay with buckets, drums, tires, truck parts—anything, really. His "warehouse" is a vast pile of open-air junk, onto which Bird tosses anything that looks interesting and from which he assembles his creations.

When he started, he vowed to his wife, Lib, that he would spend no more than $5.00 per sculpture. Since then he has fudged occasionally. The Tin Man that perpetually waves to motorists cost $45.00, mostly for aluminum paint. "I just want to give bored motorists a little something to look at," Bird told the *Auburn Plainsman*. The Bird ranch is on U.S. Highway 43 north of Demopolis.

What better use for a hay bale could one imagine? Jim Bird is a pioneer in "agritainment." NIKI SEPSAS

She Was on a Mission . . . at Age Fifty-Six

Gainesville

Maria Fearing—whose first name was pronounced with the long *i*, as in "Mariah Carey"—was born a slave in 1838 on Oak Hill Plantation near Gainesville. She didn't learn to read and write until age thirty-three, but she eventually graduated from Talladega College and became a schoolteacher in Calhoun County.

At age fifty-three she attended a lecture at her alma mater by William Sheppard, a Presbyterian missionary in Africa. She was so moved by his appeal for help that she volunteered on the spot to return with

207

him. Sheppard and everyone else tried to dissuade her, but she was determined. At age fifty-six she sold her house, collected $100 from church ladies, and paid her own way to Africa. She reached the coast, traveled 1,200 miles farther inland, and arrived at the Luebo mission in the present-day Democratic Republic of the Congo, where she lived and taught for the next twenty-one years.

Her students nicknamed her *mama wa Mputu*, meaning "mother from far away." She taught them reading, writing, arithmetic, home-making, and gardening. Some of them were young girls whom Fearing had bartered out of slavery in exchange for trinkets, tools, and salt. Fearing became perhaps the only Alabamian fluent in the language of the Baluba and Lulua tribes. An old photo shows her and her fellow missionaries in wide-brimmed hats, playing croquet.

Poor health and advancing age eventually forced Fearing to leave Luebo and come home to Alabama, where she resumed teaching school. She died at age ninety-nine and was buried in Oak Hill Cemetery.

Her grave site is on private property, but Gainesville Presbyterian Church, which Fearing attended, is still standing and still holds services once a month. It shares its small congregation with Gainesville's Baptist, Episcopal, and Methodist churches; the same people attend a different church each Sunday, in rotation, and jokingly call themselves "Metho-bapti-presby-palians."

Gee, Nice Quilts
Gee's Bend

Gee's Bend is an African American community of 700 or so people, most of them named Pettway, the name of a long-gone plantation owner. The town is located at the tip of an inland peninsula formed by a sharp bend in the river, which has no bridge at that point. Reached only by Wilcox County Road 29, which dead-ends there, the people of Gee's Bend lived in isolation for many years. As a result generations of women of Gee's Bend, working with no outside influences, developed quilt patterns unique in the United States.

The free-form patterns were born partially of desperate living conditions. The quilts had to be made quickly, lest the children freeze in wintertime, never mind right angles and formal perfection. But the women also knew they were creating things of beauty, and they learned from one another. As quilter Lucy Pettway recalls, "I used to pass by quilts out on a line, get me a piece of paper and draw a pattern from it, make me my quilt."

Gee's Bend made the news only occasionally and not for quilts. In the 1930s it was the site of a New Deal agricultural co-op, and its poverty and beauty were documented in a famous set of photographs by Arthur Rothstein. In 1965 Martin Luther King Jr., en route to Selma, preached in Gee's Bend; Gee's Bend mules later would pull the wagon containing the casket at King's funeral.

The quilts finally received notice on December 8, 1965. While driving through the area, an Episcopal minister and civil rights activist named Francis X. Walter saw three beautiful quilts hanging on a clothesline, so beautiful that he stopped the car to meet the woman who made them. The sight of an approaching white man sent the woman fleeing into the woods.

It was an inauspicious start for a business enterprise, but Walter convinced a group of local women, led by Estelle Witherspoon, that a market for their quilts existed in New York and that through their quilts they could generate money for their families independent of the whims of local landowners. At the time African Americans in many parts of rural Alabama risked financial ruin—through firings and evictions—if they exercised their newly guaranteed right to vote.

A June 21, 1966, auction in New York City sold eighty Gee's Bend quilts at a profit of $2,200. This was big money, considering that many Gee's Bend residents paid only $5.00 a month in rent. More important, big stores such as Bloomingdale's and Sears said they wanted more quilts. To meet the demand, the newly organized Freedom Quilting Bee, with help from churches and other charities, bought twenty-three acres in Alberta, the nearest town of any size. The Bee built a production facility and a day-care center and went to work.

Demand from major retailers for individual, handmade quilts didn't last long, however. Big textile mills, in the United States and overseas, could mass-produce quilts much more cheaply. Though the Freedom Quilting Bee still operates at 4295 County Road 29 (www.rural development.org/FQB.html) and is still the largest employer in Alberta, it has diversified its operation to include potholders, place mats, napkins, and customized tote bags for conferences. In 1999 it signed a contract to make aprons, baby bibs, and bandanas for the Ben & Jerry's ice cream company.

A generation after Walter's brainstorm, however, Gee's Bend quilts were rediscovered in a big way. A 2002 exhibit of seventy Gee's Bend quilts—dating from 1930 to 2000—at New York City's Whitney Museum became the talk of the art world. The *New York Times* called the quilts "some of the most miraculous works of modern art America has produced. . . . It's as if something in the local water has produced a whole villageful of Paul Klees who create their vibrant work on a bed-size scale."

The museum tour that included the Whitney exhibit was organized by a nonprofit arts organization, the Tinwood Alliance, based in Atlanta (www.tinwoodmedia.com/ExARCH.html). So far, Tinwood's ongoing marketing effort has produced a coffee-table book, a video documentary, note cards, calendars, art prints, and even a two-CD set of Gee's Bend gospel music. Former supermodel and housewares entrepreneur Kathy Ireland has contracted with Tinwood to reproduce the designs on wall art, rugs, furniture, and clothing.

Bill Arnett, Tinwood's founder, says $1 million of the proceeds from these enterprises already has gone back into the town via the newly formed Gee's Bend Foundation. To many inside and out of the art world, Arnett is a controversial figure; Andrew Dietz's 2006 book *The Last Folk Hero: A True Story of Race and Art, Power and Profit*, is a fascinating look at that controversy.

All the living Gee's Bend quilters, more than fifty women, have united as the Gee's Bend Quilters Collective, led by Mary Ann Pettway (334-573-2323; www.quiltsofgeesbend.com). Their asking prices for new quilts range from $500 to $15,000, and they're getting what they ask for.

As a side note, in 1949 Gee's Bend was officially renamed Boykin after a white congressman for whom Gee's Bend residents, at the time, were not allowed to vote (but then, Gee himself had been a white landowner, long ago). To quilt enthusiasts, however, it remains Gee's Bend forevermore.

PAckRaT Inspires ART-ful Legacy

Gordo

Ma'Cille's Museum of Miscellanea once was one of America's great backroad wonders, drawing hundreds of visitors a week to a half-dozen sagging outbuildings off Highway 86 outside Gordo. Now it's only a memory, and a hard-to-describe memory at that.

The museum was the life's work of the late Lucille House, a.k.a. Mama Lucille, or Ma'Cille for short. Inspired by reports of the Alabama Museum of Natural History, one county and one world away in Tuscaloosa, she was a lifelong collector, what some would call a "pack rat." She liked to say, "I want one of everything," but she had dozens, hundreds, and even thousands of some things—bottles, bones, buttons, bird carcasses, broken and castoff furniture and farm equipment. She gathered stranger things, too: a deformed pig pickled in a jar; two stuffed possums playing checkers; a mummified "Indian princess"; a world-class collection of used chewing gum.

After thirty-plus years of nonstop acquisition, Ma'Cille grew old and feeble, and rot, dust, and termites gnawed at her vast hoard of treasures and junk. The whole lot was auctioned off in 1998, as thousands of gawkers wandered open-mouthed through the remains.

Though Ma'Cille House is gone now, she lives on in the works of the Alabama artists and writers who made her museum a place of pilgrimage through the years. Three of them have set up shop in an old NAPA Auto Parts store; they painted over the sign except for the *A-R-T*. This gallery devoted to the "Southern Surreal" showcases the work of Glenn House, Ma'Cille's son, who makes funny, grotesque faces out of clay

(and who designed the Moon Winx sign in Tuscaloosa); his wife, Kathleen Fetters, who takes black-and-white photographs and hand-colors them with oils; and their friend Barbara Lee Black, who puts densely patterned still lifes in fragmented frames. All the works are both creepy and wonderful, like heirlooms of an Alabama Addams Family, like the legacy of Ma'Cille herself.

The gallery is located at 121 North Main Street downtown, but call first: (800) 718-5893.

Not One, but Two Mule Cele-BRAY-tions
Gordo and Winfield

As readers of the "cl-ASS-ifieds" in *Mules and More* magazine well know, Alabama has not one but two Mule Day festivals, 50 miles and more than three months apart. Both feature a mule parade and much else besides.

- Mule Day in Winfield, the older of the two festivals, is the fourth Saturday in September and draws 25,000 people. Its attractions include a duck race ("Buy a duck and win a buck!") and muzzle-loading demonstrations. For details call the Winfield Chamber of Commerce at (205) 487-8841 or visit www.winfieldcity.org/mule_day.htm.
- Mule Day in Gordo is the first Saturday in June and draws 18,000 people. It may be the odder of the two festivals, as its attractions include a Barney Fife impersonator, a balloon-blowing goat, and a stand that sells alligator kebabs. Plus, it's in Gordo, one of those American towns that for unaccountable reasons is viewed with amusement by all its neighbors, so much so that "I'm from Gordo" is a reliable laugh-getter. To learn more call the Gordo Chamber of Commerce at (205) 364-7870.

For more information, *Mules and More* (based in Missouri) is highly recommended, especially its annual "jack" issue. Visit www.mulesandmore.com.

Hueytown Hum

Mysterious low-pitched sounds of no identifiable origin, often described as sounding like the throb of distant diesel engines, are reported periodically in many parts of the world. To some people they're a phenomenon "unknown to science"; to skeptics they're just, well, distant diesel engines, highways, or air conditioners—the countless white-noise generators of the twenty-first century, noticed only when things are otherwise very quiet.

Some of these hums are reported so often, they gain proper names: the Bristol Hum, the Taos Hum, the Kokomo Hum. In 1992 the Hueytown Hum briefly made the national news when residents of this Birmingham suburb were unnerved by a mysterious new noise.

The engineers who investigated concluded that the noise was nothing more than a ventilator fan at a nearby coal mine. The ventilator fan did not make national news, but the Hueytown Hum still gets mentioned occasionally in online roundups of the "inexplicable." Did you hear something?

"Sandman" Follows Celestial Directive
Harpersville

Lonnie Holley, born in Birmingham in 1950, grew up in foster homes and reform schools and worked primarily as a short-order cook until 1977, when his two nieces died in a house fire. Suicidal with grief, he heard the Lord tell him: "Make art!"

He started with his nieces' two gravestones, since the family couldn't afford store-bought granite slabs. He molded and carved two gravestones out of core sand, an industrial byproduct discarded by foundries,

★ ★

and he's been making sandstone sculptures ever since, sometimes with the addition of bent wire and other found objects. Recently he has taken up painting as well. He teaches many hands-on workshops to children, who scrape the sandstone into designs of their own creation as Holley looks on, beaming.

For eighteen years Holley's quarter-acre sculpture garden surrounding his house was a Birmingham landmark, but an airport expansion forced him to move. The airport appraised his property at only $14,000, ignoring the presence of tons of prized sculpture that had been exhibited at the Smithsonian, Howard University, the High Museum of Art in Atlanta, the Philadelphia Museum of Art, the 1996 Summer Olympics in Atlanta, and the White House. After much bad publicity for the airport, Holley settled in 1998 for $165,700 and moved to Harpersville, 25 miles southeast of Birmingham—where he promptly got shot and wounded by an unwelcoming neighbor. Holley is one of the major figures profiled in Andrew Dietz's 2006 book *The Last Folk Hero: A True Story of Race and Art, Power and Profit*.

Irondale Cafe: Food for the Imagination

Irondale

The Irondale Cafe was run for forty years by the late Bess Fortenberry, whose niece, a Birmingham native, grew up to be writer-actress Fannie Flagg. Flagg's novel *Fried Green Tomatoes at the Whistle Stop Cafe* paid tribute to Aunt Bess, her partner, Sue Lovelace, and their cafe, which has been continuously open since 1928.

The 1991 movie *Fried Green Tomatoes* brought a fresh influx of tourists to the restaurant, and they haven't stopped coming since. The cafe Web site, www.irondalecafe.com, lists all the daily meats and vegetables. Fried green tomatoes are always on the menu; the cooks go through seventy pounds a day.

The cafe is at 1906 First Avenue North, beside the railroad tracks in downtown Irondale, just off I-20/59. Hours are 11:00 a.m. to 7:30 p.m., Monday through Friday, and 11 a.m. to 2:30 p.m. on Sunday. Check the Web site or call (205) 956-5258 to see what the day's specials are.

While the house specialty is fried green tomatoes, don't overlook the tasty fried chicken at the Irondale Cafe.

★ ★

The Face on the Door
Jasper

In April 1983 at the Walker County Medical Center, a man praying for his critically injured son saw the face of Jesus in the grain of a wooden door. The man took this as a sign that his son would live, and his son did, indeed, recover.

In the meantime, so many thronged to see the miraculous door, month after month, that the hospital put Plexiglas over the wood to protect it. Finally the door was moved to the hospital chapel, where it remains to this day.

Now Walker Baptist Medical Center, the hospital (205-387-4000) is located at 3400 U.S. Highway 78 East in Jasper. From the main lobby take the elevator to the second-floor lobby and go through the double doors on the right. The chapel, with the celebrated door beneath Plexiglas, is the last door on the left.

Ancient Footprints Are Everywhere
Jasper

In 1999 an Oneonta High School science teacher named Ashley Allen discovered a paleontological marvel in an abandoned surface coal mine near Jasper in Walker County: fossilized tracks marking the progress of a host of creatures as they walked, slithered, flopped, and crawled through a tidal flat 310 million years ago.

Between 2000 and 2004, Steven C. Minkin and the other members of the Alabama Paleontological Society (or APS) painstakingly retrieved from the old Union Chapel Mine more than 2,000 specimens—invaluable evidence of ancient fish, amphibians, shellfish, worms, insects (even insect larvae), and, yes, maybe reptiles, too. The specimens contain the earliest evidence, anywhere in the world, of group behavior in fish and amphibians.

The site of this treasure trove was at risk, interestingly enough, because of a federal conservation law that requires abandoned mines to be restored to their natural state. In this case, that would have

★ ★

meant reburying the fossils and planting a forest over them. With the help of Congressman Bob Aderholt, the Geological Survey of Alabama, and other groups, the APS managed to save the property, which was acquired by the state in 2004. It's now open only to scientists and school groups.

The Alabama Department of Conservation has designated it the Steven C. Minkin Paleozoic Footprint Site, in honor of the amateur geologist who worked tirelessly to preserve it but died in an accident before the March 2005 dedication.

Photographs of the fossils abound at an online database compiled by Ronald J. "Ron" Buta: http://bama.ua.edu/~rbuta/monograph.

An illustrated book on the site is *Pennsylvanian Footprints in the Black Warrior Basin of Alabama*, edited by Ron Buta, Andrew K. Rindsberg, and David C. Kopaska-Merkel. It's $49 (plus $5 shipping) from the Alabama Paleontological Society, www.alabamapaleo.org.

Haunted Radio Station

Jasper

Since the 1970s a series of Jasper radio stations have had their headquarters in an old house that once was owned by a car dealer named George Vines. When Vines died, the wake was held at the house, and his body supposedly lay in state in the bay window of the front room, where the station's control board is now.

Unsurprisingly, decades of station employees say George Vines continues to haunt the place. Whether he has ever spoken over the air is unrecorded, but employees swear that doors open and shut, toilets flush, doorknobs and blinds are rattled, lights are flipped on and off, and figures walk past doorways—all with no one around. People hear someone calling their names or feel someone stroking their hair. Alan Brown devotes a chapter to the station in his fine book *Stories from the Haunted South* (University Press of Mississippi, 2004).

For years the house at 409 Ninth Avenue housed WZPQ; today it houses WIXI, phone number (205) 384-3461.

★ ★

John Henry Was a Steel-Drivin' Man, but Where?
Leeds

Many American schoolchildren learn, in story or in song, the legend of John Henry, the nineteenth-century steel-driving man who killed himself outworking a steam drill. To many people it's just a tale, but some historians and folklorists through the years have speculated about whether the tale has a basis in fact—whether there ever was a real John Henry, where he might have died, and how.

West Virginia has long claimed John Henry. A historical marker at the Big Bend Tunnel, a nineteenth-century engineering marvel, reads: TRADITION MAKES THIS THE SCENE OF THE STEEL DRIVERS' BALLAD, "JOHN HENRY." West Virginia has a much-photographed John Henry statue and a well-attended John Henry festival, as depicted in Colson White-head's acclaimed 2001 novel *John Henry Days*. What West Virginia never had, according to some recent research, is John Henry.

In a 2002 article in *Tributaries*, the journal of the Alabama Folklife Association, John Garst of the University of Georgia argued that John Henry's fatal contest with the steam drill actually occurred on the old C&W Railroad in Alabama, 15 miles east of Birmingham, between the Coosa and Oak Mountain tunnels, near Leeds.

A man named C. C. Spencer wrote folklorist Guy Johnson in the 1920s, claiming to have witnessed the contest and John Henry's death, on September 20, 1887, when Spencer was fourteen years old. Spencer said it happened at "Cruzee Mountain" in Alabama. He identified John Henry as a former slave from Holly Springs, Mississippi, who worked for the railroad contractors Shea and Dabner. Spencer said John Henry's own surname was Dabner, suggesting his family had been slaves of the Dabner family before the war.

Johnson dismissed Spencer's account largely because he could find no Cruzee Mountain in Alabama. He didn't know that Coosa Mountain, east of Birmingham, is pronounced "coo-see" locally. Garst believes Spencer meant Coosa Mountain, and he has found other evidence, albeit circumstantial, backing up Spencer's story:

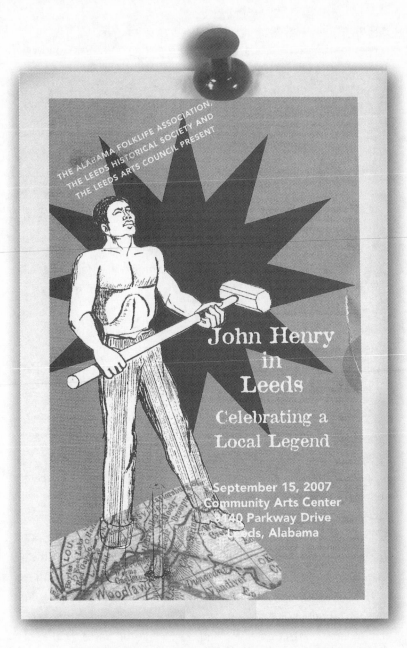

THE ALABAMA FOLKLIFE ASSOCIATION,
THE LEEDS HISTORICAL SOCIETY AND
THE LEEDS ARTS COUNCIL PRESENT

John Henry
in
Leeds

Celebrating a
Local Legend

September 15, 2007
Community Arts Center
8140 Parkway Drive
Leeds, Alabama

The drawing on the 2007 program is by local artist
Revis Brasher (1916-2001), who long supported John
Henry's connection to Leeds. ALABAMA FOLKLIFE ASSOCIATION

★ ★

- A man named Frederick Yeamans Dabney was, indeed, chief engineer for the C&W Railway during the construction of the Goodwater-Birmingham link in 1887–1888.
- Dabney was, moreover, from Crystal Springs, Mississippi, where his uncle had owned slaves. One of those slaves, according to an old census, was one Henry, born in 1844.
- Two other letter writers independently wrote Johnson in the 1920s with the same basic information, that John Henry died on the railroad near Birmingham in the 1880s. One said her uncle was a witness; the other said he remembered it because he was a steel driver in Birmingham at the time.
- At least two pre-1930 versions of the song "John Henry" place the incident on "the Georgia line" or "the Central o' Georgia" line—the later name of the C&W. (The same track is still there, but today it's the Norfolk Southern line.)
- Finally, many people in Leeds grew up hearing claims that John Henry died there—though no one, not even Garst, has found the all-important newspaper article or contemporary letter or diary that would confirm it.

   Still, Garst is convinced. "They have a [John Henry] postage stamp, a festival, and a historical monument in Talcott, West Virginia," he said. "I now think all of that belongs in Leeds."

   In the meantime visitors can see one of the two tunnels John Henry supposedly worked on at the end of his life. From US 78 in Leeds, take Highway 25 south. Cross the railroad tracks twice, then follow Highway 25 into a sharp right turn, and take the dirt road to the right. This is Tunnel Road, and it takes you past the north entrance of the Coosa Mountain Tunnel, on which John Henry is said to have worked in 1887. His fatal contest with the steam drill supposedly happened on the Oak Mountain Tunnel, 2 miles away, but getting within sight of that tunnel involves trespassing and walking on the tracks, neither of which is encouraged.

   Exhibits on John Henry and on better-documented locals such as former NBA star Charles Barkley can be seen on Highway 119 at the Bass House Museum, run by the Leeds Historical Society. For more information call (205) 699-2721 or visit www.leedshistoricalsociety.org.

How Would Monster.com List "Mob Moll?"
Lipscomb

Many Alabama towns are proud to be celebrity birthplaces, but this blue-collar Birmingham suburb, just northeast of Bessemer, is unlikely to erect a monument to one native daughter: gangster's moll Virginia Hill, best known as the mistress of Bugsy Siegel, the murderer who was instrumental in developing Las Vegas.

At birth in Lipscomb in 1916, Virginia was named Onie Hill, one of ten children of a dirt-poor family. Sources describe her father variously as a marble cutter, a mule trader, and a drunk. As a teenager she resolved to get out of Alabama as soon as she could.

She came to Chicago at age seventeen, hoping to find work in or around the 1933 World's Fair. The work she readily found was prostitution, which in Chicago was a mob-dominated industry. Soon she consorted with the town's high rollers, earning the nickname the Flamingo for her long legs and flamboyant ways.

When she took up more or less full-time with Benjamin Siegel, nicknamed "Bugsy" behind his back for his insane outbursts, Hill already had slept with a host of famous mobsters, including Joe "Joey Epp" Epstein, Frank Nitti, and Joey Adonis. Decades later, in characteristically earthy terms, she bragged to a U.S. Senate investigating committee about her sexual talents.

She also was in demand as a courier, lugging suitcases of mob money wherever they needed to go. By then her family was living in Marietta, Georgia; according to legend, on one trip home she bought them a new house with $11,000 in cash.

Her temper was almost as bad as Siegel's, and she was known for slugging women who angered her—reporters, Siegel's other girlfriends. Some people believe she was spying on Siegel for the Chicago

mob all along, letting them know that Siegel was skimming a fortune from the out-of-control expenses of his pet project, a gambling mecca in the dusty Nevada backwater of Las Vegas. That would have been ungrateful indeed, since Siegel named the place the Flamingo Hotel in her honor.

She was in France when Siegel was murdered on June 20, 1947. Some people say Chicago had tipped her off. By age forty she was a mob has-been. She lived her last years in obscurity in a small town in Austria, near Salzburg. Having attempted suicide repeatedly through-out her life, sometimes seriously and sometimes not, she finally suc-ceeded in overdosing in 1966. Her body was found in a snowdrift beside a brook.

Conspiracy buffs believe she was murdered because she knew too much, in which case it's odd she wasn't murdered sooner; by then she had been off the mob payroll for sixteen years. More likely the mob, like everyone else, had forgotten her.

Tonya Butler, We Get a Kick Out of You
Livingston

The leading scorer for the University of West Alabama football team in 2003 was a woman: place kicker Tonya Butler, the first woman in NCAA history to successfully kick a field goal.

Butler's career record at West Alabama was forty-eight of fifty-three extra-point attempts. Her all-male teammates twice elected her special-teams captain. In 2006 Butler's jersey (No. 37) and cleats went on display for six months in the NCAA Hall of Champions in Indianapo-lis, as part of the NCAA's celebration of twenty-five years of women's championships.

Before coming to West Alabama, Butler was an all-state star of the football team at Class AAA Riverdale High School in Georgia. From there she got a two-year athletic scholarship to Middle Georgia Junior College in Cochran. Her hopes for a Division I scholarship didn't pan out, but when the Middle Georgia coach moved to West Alabama, he told his former place kicker: "Hey, you have eligibility left. Are you looking for a free master's?"

Butler graduated from West Alabama in 2005 with her master's in psychology and counseling. At press time she was working as a corporate recruiter in Atlanta—and playing amateur soccer on the side, of course.

Save the Sturgeon!
Marion

Perry Lakes Park was closed for twenty-eight years because it posed a security risk—to the sturgeon.

Built in 1935 by the federal Civilian Conservation Corps, the park is

Haunted Football Field

Every high school has its own set of spook tales, told to credulous freshmen down through the years, but Marbury High's is especially interactive.

The story goes that a cheerleader was killed when she fell off the goalposts during a homecoming photo shoot. To this day (the freshmen are told), if you stand on the 50-yard line of the football field on homecoming night, the cheerleader's ghost appears between the goalposts and sashays toward you.

The teenagers of Marbury must have spent many an enjoyable homecoming night testing (or staging) that one. Marbury High (www .marburyhighschool.org) is at the northern edge of Autauga County, east of I-65 at 210 County Road 20, about 2 miles east of US 31.

next to the Marion State Fish Hatchery, headquarters of research into the endangered Alabama sturgeon. After a sturgeon was stolen from the hatchery in 1974, authorities mistrustful of hikers and picnickers closed Perry Lakes Park. Not until 2002 did Perry County reopen it.

Coincidentally, 2002 also marked the death of Bubba, the last Alabama sturgeon in captivity and perhaps the last Alabama sturgeon, period. His body was sent to the fish collection at the University of Alabama. His sperm, frozen in liquid nitrogen, was sent to a lab in Georgia, where it awaits the capture of a female Alabama sturgeon.

Perry Lakes Park is on County Road 175, 5 miles northeast of Marion. It includes a number of remarkably designed structures—a pavilion, restrooms, a bridge, and a unique 100-foot-high birding tower—all built by the student architects of Auburn University's Rural Studio Program. A 400-yard footpath leads to Nature Conservancy land and the bright white sand of Barton's Beach, the largest gravel bar on the Cahaba River. For more information log onto www.perrylakes.org.

The Stars and Bars Sews Confusion
Marion

The first flag of the Confederacy was not the famous design that causes so much controversy nowadays. The first Confederate flag, raised over the Alabama State Capitol on March 4, 1861, was the Stars and Bars. It had a circle of seven white stars on a blue square in the upper left-hand corner; the rest of the flag was a white stripe between two red stripes.

In other words, it looked a lot like the U.S. flag, so much so that battlefield commanders feared fatal confusion. Hence the separate Confederate battle flag, which is still contentious today.

Also contentious is who should get the credit for the first flag. Alabamians contend German-born artist Nicola Marschall (1829–1917), who taught art at Marion Female Seminary in Marion, designed the flag. A historical marker to this effect stands in front of the building, which later became Perry County High School, at 202 Monroe Street.

Skeptics find it odd that in all the heady flag-waving of the early Confederacy, Marschall's name never is mentioned in any 1861 newspaper accounts of the flag. Nor is it mentioned in the records of the Confederate congress. It's not mentioned even in the letter of recommendation from the flag committee. Some believe that Marschall was only one of many who sent in flag designs and that the resulting not-terribly-inspired flag was the work of, well, a committee.

The town wouldn't let Tim Tingle take the cedar wood home, so he decided to carve it where it stood. NIKI SEPSAS

Confederate president Jefferson Davis, incidentally, opposed a Confederate flag. He believed the new country should keep the U.S. flag. He argued that the Confederates were the rightful heirs to the ideals of 1776 and that the world eventually would recognize that fact. No one listened to Jefferson Davis on that point.

Carving Tinglewood
Montevallo

In his spare time coal miner Tim Tingle is slowly carving all the dead cedars of Orr Park in

★ ★

Montevallo into fantastic shapes—fire-breathing dragons, prancing unicorns, stern-faced wizards, gnarled Treebeard-like faces. There are thirty or so carvings so far, and the walkway that connects them is known as the Tinglewood Trail.

This all started in 1993, when Tingle asked the town for some of the old cedar wood so that he could whittle on it at home. When the town refused, Tingle offered to whittle on it right there where it was. The town was dubious at first, but now the Tinglewood Trail is a tourist attraction and a source of local pride. Kids leave grass in the horse's mouth and practice throwing balls into the gaping old-man faces.

The Orr Park entrance is on Vine Street. Call the Montevallo Chamber of Commerce at 205-665-1519 for more information.

American History, Lilliput Style

Montevallo

In the early 1960s the late Tuscaloosa book publisher Pettus Randall had a brainstorm: a traveling exhibit of historical miniatures that would bring American history to schoolchildren in every town in the country.

To realize his dream Randall commissioned dozens of artists, historians, and craftspeople. Thousands of hours went into designing and constructing the thirty-five desktop-size dioramas, the seventy-two tiny American presidents and first ladies. Randall demanded that every ornament on Christopher Columbus's robe, every instrument in George Washington Carver's laboratory, every whisker on Ulysses S. Grant's face be as detailed and authentic as possible.

When it was finally complete, the Miniature Museum of American History toured twenty-five states, but it never attained the smashing success Randall had hoped for. To many Americans preoccupied by television, Vietnam, urban riots, and the Apollo space program, Randall's little soldiers and presidents looked quaint at best. Eventually, Randall sadly brought the trailer full of miniatures back to Tuscaloosa and parked it for good.

Forty years later, long after Randall's death, his son and successor at

Randall Publishing, Pettus Randall III, resolved to rescue and repair the collection and to put it on exhibit somewhere. Dozens of friends and employees spent long volunteer hours unpacking the crumbling boxes, washing and mending the fabrics, and repainting the heads.

Today the Pettus Randall Miniature Museum of American History, restored to its LBJ-era glory, is a must-see attraction at the American Village, a historical park with a Founding Fathers theme. Catering mostly to school groups, the park offers replicas of Federalist-style buildings, audience-participation trials at the Colonial Courthouse, costumed interpreters portraying Patrick Henry and Ben Franklin, a Continental Army encampment, a replica of the Oval Office, and a Patriot Gift Shop—but many visitors head straight to the Randalls' beloved miniatures.

The American Village is on Highway 119, 4 miles off I-65 at exit 234. Hours are 10:00 a.m. to 4:00 p.m., Monday through Friday; the park is open Saturday and Sunday only for special events. Each July 3–4, there's a two-day Independence Day 1776 celebration. Admission is charged. For more information call (877) 811-1776 or log onto www.miniaturehistorymuseum.com or www.americanvillage.org.

Dueling Show Tunes
Montevallo

Whereas homecoming at other universities is dominated by a football game, homecoming at the University of Montevallo is dominated by a pair of competing musicals.

One musical is the Purple Show; the other is the Gold Show. Each makes use of the talents, or at least the allegiance, of half the student body. All school year, Purple students and Gold students compose music, write scripts and lyrics, build sets, design costumes—all in secrecy, because no Purple must know what Gold is planning, and vice versa.

In February the curtain finally goes up in Palmer Hall, and the shows are presented to faculty, staff, students, and alumni. Students claim the biggest fan of the annual show is a ghost named "Trummy," who

supposedly monkeys with cast and crew members backstage and indicates his favorite show by swaying chandeliers and so forth.

For some forgotten reason the panel of judges announces the winner not by shouting "Purple!" or "Gold!" but by reading aloud a "secret phrase" from the winning script, at which point Palmer Hall erupts in pandemonium—half in ecstasy and half in anguish.

Some form of College Night competition has taken place on the campus every year since 1919, though the full-fledged musical productions began about 1950. At press time Purple had a slight historical edge in the competition, forty-four wins to Gold's forty-one, but wait till next year.

Ticket information is available to the general public each January; call the alumni office at (205) 665-6215. For more information visit www.montevallo.edu/StuLife/CollegeNight.

It's Probably an Old Manhole Cover . . .
Montevallo

The official state artifact of Alabama is the Rattlesnake Disk, a mysterious, foot-wide sandstone disk on which are carved a pair of entwined horned snakes surrounding a hand and an eye. It was unearthed by a Moundville farmer plowing a field. What it signifies, what it was used for, no one now living can say for sure.

The disk is on display in the museum in Moundville Archaeological Park, one of the world's great archaeological sites: 320 acres of woods and fields containing twenty-six flat-topped Indian mounds, so tall and steep that climbing one takes effort.

Eight hundred years ago, Moundville was the largest city in North America. A thousand people lived in the town proper, and 10,000 more lived in its "suburbs" along the Black Warrior River. Their trade routes extended thousands of miles. Yet most of the town was abandoned in the 1500s; no one knows why. Only about 15 percent of the town has been excavated, so the answers may yet lie beneath the Hale County soil.

A more recent Moundville mystery is the 1980 theft of 264 pottery vessels from the museum. No one has ever been arrested, and none of the vessels has ever turned up. In hopes of a lead, curators have posted photographs of the objects at www.museums.ua.edu/oar/stolenartifacts.

Besides the mounds and museum, the Moundville park has a gift shop, a nature trail, and, each fall, a Native American Festival. The park is on Highway 69, about 14 miles south of Tuscaloosa. Park hours are 8:00 a.m. to 8:00 p.m. daily; museum hours will be determined after the building reopens in spring 2009 after renovation. Admission is free for Native Americans with an ID card; admission is charged for other persons. For more details call (205) 371-2234 or log onto www.moundville.ua.edu/home.html.

Recycled Materials/Grand Designs
Newbern

The Rural Studio is an Auburn University architectural outreach program founded in 1992 by the late Samuel "Sambo" Mockbee, who put students to work designing and building innovative homes and public buildings in Hale County as "shelters for the soul for Alabama's poorest residents."

Rural Studio buildings have the swoop and dazzle of sets in a James Bond movie, but they're made on dirt-cheap budgets, sometimes of actual dirt, or of equally humble recycled materials. One house is made of 72,000 stacked carpet squares, another of telephone poles and used tires, another of stacked hay bales stuccoed over with concrete; its large smokehouse, built of salvaged concrete, glass bottles, and highway signs, cost $40. Another frequent Rural Studio building material is "rammed earth," a mixture of soil and cement that hardens into man-made rock.

Public buildings erected by the Rural Studio can be seen in the following places:

Akron. The beams of the Akron Boys and Girls Club were salvaged from a train trestle, and the Akron Senior Center was outfitted with an aircraft-hangar door. Akron is on Hale County Road 42 near the Black Warrior River.

Greensboro. For the Hale Empowerment and Revitalization Organization (H.E.R.O.), the Rural Studio built the Children's Center and adjoining playground and the Knowledge Café for classrooms and eventual Internet access. The Hale County Animal Shelter is two enclosed air-conditioned spaces inside a semicircular, hangarlike structure that's open to the elements, naturally illuminated and ventilated. Lion's Park and the Hale County Hospital courtyard are the Rural Studio's work, too. Greensboro, the county seat, is at the intersection of Highways 69 and 25.

Mason's Bend. The Mason's Bend Community Center is made of rammed earth, aluminum sheets, and GMC car windows. Cathedral-like, it doubles as a chapel. The Rural Studio built a basketball court in this community, too. Mason's Bend is on the Black Warrior River on a dirt road west of Sawyerville; best to call the Rural Studio (see below) for directions.

Newbern. The Little League backstop at Slippery Elm Park is made of old catfish netting, while the Newbern Tigers Baseball Club backstop is chain-link fencing hung from suspension wires, so no horizontal structure blocks the view. The Newbern Volunteer Fire Department and Town Hall, a 2003–2004 thesis project, is the town's first new public building in 110 years. The Rural Studio's headquarters are in Newbern, too; Mockbee liked to call it the "redneck Taliesin," after Frank Lloyd Wright's Wisconsin headquarters. Newbern is on Highway 61 at the Perry County line.

Perry County. The vegetable stand for the Avery family's organic farm features "hog-wire" fencing designed by folk artist Butch Anthony—artwork that also serves as lockable gates after hours. When the Antioch Baptist Church was found to be in such bad shape that it had to be demolished, the Rural Studio students recycled everything they could from the old church in building the new one, including joists, paneling, boards, and corrugated metal.

Thomaston. The Thomaston Farmers' Market is at the intersection of Highways 25 and 28 in Marengo County, and the Rural Heritage Foundation headquarters (www.pepperjelly.org) is the Rural Studio's largest and most complex project to date.

Rural Studio designs have been exhibited at the Metropolitan Museum of Art, the Whitney Museum, and the Cooper-Hewitt Museum in New York City. Mockbee's many awards included a Mac-Arthur Foundation "genius grant" and, posthumously, the Gold Medal of the American Institute of Architects, a peer honor previously given to Thomas Jefferson, Frank Lloyd Wright, Louis Sullivan, Le Corbusier, Louis Kahn, I. M. Pei, and Cesar Pelli. Mockbee died of leukemia in December 2001, having just begun to sketch ideas for a new World Trade Center.

For more information log onto www.cadc.auburn.edu/soa/rural-studio/. Call the Rural Studio at (334) 624-4483 to request a map of project locations.

Roadside Front-Yard Jesus
New Lexington

A 6-foot wooden statue of Jesus Christ stands in a glass case in Johnny Williamson's yard.

A retired logger, Williamson resolved, after his mother's funeral, to build a representation of the Twenty-third Psalm. It was her favorite scripture, and he couldn't seem to get it out of his head. He worked alongside wood-carver Willie Logan, whose other public artworks include the statue of Chief Tuscaloosa in the Tuscaloosa Public Library.

They used a cypress log because of the long-standing folk belief that cypress is the biblical "gopher wood" that Noah used to build the Ark. (Some biblical scholars believe it's just a typo for *kopher*, the Hebrew word for "pitch": hence, *kopher wood* meaning waterproofed wood.)

The finished Jesus, erected in 1999, has scars carved into his hands. He holds a wooden shepherd's staff ("The Lord is my shepherd; I shall not want"), and beside him is a wooden lamb. At night the statue is illuminated by a 500-watt floodlight, so it's hard to miss.

The front-yard Jesus is on rural US 43 at Fondren Road, between Northport and Fayette.

Tower-of-London Timber
Nicholsville

Thanks to William N. Nichols, for whom Nicholsville is named, there's Alabama pine in the Tower of London.

Nichols was an early pine baron in Marengo County. His thousand-acre farm included a cotton gin, gristmill, country store, and post office, but pine lumber was his chief business. It is said he contributed the lumber for seventeen churches between Selma and Demopolis.

In the 1880s he saw a newspaper ad that said Queen Victoria's government was looking for 100-foot-long pine logs to shore up the Tower of London, then under renovation. Nichols quickly let Her Majesty's government know that he owned 200-foot-tall virgin pines on Hudson Hill in Clarke County. Soon a British envoy was sent from New Orleans to see the trees and close the deal.

The whole extended Nichols family—he and his wife had twelve children and adopted, through the years, eleven more—felled, cut, and hauled Queen Victoria's trees to the Tombigbee River for their long journey to Mobile and then across the Atlantic. Nichols bragged for the rest of his life that he personally had kept the Tower of London from falling down.

Nicholsville is on Marengo County Road 20, between US 43 and Highway 69.

★ ★

Kentuck—It May Not Have a *Y*, but It Sure Has Art

Northport

Kentuck was the original nineteenth-century name of Northport, though no one is sure why. Some say it was short for Kentucky, others that the settlement was near a "cane tuck," or cane thicket. Today, Kentuck means the biggest folk art festival in the Southeast.

The two-day Kentuck Festival of the Arts is always the third weekend in October. In a park just west of downtown Northport, more than 250 artists set up shop, all of them either invited big names of folk art or up-and-comers selected in a juried competition. More than 30,000 patrons wander the pine-straw-strewn pathways for hours, browsing and haggling and eventually buying something. Or several somethings.

Every self-taught visionary artist in Alabama comes to Kentuck: Butch Anthony, Lonnie Holley, Charlie Lucas. Many come from other states as well. Much of this work is as vibrant, bold, and bizarre as a child's drawing, and some of it is just inexplicable. North Carolina artist Robert Frito Seven, for example, always brings hundreds of hand-lettered signs, no two alike. A typical one reads:

THESE ARE MY BE-
ANS. LOOK AT THEIR
RESEMBLANCE, THEN
THINK ABOUT WHAT
YOU HAVE DONE. IF
YOU COME TO A CON-
CLUSION, EAT THE BEANS.
IF YOU SMELL RUM, LEAVE
THE AREA, BUT DON'T GO
HOME.

The Kentuck Festival has a year-round presence in downtown Northport at the Kentuck Art Center, which features a funky, eclectic shop and two galleries that house temporary exhibits. The first Thursday of every month is Art Night downtown, as Kentuck and the other Main

**More giant statues:
The huge red dog,
top, and frightening
fire ant, bottom,
are Kentuck Court-
yard landmarks.**

Avenue galleries stay open late, with refreshments and live music.

The Kentuck courtyard is notable for two pieces of permanent outdoor artwork: a giant fire ant and a tremendous red dog on the roof. No, it's not supposed to be Clifford.

The Kentuck Art Center is at 503 Main Avenue. For more information call (205) 758-1257 or visit www.kentuck.org.

Old Fixer-Upper Needs Fixing Up Itself

Northport

For generations of Tuscaloosa County teenagers, the building with the worst reputation, the ultimate haunted house, and the setting for a thousand gruesome campfire tales is the decaying former mental hospital known as "Old Bryce."

It's easy to see why, even in daytime. The only approach, from Fifth Street just west of U.S. Highway 82, is a long, shaded driveway leading straight to the columned front porch. Visitors tend to drive slower and slower as they near the entrance, and not only because of the potholes in the

Old Bryce is creepy even by day. By night—forget it! CONNIE D. JOHNSTON

untended asphalt. Old Bryce casts an inexplicable chill, like Poe's House of Usher: "I know not how it was—but, with the first glimpse of the building, a sense of insufferable gloom pervaded my spirit."

Even to drive up to the front porch constitutes trespassing, and

235

★ ★

security guards in unmarked cars are quick to shoo away the curious. This, of course, hasn't stopped countless people from slipping through the front door into the dank, strangely echoing corridors, heaped with old desks and mattresses. That the interior looks as if it were trashed by rioting inmates adds to the *Blair Witch Project* feel of the place.

The main campus of Bryce Hospital (named for its founding superintendent, Peter Bryce) is in Tuscaloosa, off University Boulevard on land adjacent to the University of Alabama, and it has been there ever since its founding in 1860 as the Alabama Insane Hospital. The abandoned building in Northport was Bryce No. 2, used in the mid-twentieth century as an annex. Though it's known as Old Bryce, it's actually newer than the oldest buildings on the main campus.

This Tin Man Has a Heart
Pink Lily

It's easy to see, looking around Charlie Lucas's place, why he's known as the "Tin Man." Metal sculptures large and small, recognizable and abstract, surround the house.

Lucas was born in Birmingham in 1951, one of fourteen children who made their own toys from scavenged materials. He had no formal art training but learned about metal and machinery from his auto-mechanic father. Not until adulthood, when a severe back injury laid him up in bed for a year, did he seriously start making metal art.

Since then, he has exhibited at Yale University, the New Orleans Museum of Art, and the High Museum in Atlanta, and his work was prominent in the landmark 1994 touring exhibit Passionate Visions of the American South: Self-Taught Artists from 1940 to the Present. He also is a regular at the Kentuck Festival of the Arts in Northport each October.

Lucas lives on Autauga County Road 82 northwest of Prattville, between I-65 and U.S. Highway 82.

★ ★

Panda Heaven
Prattville

Wilderness Park in Prattville has a three-acre bamboo forest with stalks
that can reach as high as 65 feet tall. Walking through the rustling
stalks, one expects to see a munching panda at any moment.

The bamboo was planted by landowner Floyd Smith in the 1940s.
A later owner of the land, William Butler, was a general at nearby
Maxwell Air Force Base, so pilots did Vietnam survival training in the
bamboo in the 1960s.

To get to the park, take exit 186 from I-65, then turn right on US
31. After a mile turn right on Autauga County Road 85, then left on
Upper Kingston Road. Parking is on the left. For more information call
the town Parks and Recreation Department at (334) 361-3640.

Eat Your Broccoli or I'll Take You to the Cross Garden
Prattville

Turn off US 82 onto Autauga County Road 86, just north of Prattville,
and you soon find yourself driving between hundreds of crude wooden
crosses on eroding clay hillsides. Amid the crosses are dozens of
whitewashed signs, some mounted on rusting refrigerators and washing machines, that shout in a black and red scrawl: HELL IS HOT; REPENT;
YOU WILL DIE; TO [sic] LATE IN HELL; FIREWATER; SEX PIT; HELP ME; JESUS; DIED
DRUGS; SIN SEX; SOUL IN HELL; HELL IS HOT HOT HOT; YOU WILL DIE!

The Cross Garden is creepy even by day. By night, with stray
breezes scraping tin against tin, it's the scariest half mile of highway in
Alabama.

The forbidding landscape is the creation of the late W. C. (William
Carlton) Rice, who erected the first cross in 1976, after his mother's
funeral. His goal was ministry, in the best hellfire and brimstone tradition: "They told Noah to build the Ark, and he saved all those families,
so I built it like they told me so I can save all my families."

As Rice aged and was slowed by diabetes, he wasn't able to

Mr. Rice's Cross Garden is creepy even by day.

maintain the Cross Garden as he wanted, but its deterioration only added to the effect. Rice died in January 2004. His widow, Marzell Rice, told the *Montgomery Advertiser* that the family intended to keep the garden intact. "We promised him that." Judging from the deterioration evident on a recent visit, however, people should go see the Cross Garden as soon as possible, before the single greatest man-made thing in Alabama becomes only a memory.

Tomb of William Rufus King, Vice President and Gay Icon

Selma

William Rufus King (1786–1853) was the only Alabamian ever to be vice president of the United States. He also was "about as flaming a queen as the 1840s would allow," writes Bill Kauffman in *The American Enterprise* magazine. He says King "made Oscar Wilde in full flower look like Ernest Borgnine."

In his 1999 book *Lies across America: What Our Historic Sites Get Wrong*, sociologist James Loewen "outs" both King and his longtime companion, future U.S. President James Buchanan. The two men were housemates for years.

Countless gay Web sites note that Buchanan is the only bachelor president in U.S. history, King the only bachelor vice president. One site says, "Now we're not talking just good buddies here, sweetie."

These are not new assessments. Andrew Jackson called King "Miss Nancy." A Tennessee governor called King "Aunt Fancy" and "Buchanan's better half." One of James K. Polk's law partners called them "Mr. and Mrs. Buchanan."

We also have the evidence of a letter Buchanan wrote to a female friend, while King was away on a years-long diplomatic assignment to France: "I am now 'solitary and alone,' having no companion in the house with me. I have gone a wooing to several gentlemen, but have not succeeded with any one of them. I feel that it is not good for man to be alone; and should not be astonished to find myself married to some old maid who can nurse me when I am sick, provide good dinners for me when I am well, and not expect from me any very ardent or romantic affections."

One wonders what letters King and Buchanan wrote each other, but we'll never know, because Buchanan had all his correspondence burned upon his death.

After thirty years in the U.S. Senate, King was elected vice president in 1852, on the Democratic ticket with Franklin Pierce. Sadly, King held the office only six weeks before he died of tuberculosis; indeed, he was

★ ★

sworn in not in Washington but in Havana, Cuba, where his doctor had sent him for his health. He managed to make it back to Alabama to die at home in Selma, and he was buried there, in Live Oak Cemetery, 110 West Dallas Avenue.

Mild-Mannered Photographer by Day Was Psychic Healer at Night

Edgar Cayce (1877–1945) was America's most celebrated psychic, known as the "Sleeping Prophet," whose pronouncements, or "readings," during self-induced trances are revered by hundreds of thousands of followers to this day. Often called the founder of the New Age movement, he spent more than ten years in Alabama, running a Selma photography studio by day and doing readings in the evening.

Cayce was born and raised in Hopkinsville, Kentucky, where he first reported seeing visions and speaking with the dead at age six. This sort of thing wasn't unheard of in Cayce's family; his grandfather had been a well-known dowser, or "water witch."

As an adult Cayce turned to hypnosis in hopes of curing a case of laryngitis that had plagued him for more than a year. Under hypnosis he performed his first reading, instructing the hypnotist on what to say so that the laryngitis might be cured. Cayce awoke speaking normally, with no memory of what he had said during the trance.

Soon people from all over Kentucky were flocking to Cayce's parlor in hopes of being cured by the psychic healer. Enough left satisfied to keep the crowds coming. But Cayce considered himself a

A lot of U.S. presidents and vice presidents have been the subject of scandalous rumors, in life and in death. Sometimes the rumors are proven true, for example, the Thomas Jefferson–Sally Hemings liaison.

Some historians denounce as baseless the claims of a King-

photographer by trade, not a healer, and a job as a traveling school photographer brought him to Gadsden, Alabama, in 1909.

In 1912 he moved to Selma and opened a photography studio. He told no one of his apparent psychic abilities. But just as fugitive safecracker Jimmy Valentine in the O. Henry story "A Retrieved Reformation" was forced to reveal himself when a child was locked in a vault, so Cayce's cover was blown when his own six-year-old son burned his eyes playing with flash powder in his father's studio. Dissatisfied with the doctor's diagnosis, Cayce put himself in a trance and dictated the treatment that ultimately restored his son's sight.

Soon Cayce was even more famous than before, and he did more psychic business than photography business. For several busy months he set up shop in the Tutwiler Hotel in Birmingham. He traveled extensively out West, trying unsuccessfully to recruit investors to fund his psychic search for oil. He and his family finally left Alabama for good in 1923. Thereafter, Cayce's readings went beyond the diagnosis and treatment of illness to describe people's past lives, the experience of life after death, and the true nature of Atlantis.

Thousands of Cayce's readings, indexed by his longtime assistant, Gladys Davis, are archived at the Association for Research and Enlightenment in Virginia Beach, Virginia, which Cayce founded in 1931. For more information visit www.edgarcayce.org.

★ ★

Buchanan affair, saying it never can be proven. Other historians question the need to denounce the claims. Suppose a president and vice president were gay, they ask. What's the harm?

King suffered a posthumous indignity in 1986. Upon King's death the territorial legislature had named King County, Washington, where Seattle is located, in his memory. More than a century later, the county council voted to make Martin Luther King Jr., not the long-dead Alabama slave owner, the official namesake of King County. They didn't even have to change the signs.

Among those who opposed the move were some Seattle gay-rights activists, who accused the council of homophobia.

Sisters Run into Each Other . . . Literally

It's an eerie coincidence worthy of the movie *Magnolia*, but this really happened in Six Mile.

In November 2002 Sheila Wentworth, forty-five, left her Montevallo home in her Jeep to visit her sister, who lived a few miles away. Unknown to Sheila, her sister, Doris Jean Hall, fifty-one, was at the same time getting into her Jeep at home in Centreville to visit Sheila. Behind the wheel was Doris's husband, Billy Joe Hall Jr., forty-five.

Neither sister made it. The two Jeeps collided head-on on Highway 25 near the community of Six Mile—no one knows why—and all three family members were killed.

Coming Soon for a Limited Engagement
Sterrett

Every few years, most recently over the July 4 weekend in 2008, thousands of pilgrims converge on a field near Sterrett so they can be present during a Yugoslavian mystic's visions of the Virgin Mary.

Marija Lunetti was one of the six children whose vision of Mary on a hillside in Medjugorje, Yugoslavia (now Bosnia-Herzegovina), was worldwide news in 1981. Marija says that thereafter, she has spoken with Mary thousands of times—daily, in fact.

The visions continued during Lunetti's first visit to Alabama in 1988, when she donated a kidney to her brother in a Birmingham hospital. Lunetti visits Alabama as the guest of Caritas of Birmingham, a religious community founded in 1987 to promote the Medjugorje visions.

The Vatican tends to be skeptical of visions of Mary, weeping statues, and the like. Its policy is that public revelations ended with the New Testament and that private revelations are not meant for the church as a whole. Caritas is regarded by some outsiders and former insiders as little more than a lucrative cult, but it draws large numbers of pilgrims each year, and not just Catholics.

Whenever Lunetti is visiting, she speaks through a translator over a public-address system to all the assembled throngs in the field adjoining the mission house. She relays to the crowd what Mary said that day, usually in the guest room known as the Bedroom of Apparitions. According to Lunetti, Mary's messages in Alabama have included these:

- "Do not forget that I am your mother and that I love you."
- "I give you my love that you give it to others."
- "Go in peace."
- "Praised be Jesus."
- "I am happy to be here."
- "Same time, same place."
- "I am here to help you." (This message was given outdoors in the field, on Thanksgiving Day 1988.)

★ ★

During Lunetti's visits crowds begin arriving at 4:30 a.m., and parked cars line the two-lane road for miles. Caritas posts online schedules of the daily events, most of which involve praise, prayer, worship, and, of course, the daily visitation. Out of reverence for Mary, visitors during Lunetti's visits are prohibited from chewing gum or smoking. Lawn chairs, cell phones, cameras, and revealing clothing are taboo as well.

Caritas and its visitation site are on Shelby County Road 43, between I-20 and US 280, southeast of Birmingham. The address is 100 Our Lady Queen of Peace Drive. For more information call (205) 672-2000 or visit www.caritasofbirmingham.org.

Townley Rest Area
Townley

This community west of Jasper has an admirably simple roadside attraction, lovingly maintained for years, that entices many a shutterbug to detour off US 78. Sitting in weeds in full view of the road are an armchair, a sofa, a commode, and a crude wooden sign that says WELCOME TOWNLEY REST AREA. It's on the west side of state Highway 124 between state Highways 69 and 102.

Kitschy Sign Moons '50s Motel
Tuscaloosa

The most famous neon sign in west Alabama is in front of the Moon Winx Lodge.

It was designed by Gordo artist Glenn House and installed in 1957, during a boom of motel building along America's blue highways. The sliver of a moon in profile faces the hotel, not the highway.

The sign has appeared on the cover of *Alabama Heritage* magazine and has been lauded in the pages of the arts journal *Loud Paper*. Geoff Schmidt's novel *Write Your Heart Out: Advice from the Moon Winx Motel* was published in 2000. "Moon Winx" is a cut on *Atomic Electric*, a 2003 CD by Microwave Dave and the Nukes. The Moon Winx is also mentioned in William Cobb's 2003 novel *A Spring of Souls*.

Behind the sign the motel doesn't do the business it once did, but it's still open at 3410 University Boulevard East, a.k.a. U.S. Highway 11, in Tuscaloosa's Alberta City neighborhood. Call (205) 553-1520 for reservations or just to say you passed by.

Where Was Chicken Little When We Needed Her?
Tuscaloosa

The Hodges meteorite, also known as the Sylacauga meteorite, is the most interesting museum exhibit in Tuscaloosa. It's the only meteorite in the history of the world known to have hit a person.

The eight-and-a-half-pound space rock landed on Ann Hodges in Sylacauga in the early afternoon of November 30, 1954. It came through her roof, smashed a Philco radio, and bounced off her hip while she was napping on the living room couch.

The rock was quickly identified by state geologist Walter Jones, who luckily was doing fieldwork in the Sylacauga area. By nightfall hundreds of reporters and curiosity seekers had gathered at the Hodges house, to the dismay of Hodges and her husband, a tree surgeon. Hodges became briefly famous. A photo of the big bruise on her hip appeared in *Life* magazine, and she appeared as a guest on the TV quiz show *I've Got a Secret*.

At the time, the U.S. Air Force, spooked by the Cold War and by a wave of "flying saucer" sightings (including many in Alabama), routinely confiscated everything that looked even vaguely extraterrestrial, and they confiscated the Hodges meteorite, too. Only the intercession of an Alabama congressman, Kenneth Roberts, got it returned.

The Hodgeses' landlord, Birdie Guy, sued Ann Hodges for possession of the meteorite, on the grounds that a landowner owns any minerals found on the property, whether they bubble up from below or rain down from space. The Hodgeses threatened to countersue for Ann's injuries. The case was settled out of court. Ann wound up with the meteorite, and she donated it (against her husband's wishes) to the Alabama Museum of Natural History at the University of Alabama,

where it remains today, on display on the second floor of Smith Hall. Hodges died in 1972 and was buried in the Charity Baptist Church cemetery in Hazel Green in Madison County. The museum is in the center of campus at Sixth Avenue and Capstone Drive, a block north of University Boulevard. For more information check www.amnh.ua.edu.

The Hodges meteorite is famous in Alabama, but few people know about the McKinney meteorite, a fragment of the same meteor that had Hodges in its crosshairs. A Sylacauga farmer named Julius K. McKinney found it the day after Hodges was hit, when his mule shied away from a strange black rock in the road. He sold the meteorite for enough money to buy a car and a new house. It's in the Smithsonian now.

Inventor of the Thing That Makes Your Hair Stand on End
Tuscaloosa

Have you ever encountered, at a science museum or a science fair, a big aluminum ball on a pedestal that makes your hair stand on end when you touch it?

That kind of thing is called the Van de Graaff generator, which is basically a particle accelerator for static electricity, generating high voltage at low levels of current. And the inventor was from Tuscaloosa.

Robert J. Van de Graaff (1901–1967) realized higher ambitions, though, than just making people's hair stand on end. Developed in the late 1920s and early 1930s, his generator was an important device in early atom-smashing and X-ray experiments. The largest Van de Graaff generator ever built is now used for demonstrations at Boston's Museum of Science: two spheres 15 feet in diameter, mounted on 25-foot-tall columns 6 feet in diameter. When that baby was turned on in November 1933, the headline in the *New York Times* placed Dr. Van de Graaff among the gods: "Man Hurls Bolt of 7,000,000 Volts." Classroom models typically produce only 100,000 to 500,000 volts.

Van de Graaff got his degree in mechanical engineering in his hometown, at the University of Alabama, and then went on to study physics at the Sorbonne in Paris and Oxford University in England, where he was a Rhodes scholar. For years he was on the faculty at the Massachusetts Institute of Technology.

The Civil War–era Tuscaloosa mansion that was his boyhood home is at 1305 Greensboro Avenue, just south of downtown. The Jemison–Van de Graaff mansion, once the public library, now houses the Greater Tuscaloosa Convention and Visitors Bureau and is open to the public; admission is free. For more details call (205) 758-2906 or visit www.jemisonmansion.com.

Tuscaloosa, Hollywood South

Tuscaloosa

The low-budget 1958 exploitation movie *Lost, Lonely and Vicious* was billed as a "Confidential Exposé of Boys and Girls Clawing Their Way to Success in Hollywood!"—but it was filmed in Tuscaloosa, Alabama.

The movie stars Ken Clayton as a sensitive, James Dean–like matinee idol with a death wish. It features vicious fistfights and street racing, just like those in *Rebel Without a Cause*, sort of. (One unkind reviewer called it *Rebel Without a Point*.) See if you agree, after reading this sample dialogue:

- "Against this Hollywood backdrop of fantasy, yesterday's teenager, now grown up, faces tomorrow still searching for kicks, but deeply searching for meaning."
- "I read a book. It was all about the human mind. The book called it a dark continent of motive and desire. It's about guys like me."
- "Every so often I find myself walking along a street, and I look up and see a tree. You ever really look at a tree? Ever notice the leaves? They make a funny little laughing sound."
- "I'd like to bash your head in! There's nothing funny about being kidnapped."

The Internet Movie Database (www.imdb.com) lists *Lost, Lonely and Vicious* as the only film credit for director Frank Myers and one of only two film credits for screenwriter Norman Graham. The other was

the 1960 voodoo movie *Macumba Love*, directed by the guy who only played the director in *Singin' in the Rain*; it grossed $3 million.

Only true obsessives need read this paragraph: The cast of *Lost, Lonely and Vicious* includes Barbara Wilson, who was in Roger Corman's girl-delinquent classic *Teenage Doll* (1957), and Richard Gilden, who later played the title role in *The Black Klansman* (1966). The cinematographers, Ted and Vincent Saizis, also filmed the infamous *Poor White Trash* (1957), a.k.a. *Bayou*.

For years *Lost, Lonely and Vicious* was merely a fondly remembered title among connoisseurs of schlock movies, but recently Something Weird Video has reissued the picture on DVD, as a double feature with the prison movie *Jacktown* (1962) and three "educational" short subjects of the period: *Crisis in Morality* ("Sin infiltrates, impregnates and pollutes!"), *Hell Is a Place Called Hollywood*, and *Little Miss Delinquent*. To order visit www.somethingweird.com.

The scene of the "movie premiere" in *Lost, Lonely and Vicious* was shot outside the Bama Theatre at 600 Greensboro Avenue downtown, just south of University Boulevard. The distinctive marquee is still there. The "drag race" was filmed on rural US 82 south of town, which is just that deserted in real life, even fifty years later.

Maybe Professor's Ghost Could Reveal an Exam Answer Every Once in a While
Tuscaloosa

Clarence Cason (1896–1935) was a teacher and newspaper reporter hired in 1928 by his alma mater, the University of Alabama, to create its first journalism curriculum. During his seven years at the university, he became well known for his many essays and editorials, and he was recruited by the University of North Carolina Press to write a book about the social ills of the South and how they could be remedied.

The book was *90 Degrees in the Shade* (1935), widely regarded as a classic of its type. "On the whole," Cason wrote, "the South would profit from a nice, quiet revolution." But Cason wouldn't be around to see it. Distraught by the potential reaction to his book, on the eve of its publication, he shot himself to death in his office in the campus student union.

Today the old Union Building is Reese-Phifer Hall, home of the university's College of Communication, which named its annual prize for nonfiction writing after Cason. But the journalism students who labor in the Reese-Phifer labs late at night claim that Cason's influence is felt in a more tangible way.

In the vicinity of Cason's old office, they hear footsteps where no walker is visible. Sometimes they hear a commotion in the corridor and run out to find the deserted hallway littered with torn fliers from the stripped-bare bulletin boards. They blame the ghost of Clarence Cason, still brooding in his office after seventy years.

The Mount Olympus of Mounting

Tuscaloosa

Woods & Water is a sporting-goods superstore perched on a hilltop in south Tuscaloosa, from which you can see the whole town. But the sights inside the store, constructed as a vast, wood-beamed atrium, are pretty impressive, too: a living-room-size aquarium, an extensive (and expensive) collection of antique rifles and pistols, and a mural of a mountain landscape that takes up the entire back wall.

Most surprising are the dozens of museum-quality mounted animals all over the store: deer, elk, geese, a snarling bobcat, a bear with a salmon in its mouth, even a rhinoceros. Regulars who pop in for a pocketknife or fishing lure bring the whole family so that the kids can gawk at the mounted elephant's head. One of the regulars is country singer-songwriter Hank Williams Jr., who does occasional autograph signings among the beasts of the field and birds of the air.

Woods & Water is at 5101 Summit Ridge, off Skyland Boulevard just south of I-20/59. Store hours vary by season. For more information call (800) 383-9020 or visit www.woods-n-water.com.

The Bondsmobile

Tuscaloosa

Jail Busters Bail Bonds on Fifteenth Street advertises itself with this vintage Cadillac ambulance, painted to suggest the Ectomobile in the movie *Ghostbusters*.

The Jail Busters logo replaces the startled spook in the famous "no-ghosts" logo with a sorrowful guy peering through the bars of a jail cell. On his left side is the number 24, on his right side the number 7, indicating that Jail Busters is always ready to take your call. "Who do ya' call . . . When ya' take a fall? Our number's on the wall! We-Bust-U-Out."

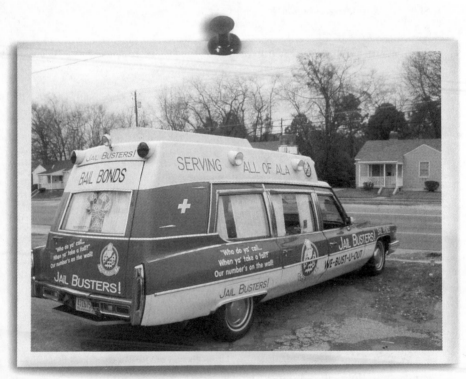

Jail Busters Bail Bonds in Tuscaloosa advertises itself with this vintage Cadillac ambulance, painted to suggest the Ectomobile in the movie *Ghostbusters*.

The front view shows the reversed ambulance-style type that reads JAIL BUSTERS in a rearview mirror. That's clearly a vintage Cadillac logo above the grille, with the pearl-topped crown that Cadillac recently scrapped, alas. But the obsessive fan site www.geocities.com /ectomobiles suggests the Bondsmobile probably is not the same make as the 1959 Miller Meteor driven in the movie by Venkman, Stantz, Spengler, and Zeddmore. The Ectomobile had limo-style windows all the way down the side, whereas the Bondsmobile has a landau-style design, with no side windows in the back—more typical of a hearse than an ambulance. The Ectomobile also had more pronounced, upswept tail fins. But the Bondsmobile is still very, very cool.

Tripping with Dr. Osmond

Tuscaloosa

One of the most interesting doctors to work at Bryce Hospital in modern times was the late Humphry Osmond, a native of England who was on staff from 1971 to 1992. Osmond was a pioneering researcher into LSD and mescaline. He argued for years that if doctors were to take hallucinogenic drugs, they would understand their schizophrenic patients better. He also used the drugs to treat schizophrenics, chronic alcoholics, and other unfortunates.

Osmond's most famous LSD research volunteer was the British novelist Aldous Huxley, author of *Brave New World*, who wrote about his mind-blowing experiences in *The Doors of Perception*. At one point in their correspondence, Huxley wrote Osmond a little poem:

TO MAKE THIS TRIVIAL WORLD SUBLIME
TAKE HALF A GRAMME OF PHANEROTHYME.

Osmond replied:

TO FATHOM HELL OR SOAR ANGELIC
JUST TAKE A PINCH OF PSYCHEDELIC.

Psychedelic was a word Osmond made up, from *psyche* and the Greek for "to make visible," and it quickly entered the English

★ ★

language. The *American Heritage College Dictionary* gives this definition: "Of, characterized by, or generating hallucinations, distortions of
perception, altered states of awareness, and occasionally states resembling psychosis."

By the time Osmond came to Bryce, the United States had made
hallucinogenic drugs illegal, which he regarded as a misguided setback
for science. When he died in 2004, a colleague wrote: "Humphry was
intelligent, calm, kind, full of creative ideas, and undeterred by conser-
vative psychiatric opinions."

Does He Have a Little Man on His Shirt?
Tuscaloosa

Since 2002 an unnamed, 7-foot-long alligator has lived at the Country
Club of Tuscaloosa, in the pond beside—what else?—the thirteenth
hole.

Occasionally visible, the gator swims, suns itself, and sometimes
crawls out of the water with a squirming muskrat in its mouth. Though
it's unusual to find a gator this far north, it's not unheard of. Since
publication of our first edition, in fact, a second gator has moved onto
the same golf course; it hangs out in the water by the third hole.

Even before the first gator showed up, golfers had nicknamed the
thirteenth hole the "Beast," because it has railroad tracks on one side
and the pond on the other. Now golfers have more incentive to err on
the side of the railroad.

Only members and their guests are permitted on the private golf
course.

The Reverend Fred Lane and "French Toast Man"

The college town of Tuscaloosa has a lot of live music, and some of it, through the years, has been strange. (Two examples are listed below.) But its strangest musical act by far, one of the strangest musical acts anywhere, was the Reverend Fred Lane, a grinning, bespectacled fiend with a handlebar mustache and a face covered in Band-Aids.

The Reverend Fred Lane can be heard on three CDs: *Raudelunas 'Pataphysical Revue* and *From the One That Cut You*, both recorded live in Tuscaloosa in the mid-1970s, and his long-dreaded studio album, *Car Radio Jerome*, released in 1983. Song titles include "Danger Is My Beer," "I Talk to My Haircut," "Rubber Room," "Meat Clamp Conduit," "Upper Lip of a Nostril Man," "Hittite Hot Shot," "Dondi Must Die," and "Dial 'O' for Bigelow."

The highlight of *Car Radio Jerome* is the surreal ditty "French Toast Man," about the sinister distribution of French toast to unwary children; it's a two-and-a-half-minute jaunt into a new and terrible world. If Walt Disney's Goofy had a bad acid trip, he would babble something like "French Toast Man."

The Reverend Fred Lane was born of the experimental, improvisational music of the hippie era, which in Tuscaloosa peaked late, about 1975. *Raudelunas 'Pataphysical Revue* was a surreal campus "happening" devised by various local talents, including T. R. (Tim) Reed, Craig Nutt, Davey Williams, Roger Hagerty, Anne Le Baron, LaDonna Smith, and Nolan Hatcher. "Quite a lot of people came," Williams recalled. "Of course, quite a lot of people left immediately." Because the show needed a master of ceremonies, Tim Reed donned Band-Aids and boxer shorts and became the Reverend Fred Lane.

(Continued)

Reed and company had other projects, too: For example, the Raude-lunas Marching Band enlivened University of Alabama Homecoming parades from 1973 through 1977. One year it was the Marching Vegetable Band, another year the Marching Appliance Band, and so on, with costumes to match. The Marching Vegetable Band showed up at a 1973 Randy Newman concert in Tuscaloosa, in honor of the singer-songwriter's thirtieth birthday; the future Oscar winner termed them "weird."

There has been no new Reverend Fred Lane material in twenty years, but thanks to CDs and the Internet, he has a fervent and growing cult following around the world. The best Reverend Fred Lane fan site, www.craignutt.com/raudelunas/russell/fredlane, is the work of Stewart C. Russell, a Scot now living in Canada. *Mojo* magazine devoted a June 2001 article to Lane and the 1970s Tuscaloosa music scene. Fans who weren't born in 1975 swap tantalizing rumors of unreleased Fred Lane material, including a feel-good campfire sing-along titled "We're Going to Hell."

With the exception of late painter and poet Nolan Hatcher, all the other members of the Raudelunas crowd are still around, scattered around the country, ripe for a reunion show: Hagerty at Tuskegee University, Le Baron at the California School of the Arts, Williams and Smith in Birmingham. Craig Nutt is a nationally known wood sculptor in Tennessee; his Web site, www.craignutt.com/raudelunas, is a trove of Fred Lane–related material.

And what of Fred Lane himself? Tim Reed still lives in Tuscaloosa, where he, too, is a nationally known wood sculptor. Every year at the Kentuck Festival of the Arts in Northport, Reed exhibits a new set of intricate and whimsical "whirligigs," moving sculptures with titles such as *Salad Shooter* and *Electric Bathtub*. Who can say, however, whether his maniacal alter ego will ever be heard from again?

The Reverend Fred Lane may be Tuscaloosa's strangest musical act, but two close contenders deserve mention here:

- Hooper called itself "The World's Greatest Stunt Band." It also was the world's only Burt Reynolds tribute band: The 1978 Burt Reynolds movie *Hooper*, about a movie stuntman, was partially filmed in Tuscaloosa. Hooper concerts included mock fights, leaps into the audience, that sort of thing. Hooper played only four shows, the last in 1999, but it has not been forgotten.

- D.C. Moon and His Atomic Supermen is a rocking science fiction band, with song titles that set off photon torpedoes of nostalgia: "They're Coming After You," "I Married a Woman from Outer Space," "Colossal Man," "Number Twelve Looks Just like You." Moon and company perform at science fiction conventions in addition to their Tuscaloosa gigs. For updates visit their Web site at www.dcmoon.com.

★ ★

Alabama's Shortest Interstate

Interstate 359, which connects I-20/59 to downtown Tuscaloosa, is only 2.3 miles long and thus is Alabama's shortest interstate highway. That still makes it more than twice as long as the shortest interstate highway in the nation, Interstate 375 in Detroit, which is 1.06 miles.

More interstate trivia: Although I-59 runs through four states, all its three-digit spurs are in Alabama: Interstate 359 in Tuscaloosa, Interstate 459 in Birmingham, and Interstate 759 in Gadsden.

Randy "Woody" Randall
Tuscaloosa

After many years as a fixture in the front lobby, Randy "Woody" Randall, a plastic dummy in a night watchman's uniform, "retired" in April 2006 from Randall-Reilly Publishing in Tuscaloosa.

According to CEO Mike Reilly, the dummy was brought to Tuscaloosa by his predecessor, the late Pettus Randall III, who encountered it at an American Rental Association trade show. An exhibitor had rigged the dummy with a loudspeaker so that as people walked past, the dummy seemed to greet them by name: "Hi, Pettus!"

Enthralled, Randall bought the dummy for $2,200, hoping to take it on the trade-show circuit. When that didn't work out, Randall decided to dress the dummy in a night watchman's uniform and set it in the window as a deterrent to burglars. "Hello, Woody," Randall would tell the dummy each morning as he walked in.

In a celebrated incident one Halloween, Randall employee Tim Cooper, then art director of *Overdrive* magazine, disguised himself as the

"Woody" Randall, longtime fixture in the lobby of
Randall-Reilly Publishing, was a bargain at $2,200.

★ ★

dummy and sat frozen in position in the lobby until an unsuspecting Mike Reilly walked past, whereupon the "dummy" reached out and goosed him. Excitement ensued.

Randall-Reilly Publishing honored the dummy's retirement from the public eye with cake and coffee at a company-wide meeting on April 10, 2006. The first job applicant to sit in Woody's chair in the lobby, at 3200 Rice Mine Road Northeast, was in for a lot of strange looks.

Turned On, Tuned In, Kicked Out
Tuscaloosa

The late counterculture guru and LSD advocate Timothy Leary, famed for his 1960s motto "Turn on, tune in, drop out," was an undergraduate in the 1940s at the University of Alabama in Tuscaloosa.

Leary was most familiar at the time with the traditional undergraduate drug, alcohol. By the time the Massachusetts native came to Tuscaloosa, he already had been kicked out of West Point for a liquor bust. But his interest in harder drugs seems to have come much later, after he left Alabama for good.

The head of the UA psychology department told Leary that he needed intelligent students, and this much impressed the young man. Leary later recalled: "This was the first time in my life that I had heard anyone imply intelligence was a desirable trait. Up to this moment being smart had always got me in trouble. Conformity was the virtue I was used to hearing about."

Leary got into trouble on the Tuscaloosa campus not for alcohol but for another time-honored reason: spending the night with a girlfriend in her dormitory. He was kicked out of school again, an act with serious consequences in the middle of World War II. Leary lost his draft deferment and was sent to artillery training at Fort Eustis, Virginia.

But the army needed psychologists as well as artillerymen, and the former head of the UA psychology department was now chief psychologist at an army hospital in Pennsylvania. Leary was allowed to complete his UA degree in the army in 1943 and transfer to his mentor's hospital, where his medical career began. Leary's interest in hallucinogens apparently dates from 1957, after his wife's suicide, when as a researcher at the Kaiser Foundation, he read an article about them in *Life* magazine.

It's interesting that the two most influential LSD proponents of the twentieth century both spent years in Tuscaloosa: Leary as a UA undergrad in the 1940s and Humphry Osmond on staff at Bryce Hospital from 1971 to 1992. Could it have been something in the water?

Bad Heir Day
Vernon

He's largely forgotten now, but for a few years in the nineteenth century, Reuben Houston "Rube" Burrows was America's most famous train robber. Between 1886 and 1890 he robbed eight passenger trains across the frontier—Texas, Arkansas, Mississippi, and Alabama—for an estimated total haul of $20,000. The Pinkertons put a $7,500 price on Burrows's head, and he was killed in a shootout near Linden, Alabama, in 1890, age thirty-six. He's buried just outside of Vernon.

According to legend Burrows was "the Robin Hood of train robbers," sharing his loot with the poor, but this story was told about most every train robber in the nineteenth century, when railroad magnates, being rich and powerful, were widely hated. For a handful of men with guns to stop a train and rob it, moreover, seemed a pretty dashing exploit. So many an ignorant, selfish thug got romanticized, by the poor and downtrodden, as a sort of backwoods Lancelot. Several dime novels were written about Burrows, such as *Rube Burrows, King of Outlaws* by George W. Agee (1890).

Mark Hughes Cobb of the *Tuscaloosa News* has written a one-act musical comedy, *Bad Heir Day*, about a strange incident in Burrows's career, when he purportedly used a preposterous fake mustache in an attempt to fool a postmaster who had known him all his life. Cobb is

★ ★

descended from the postmaster, hence the pun of the title. The one-act was performed at the 2003 Kentuck Festival of the Arts in Northport.

To get to Burrows's grave, take Highway 18 east from Vernon to Old Highway 18 east and then go left (north) on Lamar County Road 9 to the Fellowship Baptist Church cemetery.

Calculation of the Damned

In 1993, the *Birmingham News* delighted non-Baptists everywhere by publishing large portions of a remarkable document created—purely for internal use—by the Home Mission Board of the Southern Baptist Convention: a county-by-county estimate of how many Alabamians were going to hell. Worst off was Shelby County, which includes part of Birmingham and various well-off suburbs, and where 63.5 percent of the residents were expected to fry.

The lead of the page-one story by Greg Garrison was "More than 1.86 million people in Alabama, 46.1% of the state's population, will be damned to Hell if they don't have a born-again experience professing Jesus Christ as their savior, according to a report by Southern Baptist researchers."

A church spokesman told the *New York Times:* "If we were selling snow tires, we'd want to ask ourselves, 'Where are the people who need snow tires?' It's kind of a crass analogy, but where are the people who need the Lord? That's where we need to go."

The calculation assumed that virtually all non-Christians, including Jews and Muslims, were damned by definition, that virtually all

One Batty Temple

Vestavia Hills

The Temple of Sybil is the only remaining structure of the twenty-acre Shades Mountain estate of the late George Battey Ward, a Birmingham mayor and classics enthusiast.

Southern Baptists were saved, and that the great mass of Catholics and Protestants—including non-Southern Baptist Baptists—were on the fence.

The gagsters who sponsor the Ig Nobel Prizes—an annual dubious honor for scientific research that "cannot or should not be reproduced"—were pleased to award the Southern Baptists their 1994 prize for mathematics. No Southern Baptists showed up to accept, so Terje Korsnes, the Norwegian consul to Boston, accepted for them, with one of the great speeches of modern diplomatic history:

> I was asked to come here tonight and accept custody of this prize on behalf of the people of Hell, Norway. We were delighted to learn that so many people in the great state of Alabama will go to Hell. We have a special place in Hell for all of you.

For more Ig Nobel prizewinners, see Marc Abrahams's book *The Ig Nobel Prizes* (Dutton, 2003), and the Ig Nobel Committee's page saluting the Baptists at http://improbable.com/ig/1994/1994-math.html.

★ ★

U.S. Highway 31 commuters pass the last remnant of the George Battey Ward estate.

Some whispered that Ward's middle name was apt. He based the design of his house on the Temple of Vesta in Rome, home of the six vestal virgins who tended an eternal flame, thus ensuring Rome's safety. He called his spread Vesta Via, meaning "Vesta's Way" or "Vesta's Road." There he threw the most elaborate toga parties in Alabama history. Well-to-do guests strolled about the grounds wearing sheets, sandals, and laurel wreaths, watching Ward frolic with his hound dogs, all of which were named for Greek and Roman gods.

Ward never married and left no children when he died in 1940, and Vesta Via became the nucleus of the upscale Birmingham suburb of Vestavia Hills. The big house was demolished in 1971. All that remained was the pretty gazebo, which was moved to its present site, the town's north entrance, in 1975.

The sybils, in ancient times, were priestesses who uttered the sometimes cryptic messages of the gods. The ancient world had many sybils and many temples dedicated to them. Ward based his on the Temple of the Sybil at Tivoli, Italy.

Today his Temple of Sybil is maintained by the Vestavia Hills Garden Club. It's at the intersection of Shades Crest Road and US 31.

index

index

index

index

index

index

index

index

About the Author

Andy Duncan lived for ten years in Alabama, earning an M.F.A. in fiction writing from the University of Alabama in Tuscaloosa and working as a senior editor at *Overdrive* magazine, "The Voice of the American Trucker." He continues to teach in the Honors College of the University of Alabama, but he now lives in Maryland, where he is an assistant professor of English at Frostburg State University. His other books include *Beluthahatchie and Other Stories,* a fiction collection, and *Crossroads: Tales of the Southern Literary Fantastic,* a fiction anthology that he co-edited with F. Brett Cox. His fiction has won two World Fantasy Awards and the Theodore Sturgeon Award for best science fiction story of the year. His blog is http://beluthahatchie.blogspot.com.